INTREPID
Australia

Andrew Bain

Aboriginal and Torres Strait Islander People are advised that this publication contains the names, and may contain images, of deceased people. We apologise for any distress this may inadvertently cause.

Hardie Grant EXPLORE | Intrepid

WHAT MAKES AN INTREPID GUIDE

Intrepid, for us, means being adventurous, brave and, above all, curious. Whether you're trekking through remote countryside or trying a new-to-you dish, these kinds of experiences allow us to reach beyond our everyday to learn something new and connect with people and places.

Intrepid Guides are for the intrepid traveller – those who want to see the world in meaningful and memorable ways, rather than just push through a to-do list.

Each guide highlights places, activities and experiences that make a country special and allow us to connect to these destinations and gain life-long memories and broaden our perspective.

The contents of this guide align with everything that drives Intrepid Travel and Hardie Grant Explore – chasing adventure in new (to us) places while getting to know the people who call them home and supporting their communities along the way.

INTREPID

Australia

※ Intrepid Travel and Hardie Grant Publishing are both companies that were founded in Naarm/Melbourne, on the land of the Wurundjeri Woi-wurrung and Bunurong Peoples. We acknowledge that they are the Traditional Custodians of the land that we work on, with deep and ongoing connection to Country, and pay respect to their Elders, past and present.

We also extend our respect to all Traditional Custodians of the vast and diverse lands that we travel on throughout what we today know as Australia.

INTRODUCTION
vii

THE OLDEST LIVING CULTURES
x

THE BASICS
xii

BEST OF AUSTRALIA
1

NATURE
13

WILDLIFE
89

RESPONSIBLE TRAVEL
111

FOOD & DRINK
129

FESTIVALS & EVENTS
153

ACTIVITIES & SPORTS
179

HISTORY
207

ART & CULTURE
231

ARCHITECTURE
275

SLOW TRAVEL
287

INDEX
316

ABOUT THE AUTHOR
323

✱ INTRODUCING INTREPID TRAVEL

As the world's largest purpose-led adventure travel company, Intrepid Travel has been taking travellers around the globe since 1989.

On hundreds of trips in over 100 countries, Intrepid brings small groups of like-minded travellers together with a locally based leader. Intrepid itineraries weave the highlights into the hard-to-forget moments in hard-to-find places. From homestays to Indigenous community-led experiences, between the hidden noodle bars and backstreet bodegas, Intrepid experiences are built to keep the economic benefits of travel where they belong.

It all stems from a simple mission: create positive change through the joy of travel. As a B Corp, Intrepid is committed to balancing purpose and profit by operating equitably, sustainably and transparently. The Intrepid Foundation, established in 2002, gives travellers a way to give back to the places they've visited by supporting organisations around the world that are making a difference in their communities.

At Intrepid, travel is about more than just seeing the world, it's about experiencing it and sparking connections with Intrepid people wherever you go.

Learn more at intrepidtravel.com.

INTRODUCTION

Australia is a timeless land home to equally timeless cultures. The country's low mountains are among the oldest on the planet (the Hamersley Range in Western Australia's Pilbara region is recognised as the second oldest on Earth) and once stood as high as the Himalayas. Similarly, the Finke River, flowing through the deserts of Central Australia, is thought to be the oldest river in the world.

Dinosaur skeletons and footprints dating back 170 million years litter the land – most noticeably around western Queensland – and Australia's First Nations people form the world's oldest living cultures, dating back at least 65,000 years. Aboriginal people have a deep connection to country and waterways.

Overlaying this long history is the relatively recent arrival of settlers from other lands, which began in 1788 when the First Fleet of 11 British ships sailed into Botany Bay, now part of the southern coastline of Sydney/Warrane. Six of those ships contained convicts – prisoners sentenced to transportation to the new British colony – but almost half of the arrivals were free settlers.

Today, Australia is a highly multicultural and contemporary society made richer by the cultures – ancient and new – that make up its population of 26 million people.

For historic sights around the country, see p. 207.

Andrew Bain

TIMOR SEA

JOSEPH BONAPARTE GULF

Kununurra

KIMBERLEY

Broome/Rubibi

Fitzroy Crossing

Port Hedland

Karratha

GREAT SANDY DESERT

PILBARA

Exmouth

Newman

LITTLE SANDY DESERT

GIBSON DESERT

INDIAN OCEAN

Carnarvon

WESTERN AUSTRALIA

Mount Magnet

GREAT VICTORIA

Geraldton

Kalgoorlie-Boulder

NULLARBOR

PERTH/BOORLOO

Norseman

Margaret River

Esperance/Kepa Kurl

SOUTHERN

AUSTRALIA

Capital city: Canberra/Ngunnawal/Ngunawal/Ngambri

There are more than 250 Indigenous languages with 800 dialects, but the most commonly spoken language is English

Surrounded by water, Australia has approximately 30,000 kilometres (19,000 miles) of beaches

Australia has 6 states and 2 territories

THE OLDEST LIVING CULTURES

Australia is alive with the long history of the Indigenous people, our culture and our presence. Nowhere else in the world can you see and experience the oldest living cultures of humankind. This guide contains experiences of Aboriginal and Torres Strait Islander places, tourism adventures, art centres and galleries, guided walks and cultural events, but these are only some of the ways local and international travellers can find their way through our beautiful lands and waters and make a cultural connection with the people who know it best.

There are two distinctive Indigenous cultural groupings in Australia: Aboriginal peoples on the mainland and most islands and the Torres Strait Islanders, whose homelands are in the Torres Strait between the northern tip of Queensland and Papua New Guinea. People are believed to have settled on these islands about 20,000 years ago. Aboriginal peoples have been living on the mainland for at least 65,000 years; archaeologists have uncovered evidence of people living in Arnhem Land in the Northern Territory 65,000 years ago, with ongoing research in other parts of Australia indicating even longer periods.

The Indigenous footprint can be found across the Australian continent and its islands, but it is often invisible until it is pointed out. Once you see the evidence of Aboriginal life, a whole new world opens up. You begin to see the country around you differently. Keen to share their cultural riches, hundreds of Aboriginal people have found ways to invite tourists into their lives, even briefly, to enjoy the experience of being in Aboriginal Country with the people who know it best: the Traditional Owners. With a deep knowledge of the natural world, they are the ideal guides to show you the extraordinary range of environments across the country.

The opportunity for Indigenous Australians to share their experiences and knowledge with tourists opened up when land rights were recognised and Indigenous people became joint managers of large swathes of our Country. Now there are visitors centres, art and cultural centres, museums and festivals in even the most remote places, showcasing the fascinating history and cultures of Indigenous societies.

When you are travelling around Indigenous Australia, you will find yourself in extraordinary situations with extraordinary people, whether you are exploring by foot, vehicle, boat, horse or camel; in semi-arid areas such as the Central Desert or the Western Desert; savannah country across north Australia with its many dramatic rock outcrops, escarpments and gorges; the wet rainforests where fast flowing rivers cascade over mountain ranges; the temperate-zone coastal and riverine plains; the forests; the Great Dividing Range in its many forms; on the beaches, islands and reefs; and in the cities and towns.

Indigenous people have established cultural and natural tourism businesses and opened up their Country for tourists with great energy, determination and a love of sharing the beauty of their culture and heritage. Also, the benefits of tourism to local Indigenous people are many. In large parts of Indigenous Australia, where there are few other economic opportunities, tourism businesses are a pathway for local families to enjoy the benefits of their unparalleled ancestral heritage.

With their own tourism projects, local people have the opportunity to work on their Country with their family members. They can also teach their own young people as well as tourists about their culture, history and heritage because Indigenous tourism preserves traditional knowledge and involves the younger generations in its continuation. There are surprises, too, for even the most knowledgeable Traditional Owner. While visiting remote parts of their old estates, where threatened populations were protected from introduced predators and land clearance, Traditional Owners have discovered new species of flora and fauna and surviving pockets of species thought to be extinct.

By Professor Marcia Langton

There are more than 260 Traditional Owner Groups throughout the country, each with their own language and traditions. We have included the name of the Traditional Owners in various entries to acknowledge their ongoing connection to the land, sky and water. Where possible we have included the Traditional Names of locations throughout, following the colonial names.

This text has been extracted and updated from Marcia Langton's *Welcome to Country 2nd Edition* **(2021), where you can find more detailed information about Aboriginal and Torres Strait Islander history and culture as well as a comprehensive list of Indigenous-owned and -operated tourism businesses.**

Garma Festival (*see* p. 168) celebrates Yolŋu life and culture and is Australia's largest First Nations gathering

THE BASICS

Geography

Think of Australia and the 'outback' – a vague notion of remote and dry inland areas – likely springs to mind, but the reality for Australians is that around 87 per cent of the population lives within 50km (31 miles) of the coast, and most of those along the east coast. It's here that the country's three largest cities – Sydney/Warrane, Melbourne/Naarm and Brisbane/Meanjin – are found. Between them, these cities – the state capitals of New South Wales (NSW), Victoria and Queensland respectively – contain half of the Australian population alone. Adelaide/Tandanya (South Australia/SA), Perth/Boorloo (Western Australia/WA) and Hobart/nipaluna (Tasmania) are the other state capital cities, with Darwin/Garramilla being the capital of the Northern Territory (NT). Rivalry between Sydney/Warrane and Melbourne/Naarm in the 19th century led to Canberra/Ngambri/Ngunnawal being purpose-built as the national capital in 1913.

Australia is a massive country – the sixth largest in the world – and the only one to inhabit a full continent. Representing about 5 per cent of the world's land mass, Australia unsurprisingly has a wealth of different landscapes. Almost 20 per cent of the country is covered in desert, but there are also 34,000km (21,127 miles) of coastline and more than 8000 islands. Rainforests range from tropical wonders such as the Daintree in northern Queensland to Tasmania's takayna/Tarkine, the world's second-largest temperate rainforest.

Some of the world's tallest trees grow in Australia (see p. 78), and the beaches are typically as beautiful as they are legendary. Long coral reefs stripe both sides of the nation – the Great Barrier Reef (see p. 108) in the east and Ningaloo Reef (see p. 6) in the west. Its mountains are low on the world scale, with the country's highest peak, Mount Kosciuszko (see p. 27), reaching to just 2228m (7310ft) above sea level, but the primary mountain range, the Great Dividing Range, stretches for more than 3500km (2175 miles) along the east coast.

Climate

Stretching almost 4000km (2485 miles) from north to south, Australia straddles several climate zones. For instance, in the middle of winter, southerly Hobart/nipaluna averages a maximum of around 13ºC (55ºF), while northerly Darwin/Garramilla clocks in at an average of 31ºC (88ºF).

In the tropical north (Queensland, NT and northern WA), the best time for travel is around the winter months (roughly May to September), when conditions are at their most comfortable and the dry season is in full swing – it's still warm enough for swims, but dry enough for travel.

In the country's south, summers (December to February) blaze brightly, filling beaches with bodies and outdoor restaurants and bars with patrons. This is no time to hit the deserts, with temperatures routinely exceeding 40°C (104°F), while the north is awash in monsoon rains. Winter travel has its own beauty, even in the south (albeit minus the swims for all but the bravest), with winter menus and fireside venues warming the experience.

Top **Climbing the stairs to view the Twelve Apostles**
Bottom **Overlooking Tasmania's Cradle Mountain**

DISTANCE COUNTS

In a country as large as Australia, journeys are everything. It takes more than five hours to fly from Sydney/Warrane to Perth/Boorloo (about the same time as a flight from London to Cairo or New York to Mexico City). Attempt it by land and it's a drive of nearly 4000km (2485 miles), or a four-day journey on the *Indian Pacific* railway (see p. 294).

Amid such distances, road trips are a way of life for Australians, with even a drive from Melbourne/Naarm to Adelaide/Tandanya – the state capitals in closest proximity to each other – taking more than eight hours. But every big drive can become a great drive, with the country laced with scenic and revealing roads. Here are some of Australia's best driving routes:

✱ **Great Ocean Road (Victoria):** The most famous drive of all – a seaside spectacular along 240km (150 miles) of coastline between Torquay to Warrnambool.

✱ **Pacific Coast (NSW and Queensland):** A 1000km (621-mile) drive from Sydney to Brisbane past the Hunter Valley vineyards, Byron Bay and the Gold Coast.

✱ **Nullarbor Plain (SA and WA):** The stuff of outback legend – 1200 largely treeless kilometres (746 miles) populated by roadhouses, cliffs, migrating whales and the world's longest golf course (see p. 182).

✱ **Red Centre Way (NT):** Better red than, well, almost anything on this 1100km (683-mile) loop out from Alice Springs/Mparntwe to Uluṟu (see p. 81), Kings Canyon (see p. 35) and the waterhole-studded Tjoritja/West MacDonnell Ranges (see p. 297).

✱ **Explorers Way (SA and NT):** Go top to toe on this 3000km (1864-mile) outback continental crossing from Darwin/Garramilla to Adelaide/Tandanya.

✱ **Gibb River Road (WA):** 4WDing at its best on this gorge-lined 880km (547-mile) connection from Broome to Kununurra in the evocative Kimberley.

Be wary of cassowaries on Cape Tribulation roads!

Opposite **The Twelve Apostles viewed along the Great Ocean Road**

DRIVING SAFETY TIPS

* Keep an eye on that fuel gauge. Roadhouses (outback petrol stations) can be 200–300km (125–185 miles) apart, especially in the west.

* Break up long drives with regular rest stops – it's recommended to stop at least every two hours when driving. Highways and major roads in Australia are dotted with dedicated rest stops (often a roadside pull-out with a toilet and perhaps a picnic table).

* One of the greatest hazards on Australian roads is wildlife, particularly around dawn and dusk. Try to avoid driving at these times, especially in outback areas; if you must drive at these times, reduce your speed and be hyper-alert to wandering wildlife.

* Slow down on unsealed roads and be prepared for corrugations.

* Large trucks are plentiful on Australian roads, including 'road trains', which, in remote areas, can contain up to four trailers and be up to 60m (200ft) in length. Give them space and plenty of respect.

* If travelling remote, carry spare drinking water in case of emergency.

* Electric vehicle owners take note – more and more roadhouses are armed with charging stations; however, always check locations and plan ahead for long distance drives.

Swimming is a national pastime

SWIM SAFELY

* Swimming is arguably the most Australian of all activities, with white sands, blue seas and red-hot temperatures luring locals and visitors to the country's multitude of beaches. In 2024 alone, however, more than 300 people drowned in Australia. Avoid becoming a statistic.

* Swim at beaches patrolled by lifesavers (themselves an iconic staple of Australian beaches) and always swim between the red and yellow flags on these beaches – these are the patrolled areas.

* Learn to identify a 'rip' – currents that run fast from beaches back into the ocean – which cause even strong swimmers to struggle against their force. Rips are often darker in colour than the water around them and form a break in the waves. If you see a 'Dangerous Current' sign, it usually indicates the presence of a rip.

* Shark attacks are rare but real. Some beaches have shark nets for extra safety. Otherwise, avoid swimming near river mouths or at dusk.

* If you're stung by a jellyfish, remove any stingers or tentacles and pour warm water over the stings (take a shower if you can). The tiny Irukandji jellyfish is found in the waters of northern Australia, typically from around November to May. Its sting can be life-threatening, so wear a full-piece Lycra swimsuit if snorkelling on the Great Barrier Reef (reef tour boats often supply these suits) or swimming in tropical waters. If stung, douse the area in vinegar (bottles of which are found on many northern beaches) and call the emergency number (000) for an ambulance.

* In northern Australia, pay heed to yellow crocodile warning signs. If there is a sign, there's a chance of crocs in the water, so don't even think about swimming.

Pop Culture

Once a nation with a White Australia policy to actively prevent non-European immigration, Australia has matured into a melting pot of nationalities and cultures alongside the original First Nations populations (*see* p. x). Almost 30 per cent of Australians were born overseas, and people from almost every nation on Earth now call Australia home. These 7.7 million foreign-born residents, and the earlier migrants that preceded them, have had profound influences on Australian culture. Where international dining once meant little more than a Friday evening trip to the local Chinese restaurant, today the many and varied flavours of the world are the cornerstone of local dining.

Melbourne/Naarm has often been referred to as the largest Greek city outside of Athens and Thessaloniki, while Italian migration has been the bedrock of Australia's celebrated coffee culture.

Pub rock and stadium concerts bring world-class live music to every city, while festivals range from one of the world's largest LGBTIQ+ celebrations to ute musters (*see* p. 167), kelpie capers (*see* p. 158) and a First Nations festival of light (Parrtjima, *see* p. 175).

Cultural Festivals of Australia

Jan: Parkes Elvis Festival (*see* p. 164)
Jan/Feb: Sydney Lunar New Year (*see* p. 174)
Feb: Sydney Gay and Lesbian Mardi Gras (*see* p. 156)
Aug: Garma Festival (*see* p. 168)
Sept/Oct: Desert Mob (*see* p. 171)

AFL

When you hear a crowd of sports fans yelling 'ball' and a team scoring a point for missing a goal, you know you've entered the baffling world of Australian Rules Football (or AFL). Resembling organised chaos to the uninitiated, this home-grown sport is most popular in the southern states – Victoria, South Australia and Tasmania, along with Western Australia – though there are teams from Queensland and NSW in the 18-team national league.

The rules are as intricate and unique as the high-flying marks (catches) and handballs (punching the ball off one hand to pass it to a teammate), but it's unquestionably one of the most athletic games in the world. Take the time to understand it and you too might end up screaming 'ball' (calling for a free kick for a 'holding the ball' infringement) with tribal fervour among 90,000 footy fans at the 'G' (Melbourne Cricket Ground, or MCG).

The men's AFL season runs from March to September, while the ever-growing women's AFLW competition runs from around September to November.

CLASSIC AUSSIE MOVIES

The Castle (1997): One family's fight to save their home from an airport expansion – everything will be about 'the vibe' once you've seen it.

Ten Canoes (2007): The first Australian feature film entirely in a First Nations language, starring the late and great Yolŋu actor David Gulpilil.

Mad Max: Fury Road (2015): A dusty, futuristic dystopia that some call the greatest action movie ever made.

The Adventures of Priscilla, Queen of the Desert (1994): Three drag queens road tripping through the outback.

They're a Weird Mob (1966): An Italian migrant's comedic experience in trying to understand Australians.

Gettin' Square (2003): You'll never hear the slap of a thong (flip-flop) the same way again.

Top **Garma Festival**
Bottom **The eponymous Priscilla is driven through the outback in style in *The Adventures of Priscilla, Queen of the Desert***

BEST OF AUSTRALIA

Australia's Big Things
2
Glorious Wildlife
4
Road Trip: Pilbara and Ningaloo
6
Road Trip: Way out West
8

AUSTRALIA'S BIG THINGS

Everything's big in ... well, the Australian roadside. This is a nation that has a distinct fondness for creating larger-than-life replicas – big animals, big birds, big fruit – and plonking them down as roadside attractions. There are more than 200 big things across the nation, breaking up drives and often defying belief. There was even a new 'big' – the Big Tractor at 11.5m high and 16m long – unveiled in the WA town of Carnamah in late 2024.

Here are a few of the biggest and best to get your collection started.

Big Pineapple (Woombye, Queensland)
Arguably the most famous of the bigs, it was once claimed as Australia's most popular tourist attraction – standing 16m (52ft) high beside a pineapple plantation. Also home to a train, zoo, high-ropes course and zip line.

Big Banana (Coffs Harbour, NSW)
Motorists have been keeping their eyes peeled for the 13m (43-ft) banana beside the Pacific Highway since 1964. Starting life as an eye-catching gimmick for a banana stand, it's now a full-on fun park – think water slides, ice-skating rink, escape rooms and laser tag, for starters.

Big Gumboot (Tully, Queensland)
The 7.9m (26-ft) Golden Gumboot in the centre of Tully represents the 7.9m (26ft) of rain that fell on the town – one of a couple of claimants for the title of Australia's wettest town – in 1950.

Big Bulls (Rockhampton, Queensland)
Not one, not two, but six stocky bulls dotted around 'Rockie', celebrating its claim to be Australia's beef capital. Thieves have made a habit of castrating the bulls' balls.

Big Potato (Robertson, NSW)
Kindly people accept this 10m (33ft) replica as a potato, but others have drawn more critical comparison to a turd. We think they have a point.

Big Prawn (Ballina, NSW)
To 'come the raw prawn' is part of the Aussie lexicon, so why not really come to the prawn? This well-crafted, 9m (30-ft) crustacean atop a hardware store is one of the more elegant of the 'big' oeuvre.

Big Cassowary (Mission Beach, Queensland)
The colourful cassowary, the world's second-heaviest bird, can be difficult to find in the wild, but it can't be missed as you drive through Wongaling Beach, where there's a 5m (16.4-ft) model.

Big Galah (Kimba, SA)
Another day, another gargantuan bird. This 8m (26-ft) fibreglass galah stands outside a gem shop at the midpoint of the long drive between Sydney/Warrane and Perth/Boorloo.

Big Merino (Goulburn, NSW)
This 15.2m (50-ft) sheep, affectionately known as Rambo, might appear to have several chins, but it's the eyes that are key to its appeal. Climb inside and you can peer out of them across the world.

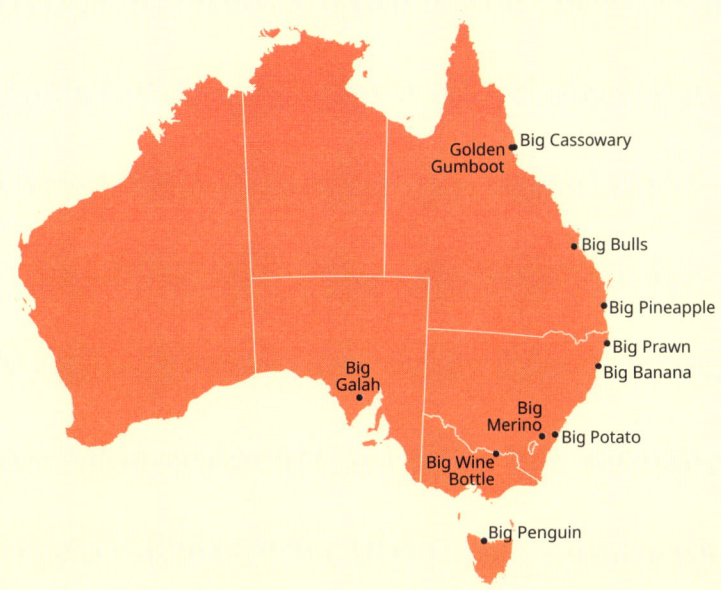

DAGGY

If there's an Australia term that best describes Big Things (and our confusing obsession with them), it's daggy. To be a dag, or to be daggy, is to be un-cool in a kind of lovable way. While the word's origins aren't quite as lovable (we'll leave you to discover that on your own), to be daggy is to embrace the un-coolness in all of us.

Big Penguin (Penguin, Tasmania)
More Pingu than penguin, this cartoonish statue of a little penguin is suitably quite small as the genre goes – just over 3m (10ft) high. It's often dressed in different costumes, though ironically the town of Penguin is one of the few spots along this coastline where little penguins don't come ashore.

Big Wine Bottle (Rutherglen, Victoria)
Repurposing at its best, this is a 36m (118-ft) brick water tower built in 1900 and later zhooshed up with a mesh top to resemble a wine bottle. Fitting for a town noted for its fortified-wine production.

The Big Merino in Goulburn

GLORIOUS WILDLIFE

If any world star is in need of a PR makeover, it's Australia's wildlife. There are plenty of visitors who arrive believing the country is crawling with risk – snakes, crocodiles, sharks, jellyfish and spiders – but the statistics tell otherwise. An average of just two people die from a snakebite each year, and since European settlement there's been one death from shark attack on average per year. This in a nation of 26 million people.

Respect the animals' power and presence, and be mindful of safety, but also admire their beauty and mystique.

Snakes
Coming across snakes on walking trails isn't uncommon, but encounters that go beyond sightings are. Snakes aren't naturally aggressive, and most bites occur when people try to pick them up or kill them. If you see a snake, leave it alone. Once it's alert to your presence, it will likely dart away. If it's having a particularly pleasant sunbake and doesn't notice you, make a bit of noise, stay at least a couple of metres away, enjoy the sighting and wait till it moves on.

Crocodiles
Saltwater (or estuarine) crocodiles are found throughout the waterways and coastline of northern Australia – from around Broome in the west to Gladstone in the east. There's an old maxim that you should never go to the water's edge at the same spot twice in crocodile country, but a more effective solution is to never approach the edge at all.

Irukandji Jellyfish
Those bottles of vinegar you might see on north Queensland beaches aren't for your chips. They're for the treatment of stings from Irukandji, a small venomous box jellyfish found along the northern Australian coast from November to May. When snorkelling on the Great Barrier, wear a full-piece Lycra suit to avoid stings (tour boats provide them). If stung, douse the area with vinegar and call an ambulance.

Furry Friends
Australia's collection of native critters is a big part of the country's charm, and spying a kangaroo, koala, wombat or platypus is atop the travel wish list for many visitors. There's no way to guarantee a sighting, but head to any of the following and the chances are very good:

Koalas
– Kangaroo Island (SA)
– Magnetic Island (Queensland)
– Noosa National Park (Queensland)
– Port Macquarie (NSW)

Wombats
– Maria Island National Park (Tasmania)
– Cradle Mountain (Tasmania)
– Wilsons Promontory National Park (Victoria)
– Kangaroo Valley (NSW)

Kangaroos
– Narawntapu National Park (Tasmania)
– Kangaroo Island ... of course (SA)
– Halls Gap (Victoria)
– Mungo National Park (NSW)

For roos on beaches, *see* p. 94.
For the best platypus possibilities, *see* p. 107.

Top **Kangaroo Island is a great place to spot koalas**
Bottom **Look out for crocodiles in Kakadu National Park**

ROAD TRIP

PILBARA AND NINGALOO

String together the planet's longest fringing reef with some of the country's most deeply etched gorges and the world's largest concentration of rock art on an 1800km (1120-mile) loop through the red sands and blue seas of Western Australia's Pilbara and Ningaloo Reef regions.

Murujuga National Park
On the tendril-thin Burrup Peninsula, Murujuga National Park contains countless First Nations petroglyphs, among them human figures and extinct animals including thylacines (Tasmanian tigers) that once roamed the mainland – it's the greatest concentration of rock art on the planet.

Exmouth

Exmouth is the gateway to Ningaloo Reef, one of the largest fringing reefs in the world. This means a mere step or two from the shoreline can have you snorkelling among a plethora of marine life. From March through September, whale sharks also cruise the waters of Ningaloo. If you're a diver, Exmouth's Navy Pier is one of Australia's best shore dives.

Yardie Creek

Though overshadowed by the World Heritage–listed reef just offshore, Cape Range National Park is framed in glorious beaches (don't miss Turquoise Bay) and chiselled with canyons and gorges. The cape road ends at Yardie Creek, where walking trails and a boat tour head along or beneath the cliffs of the gorge.

Coral Bay

Step straight off the beach into flourishing coral gardens at this small holiday town at the southern end of Ningaloo Reef. Its name comes from the amazing coral to be found in the waters here, and if you head deeper into the ocean there is plenty of marine wildlife to witness.

Tom Price

Western Australia's highest town (747m/2451ft above sea level) is a mining centre with a sideline in national parks. Tour an open-cut iron-ore mine and climb Mount Nameless/Jarndunmunha at the edge of town for vast views over the Pilbara plains before heading into Karijini.

Millstream-Chichester National Park

Winter wildflowers aplenty and spring-fed pools such as Python Pool and Deep Reach/Nhanggangunha (a sacred place that's home to the serpent Warlu in Ngarluma and Yindjibarndi stories) for cooling swims in this oasis on the red plains.

Karijini National Park

Australia's greatest cluster of gorges – deep in the earth and deep in colour – is found inside this remote and spectacular park. Delve into seven distinct gorges to find waterfalls, swim holes and scrambling challenges, all in the shadow of WA's highest mountains.

PLAN AHEAD

After rain, roads into Millstream Chichester National Park can be unpassable to 2WD vehicles, so check ahead at the park office (08 9814 5144) or the online Shire of Ashburton road report. ashburton.wa.gov.au/community/travel/road-report.aspx

Ningaloo Reef

ROAD TRIP

WAY OUT WEST

In the far west of NSW, things get wonderful, wild and sometimes weird. Immerse yourself in the outback with a 2000km (1240-mile) road trip to the very edge of the Never Never, finding the back o' Bourke and rolling through landscapes that don't just appear cinematic – they've starred on the big screen numerous times.

Dubbo
Start on the Great Western Plains, 390km (242 miles) inland from Sydney. On the drive ahead, you'll see copious wildlife – kangaroos, emus, eagles, feral goats.

Warrumbungle National Park
Summits by day, stars by night as you hike to craggy, sharp-tipped peaks – the plugs of extinct volcanoes – with names like the Breadknife and Grand High Tops inside Australia's first Dark Sky Park.

Lightning Ridge
Opal-mining towns are a world unto themselves, filled with characters and quirks. Lightning Ridge is famed for its black opals, but you'll also find sculptures inside a mine, fossicking areas for a spot of noodling, an isolated pub smack dab in the middle of an opal field and subterranean living.

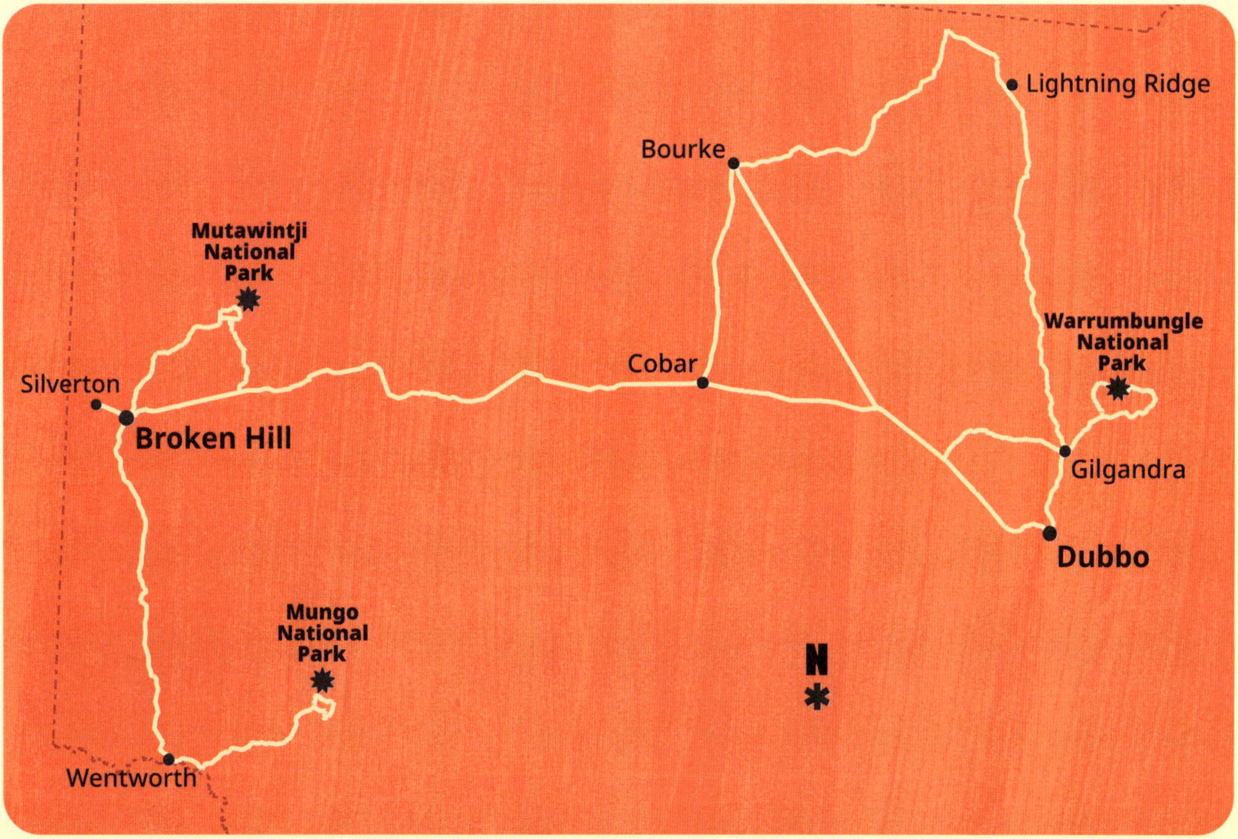

Sandstone sculptures, Broken Hill
Opposite The Breadknife, Warrumbungle National Park

Bourke
Australians have a saying for the most remote of outback country: the back o' Bourke. Make claims to having been there with a stop in Bourke, where you can take a First Nations cultural tour through town and indulge in outback stories at the Back O' Bourke Exhibition Centre.

Mutawintji National Park
Explore red gorges and rockholes on foot, and sign on for a First Nations-led tour into Mutawintji Historic Site for an exclusive look at some of the finest and most extensive rock art in NSW.

Broken Hill
Made by mining (hence that huge mullock pile in the middle of town) and since claimed by movie makers and artists, Broken Hill is the epitome of an outback town, at least until you discover that art galleries outnumber pubs.

Silverton
The ghost(ish) town at Broken Hill's edge feels like the last stop on Earth when you stand atop Mundi Mundi Lookout and note the curvature of the planet along the horizon. The photos on the pub walls and the presence of the Mad Max 2 Museum (*see* p. 241) attest to Silverton's fame as a movie starlet.

Mungo National Park

The clay pinnacles that rise so spectacularly from the Walls of China sand dunes are only the second most fascinating thing at Mungo. In these dunes, the oldest-known human remains in Australia – around 42,000 years old – were discovered. Wander the dunes on a parks-led tour.

Wentworth

Australia's two longest and greatest rivers – the Murray and the Darling – meet in what was once Australia's busiest inland river port. Climb the tower to view the confluence and then contemplate your onward journey – roads radiate from here to Adelaide/Tandanya, Melbourne/Naarm and Sydney/Warrane. Take your pick.

Top **A lone tree in Mutawintji National Park**
Bottom **Emus near Silverton**
Opposite **Lightning Ridge**

14	A Sandy Home
17	Nulla-Boring?
18	Hiking Through Australia's Largest Island National Park
20	Simply Gorge-ous
22	Australia's Only Real Mountain?
23	An Urban Gorge
24	Sleep a Night Over the Reef
27	Climb Australia's Highest Mountain
30	The White Album
32	Australia's Other Monolith
33	The Other MacDonnells
35	The King of Canyons
37	Beyond the Blue
38	Coast of Fire and Water
40	Accessible National Park Trails
42	Australia's Largest National Park
43	Think Pink
44	Sensational Swims of Litchfield
46	The Nature of Cities
51	SUP through the Outback
52	Great Hiking Expectations
54	The Turning of the Fagus

"The river is bringing us back to a normal relationship with the world"

56	Sydney/Warrane's Secret Garden
57	Soak in the Snow
58	A 'Sunday Session
60	Tall Falls
61	Stone Surf
62	Gorging on Walks and Water
64	Mungo Magic
66	Made in Australis
67	Glowing Ghost Mushrooms
68	Art and Nature
71	Blooming Good
72	In the Flow on the Franklin
75	Capital Beaches
76	The Green Behind the Gold
78	Tall Timber
79	The Giving Gorge
80	Next Door to Uluṟu
81	The Pinnacle of Landscapes
82	Pounds and Craters
84	The Lord of Islands
86	The Beehive Bungles
87	Catching the Tube

A SANDY HOME

K'GARI, QUEENSLAND
BUTCHULLA COUNTRY

To Butchulla woman Aunty Joyce Bonner, the meaning of K'gari is simple: home. 'Home amongst my people, the descendants, the ancestors, the Midiru, the Traditional Owners,' she says. 'It's our place. It's what we call home.'

Masquerading under the name Fraser Island for almost 200 years, the world's largest sand island – 123km (76 miles) from tip to toe – was returned to the Butchulla in 2022, reverting at the same time to its traditional Butchulla name of K'gari. Pronounced 'gurrie', the name comes from the Butchulla People's creation story for the World Heritage–listed island, which is almost entirely composed of sand dunes. This is no barren, sandy desert, however. This is a sandy wonderland where rainforest grows up to 50m (164ft) tall, with more than 100 lakes pooled in its sand.

Protected as K'gari, Great Sandy National Park, the island has long been a favourite 4WD destination, with visitors exploring its sandy tracks and beaches (4WDs are available for hire in Hervey Bay, the mainland town, 300km (186 miles) north of Brisbane, with ferry connections to the island).

Half the world's perched lakes (lakes that sit atop compacted sand) are found on K'gari, with some of the clearest water on Earth – most are pure rainwater. The collection includes stunning Boorangoora/Lake Mckenzie, Lake Boomanjin (the world's largest perched lake) and Lake Wabby (K'gari's deepest lake). You can go with the flow at Eli Creek, drifting downstream on your back in the gin-clear water, and effervesce in the seaside Champagne Pools, which get a bubbly, Jacuzzi-like effect when aerated by waves breaking over the rock pools.

The rusted wreck of the *Maheno*, a ship that beached on K'gari in 1935, is another favourite stop along the ocean beaches for 4WDers. From August to October, these same beaches might also provide glimpses of passing humpback whales.

Walkers too find ample reward on K'gari's sands. You might connect the lake dots with a 12km (7.5-mile) hike (one-way) from Boorangoora/Lake Mckenzie to Lake Wabby, wander through these rainforests somehow growing from sand in the Valley of the Giants or set out on the 90km (56-mile) K'gari Great Walk (*see* p. 52), threading between the island's lakes and beaches.

And with the handover of the island to the Butchulla, watch this space for new and deeper opportunities to engage with the island and its people. 'I think what we should share with visitors is the richness and the culture of our peoples and what it means to the Butchulla People, and be connected as the Butchulla people are to it,' says Butchulla elder Uncle Boyd Blackman. 'To take that away – it is something you can't buy in a shop; it's something that is given to the people by the Butchulla People.'

parks.desi.qld.gov.au/parks/kgari-fraser

❋ DOG DAYS ON K'GARI

Among the enduring images of K'gari are its dingoes (wongari), readily seen across the island and its campgrounds. Inhabiting K'gari for thousands of years, the dingoes are wild animals and need to be treated with respect. Stay dingo-safe by following these few guidelines:

- ❋ Stay at least 20m (66ft) from dingoes.
- ❋ Carry a stick (or hiking pole or umbrella) to deter dingoes from approaching.
- ❋ Don't feed dingoes, and don't picnic or eat on lakeshores or the beach.
- ❋ Don't run; this can trigger a dingo's instinct to chase.
- ❋ Don't walk alone on the island.

Beach driving in K'gari

Top **The flat expanse of the Nullarbor Plain**
Bottom **The spectacular Head of Bight cliffs**

NULLA-BORING?

◉ NULLARBOR PLAIN, SA & WA
MIRNING & YINYILA COUNTRY

Some people will tell you that the nature of the Nullarbor Plain is betrayed by the name itself – a bore. Don't believe them. Sure, it's a long journey – 1200km (746 miles) between Ceduna and Norseman – punctuated with fatiguing facts such as the world's longest straight stretch of road (146km/90 miles) and all but treeless much of the way (the name comes from the Latin *nullus* and *arbor*, meaning 'no trees'), but this infamous road trip has subtle variety and multiple reasons to linger.

Head of Bight Cliffs

The Nullarbor ends abruptly at the Head of Bight cliffs, where the planet's largest sandstone plain is seasonally replaced by the ocean's largest creatures. Each year from around June to October, southern right whales are readily seen from the clifftop lookouts at the Head of Bight Visitors Centre. Peak season is July and August, when more than 100 whales can be in the area.

Eyre Bird Observatory

Peeping out of the sand dunes south of Eucla, you'll find the beautiful ruin of the Eucla Telegraph Station, built in 1897. Today it's the centrepiece of the Eyre Bird Observatory, the oldest bird observatory in Australia. It's open for day visits and has accommodation, and more than 240 bird species have been sighted here.

Caiguna Blowhole

The limestone plain is punctured with more than 250 caves. Poke your head into the Murrawijinie Caves, 10km (6.2 miles) from Nullarbor Roadhouse, and listen to the 'breathing' of Caiguna Blowhole, an exhalation caused by changes in air pressure – air has been recorded exiting the cave at up to 72km/h (43 mph).

Balladonia

One night in 1979, Australia paused, anxious in the knowledge that NASA's Skylab space station was likely to crash to Earth somewhere in the country. Ultimately, it came down near the Nullarbor stop of Balladonia, where the motel now has a museum devoted to the nervous night.

HIKING THROUGH AUSTRALIA'S LARGEST ISLAND NATIONAL PARK

◉ **HINCHINBROOK ISLAND NATIONAL PARK, QUEENSLAND**
BANDJIN & GIRRAMAY COUNTRY

Towering out of the Coral Sea, midway between Cairns and Townsville, Hinchinbrook Island/Munamudanamy is Australia's largest island national park. The traditional land of the Bandjin and Girramay People, it rises to 1121m (3678ft) above sea level, making it also the highest island (outside of Australia's Antarctic islands) in Australia and holds one of the country's largest stands of mangroves.

They're impeccable natural credentials, enhanced by the presence of one of Australia's most rewarding bushwalking trails. Typically walked over four days, the 32km (20-mile) Thorsborne Trail is as close to a beach holiday in boots as Australia delivers. Stringing together half a dozen beaches, it's a tropical idyll with a single tropical drawback – the yellow crocodile warning signs that dot the trail and keep overheated walkers out of the otherwise tempting seas.

If it sounds like a tease, fear not. Step off the coast, as the trail does between beaches, and croc-free waterfalls and waterholes await. Campsites at Zoe Bay and Mulligan Falls (typical second- and third-night stops for walkers) are steps from cooling swims, the top of Zoe Falls is like a series of natural infinity pools and keen eyes might uncover the hidden-in-plain-sight Blue Pools beside the trail as it approaches Zoe Bay.

Ferries service the trail from Lucinda (home to the longest jetty – 5.76km/ 3.58 miles – in the Southern Hemisphere) and Cardwell, and hikers must camp each night along the trail. With only 40 people allowed on the island at a time, sites are snapped up fast. They can be booked up to six months ahead at qpws.usedirect.com/QPWS.

◉ parks.des.qld.gov.au/parks/hinchinbrook

Top **Hinchinbrook Island National Park**
Bottom left **Visitors can swim in idyllic, croc-free freshwater pools**
Bottom right **Mulligan Falls**

SIMPLY GORGE-OUS

📍 KARIJINI NATIONAL PARK, WA
BANYJIMA, INNAWONGA & KURRAMA COUNTRY

Outback gorges have a singular beauty. Typically lined with towering red cliffs and filled with waterholes as cold as the desert air is hot, they're the inground pools of the interior, and no place has a more spectacular collection of these fabulous fissures than Karijini National Park.

Western Australia's second-largest national park, covering an area one-tenth the size of Tasmania, might hold the state's highest mountains, but its true beauty spots are hidden in the cracks beneath, with seven gorges creating a subterranean labyrinth of shaded chasms. Each one is similar, and yet each one is also distinctive and unique. My recommendation for finding the best national park in the country is to take the time to explore them all – it's a 300km (186-mile) drive here from the coast at Port Hedland, so why hurry things after making that effort?

At the heart of the Pilbara park is a cluster of gorges near the Karijini Eco Retreat, run by the Gumala Aboriginal Corporation, serving the Traditional Banyjima, Kurrama and Innawonga Traditional Owners. Among them is Jijingunha, aka Joffre Gorge, one of the deepest of the park's chasms, entered by descending a long series of ladders to the edge of a waterhole, where you can swim downstream, then scramble briefly upstream into a wide amphitheatre with a seasonal waterfall (less gymnastically, there's also a lookout platform high above on the rim of the gorge).

Two of Karijini's signature scenes – Kermit Pool and Handrail Pool – are also among this cluster of gorges, though both make you work to witness them. Inside Hancock Gorge, small Kermit Pool is reached after swimming along a short channel and then descending through the Spider Walk – a slot canyon so narrow that you need to use your hands and feet like a bridge between its walls.

Handrail Pool, inside near Weano Gorge, is approached through another narrow, water-polished slot canyon, which suddenly widens into a large circular pool (reached by descending the cliffs on the said handrail).

Karijini's other signature scene – Spa Pool – is at far-flung Minthukundi/Hamersley Gorge, squeezed into the national park's north-west corner. Beneath cliffs that have been spectacularly bent, upturned and folded by geological forces, there's a great swimming hole at the base of the main waterfall, though the tear-shaped, waterfall-fed stunner that is Spa Pool sits above this main waterfall, requiring a swim across a larger pool or a scramble around its edges.

The best swims in the park are arguably in visitor-favourite Dales Gorge, home to the park's only permanent waterfall. Here, the Gorge Rim Walk provides an overhead perspective on the gorge, while a pair of pools beckon as an escape from the inevitable heat. One is at the foot of Jubula/Fortescue Falls, while a few minutes walk upstream is Jubura/Fern Pool. A swimming platform was installed at Jubura/Fern Pool in 2022, but note that this pool is a site of immense significance to the Traditional Owners, so please treat it with respect.

Book well ahead to stay at either the Karijini Eco Retreat or the popular Dales Campground – online bookings for the latter's 140 sites (parks.dbca.wa.gov.au/park-stay) open six months ahead.

exploreparks.dbca.wa.gov.au/park/karijini-national-park

Top **Weano Gorge**
Bottom **Swimming at Karijini**

AUSTRALIA'S ONLY REAL MOUNTAIN?

⊙ SOUTHWEST NATIONAL PARK, TASMANIA
PALAWA COUNTRY

Hundreds of millions of years ago, long before humans roamed the Earth, Australia's mountains stood as high as the Himalayas. Worn down by time and erosion, Australia is now the lowest continent on the planet, leading the Everest-conquering Sir Edmund Hillary to once declare Federation Peak as 'Australia's only real mountain'.

This ominous summit tops out at just 1224m (4016ft) above sea level, but is considered the most challenging climb for hikers in the country. It's not an ascent for the faint-hearted, ending in a rock scramble through the face of the peak, peering directly between your legs to Lake Geeves, around 600m (1969ft) below.

The standard hiking approach is from Farmhouse Creek, 100km (62 miles) south of Hobart/nipaluna, and it's a muddy, overgrown battle just to reach the mountain, let alone make the climb.

For a simpler glimpse that'll still give you a gulp, 'Fedders' is often passed on Par Avion flights to Melaleuca (Southwest National Park), or it can be distantly seen on a fine day from atop Hartz Peak or kunanyi/Mount Wellington.

Federation Peak is Australia's toughest climb
Opposite **Cataract Gorge**

AN URBAN GORGE

◉ LAUNCESTON, TASMANIA
PALAWA COUNTRY

Few world cities can boast the presence of a natural feature as dramatic as Cataract Gorge just 1km (0.6 miles) from the doors of its city-centre stores. But walk 15 minutes from Launceston mall, ducking beneath the 1864 wrought-iron Kings Bridge, and urban life suddenly feels aeons away.

It's here that the South Esk River squeezes for 5km (3.1 miles) between dolerite cliffs, briefly opening wide at First Basin, a natural amphitheatre with extensive lawns, a public swimming pool, restaurant and the world's longest single-span chairlift (457m/1500ft) whirring from bank to bank.

Walking trails run along both banks, wriggling through to Duck Reach, where a defunct power station drove the Southern Hemisphere's first electric street lights in 1896. And when Hydro Tasmania releases water from the upstream Trevallyn Dam, the gorge becomes one of Australia's most powerful white-water kayaking runs.

For a First Nations perspective on the gorge and its cultural significance, book a walking tour with kooparoona niara Tours.

SLEEP A NIGHT OVER THE REEF

◉ GREAT BARRIER REEF, QUEENSLAND
NGARO–GURENG GURENG COUNTRY & ALL FIRST NATIONS IN BETWEEN

Sure, you can spend the day diving on, or snorkelling over, the Great Barrier Reef, but when night falls and the crowds have sailed back to the mainland, the reef remains a marine spectacle for a lucky few.

Experience it after dark at Reefsuites, Australia's first underwater accommodation that also comes with an Advanced Eco Certification from Ecotourism Australia. Reefsuites' two rooms dangle 4m (13ft) beneath the Reefworld Pontoon on Hardy Reef, around 40km (25 miles) offshore from the Whitsunday Islands (and home to the much-photographed Heart Reef). Each room has a wall of floor-to-ceiling windows, glass panels in the floor, and a glass-walled bathroom, providing an endless view of the antics of reef life, from colourful shoals of fish drawing past the windows like curtains to languid turtles and resident grouper, George.

By day, the pontoon is busy with visitors, but when the tour boats leave in the middle of the afternoon, it becomes an exclusive island for guests, including those in another 12 beds on the ponton deck, where there's also a bar for that cherished reef sundowner.

Head south and there's another eco-certified reef-sleep opportunity at Lady Musgrave HQ, a pontoon moored off the coral cay of Lady Musgrave Island, the Great Barrier Reef's southernmost island. The three-level, solar- and wind-powered pontoon has eight glamping-style beds on the deck, while the pontoon's underwater observatory converts into a liveaboard-style bunkroom with 20 beds (available for group bookings only) arrayed along the windows. You can even become marine biologist for the day as part of Lady Musgrave Experience's citizen science programs.

◉ cruisewhitsundays.com/experiences/reefsuites
◉ ladymusgraveexperience.com.au/lady-musgrave-hq

Lady Musgrave atoll, Great Barrier Reef

BEST OF THE REST

Sure, Mount Kosciuszko is the tallest peak in the country, but what about going a step further and climbing the tallest in every state?

* **Mount Bogong (Victoria)** At the northern edge of Alpine National Park, 1986m (6516ft) Bogong can be reached on three walking trails. The shortest, Granite Flat, can only be accessed by 4WD, while the Staircase Spur is one of the most sustained climbs in Australia – 1300m (5265ft) of ascent! – which leaves many content to use the Eskdale Spur approach. Allow about six hours.

* **Mount Ossa (Tasmania)** Less famous than nearby Cradle Mountain (Tasmania's fifth-highest peak), but standing taller, 1617m (5305ft) Ossa is a scrambly side climb for hikers on the week-long Overland Track (*see* p. 298) or a lofty goal after an overnight stay at Pelion Hut for walkers on the intersecting Arm River Track.

* **Mount Bartle Frere (Queensland)** Any climb this big is going to be a sweaty slog in the humid Far North Queensland tropics, but that challenge might be nothing on the rain – this 1611m (5285ft) mountain is one of the wettest places on Earth. Allow a couple of days for the ascent.

* **Mount Woodroffe (SA)** This 1435m (4708ft) mountain in the remote Anangu Pitjantjatjara Yankunytjatjara Lands requires a permit to climb, obtained most easily by joining the annual Mount Woodroffe Climb trip run by Adelaide tour company Diverse Travel Australia (diversetravel.com.au).

* **Mount Meharry/Wirlbiwirlbi (WA)** Isolated on the edge of Karijini National Park (*see* p. 20), 1249m (4098ft) Meharry sees few climbers on foot since a 4WD trail runs all the way to the top. Most hikers prefer Mount Bruce/Punurrunha, the second-highest peak in the state, 60km (37 miles) away, with vast views all the way along its wide-open ridge.

CLIMB AUSTRALIA'S HIGHEST MOUNTAIN

◉ KOSCIUSZKO NATIONAL PARK, NSW
NGARIGO & WOLGALU COUNTRY

Reach the summit of Mount Kosciuszko on a quiet day, and you can rightly claim to be the tallest person in Australia. Peeping its head above the main ridge of the Snowy Mountains, it stands 2228m (7310ft) above sea level, making it the highest mountain in the country.

It's not a difficult climb – a road once ran to the summit, and a chairlift now does most of the grunt work, delivering hikers to the start of a steel mesh walkway from the ski village of Thredbo. From here, it's a 13km (8-mile) return hike to the top of the country, heading through snow clearings and around the rim of the cirque above Lake Cootapatamba, the highest lake in Australia (2048m/6719ft). The steepest moments come at the end, as the track climbs above Rawson Pass to the summit and the loftiest view in the land.

A second, longer (18.6km/11.6-mile return) approach to the mountain sets out from the road end at Charlotte Pass, 40km (25 miles) west of Jindabyne, following the old summit road to intersect with the Thredbo track at Rawson Pass. Bikes are permitted as far as Rawson Pass (which has bike racks), and the track is suited to mountain bikes and gravel bikes.

Whichever route you take to 'Kozzie', pay careful attention to the weather forecast and be prepared for sudden and fierce changes in conditions.

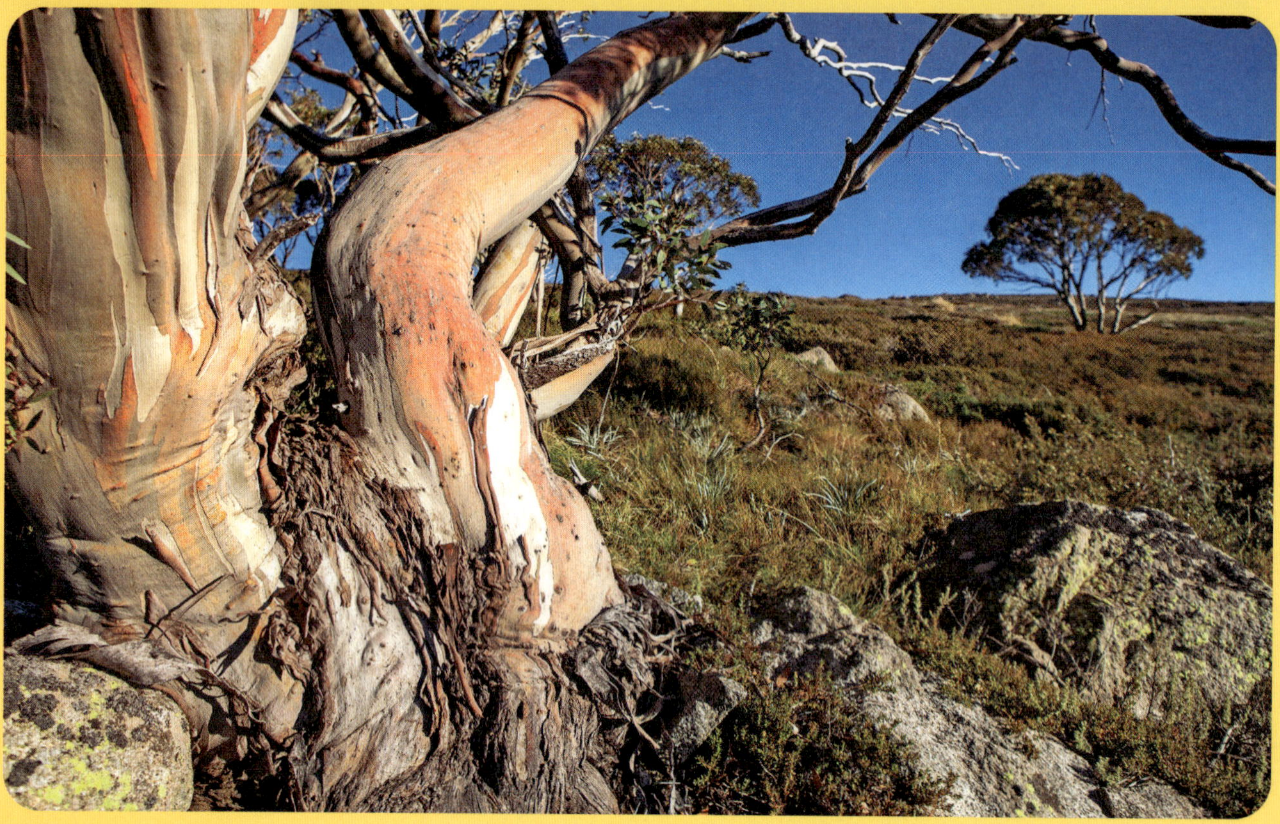

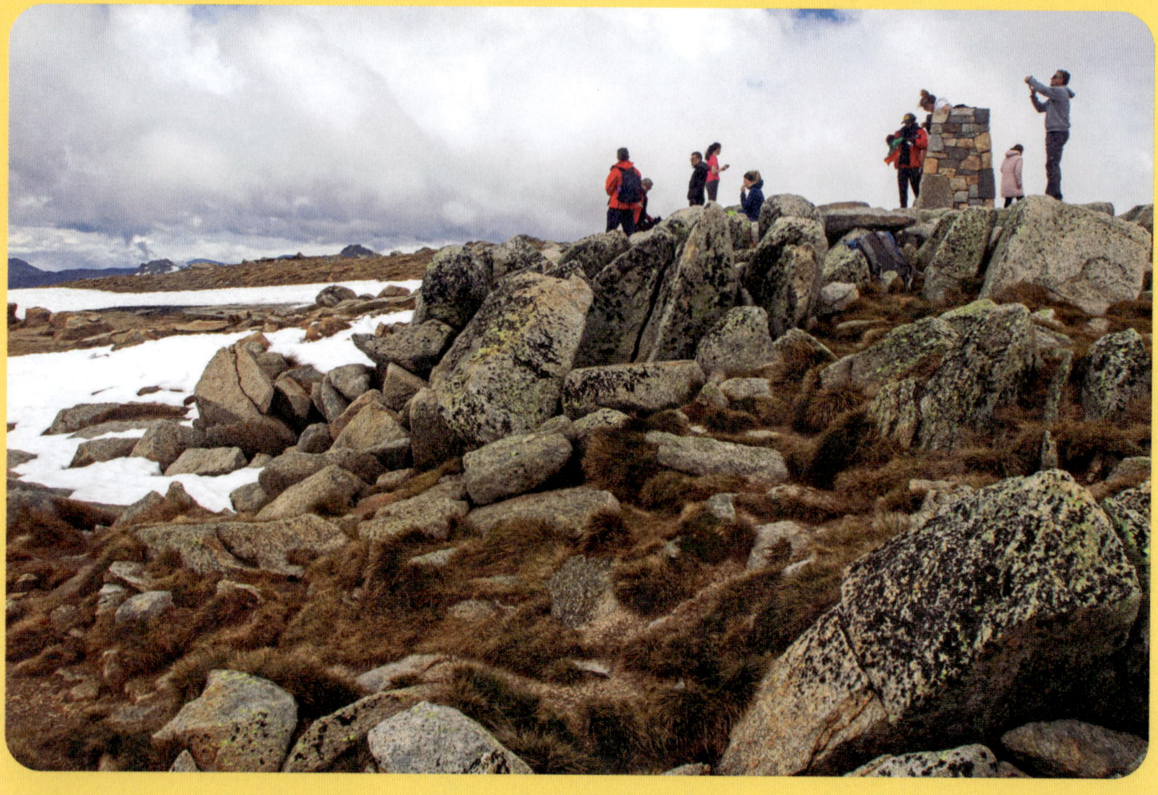

Creek flowing on a high plain in the Snowy Mountains
Opposite top **The distinctive snowy gums mark the landscape**
Opposite bottom **Atop the summit of Mount Kosciuszko**
Previous **The Cootapatamba lookout**

THE WHITE ALBUM

◉ **VARIOUS LOCATIONS**

If Australia overachieves in one thing, it's beaches. More than 10,000 ring the continent, with half of the country's population living within 7km (4.3 miles) of a beach. But not all strands are created equal. The battle to be the country's whitest and brightest beach is hard fought. Here are some of the top contenders.

Whitehaven Beach, Queensland
Popular opinion often rates this Whitsunday Island stunner the fairest and most beautiful of all. Boat trips to the beach depart from Airlie Beach and nearby Shute Harbour. Climb to Hill Inlet Lookout at the beach's northern end for the upstairs perspective.

Hyams Beach, NSW
Once spruiked (erroneously) as Guinness World Records' whitest beach on the planet, Hyams is just one of a rim of pearly whites inside Jervis Bay. The appropriate way to arrive is on the 2.5km (1.6-mile) White Sands Walk from equally dazzling Greenfield Beach.

Wineglass Bay, Tasmania
This Freycinet Peninsula beach once ran red with the blood of whales – it's how it earned its name – but these days it's more like a fine white. Its perfect curve can only be reached on foot (or seen on a boat trip with Wineglass Bay Cruises), and while most walkers ascend only to a lookout platform clipped onto the slopes of the Hazards, 200m (656ft) above the beach, the trail continues down onto the soft white sand, which you might even share with a wallaby or two.

Lucky Bay, WA
In 2017, scientific researchers determined this beach in Cape Le Grand National Park to be Australia's whitest of all. With its turquoise waters and granite headlands, it's gobsmackingly beautiful, and the 15km (9.3-mile) Cape Le Grand Coastal Trail connects it to a string of other white wonders. Lucky, indeed.

The white sand of Hyams Beach

AUSTRALIA'S OTHER MONOLITH

⦿ MOUNT AUGUSTUS NATIONAL PARK, WA
WAJARRI COUNTRY

Don't believe the hype ... Uluru isn't the largest monolith in Australia. The rocky honour of being the largest single stone in the country belongs to little-known Mount Augustus, plugged into the remote red sands of Wajarri Country in the Gascoyne region.

To get here means a drive of at least 350km (217 miles) from the nearest town (Meekatharra), but it's a compelling destination. Stretching more than 8km (5 miles) end to end and rising 715m (2346ft) above the mercilessly flat plains around it, Mount Augustus is more than twice the size of Uluru. In simple terms, this sandstone mountain known to the Wajarri as Burringurrah is the world's largest rock.

A 49km (30-mile) road (suitable for 2WDs) loops around the mountain, providing the full range of perspectives and scenes, with the sandstone changing colour with the march of the day's light. The small, encompassing Mount Augustus National Park also has 11 walking trails, including a challenging summit climb that's open (due to heat) only from March to October (the trailhead closes at 7am in March, April, September and October to prevent hikers from setting out into the heat of the day). Expect to be on the exposed slopes for five to eight hours if making the climb.

Other trails nose into gorges and springs, while the short Petroglyph (200m/0.1-mile return), Ooramboo (550m/0.3-mile return) and Flintstone Rock (650m/0.4-mile return) trails lead to First Nations rock engravings low on the mountain.

⦿ exploreparks.dbca.wa.gov.au/park/mount-augustus-national-park

Looking up at Mount Augustus

THE OTHER MACDONNELLS

◉ EAST MACDONNELL RANGES, NT
EASTERN ARRERNTE COUNTRY

Mention the MacDonnell Ranges and most people automatically think of Tjoritja/West MacDonnell Ranges with their headlining gorges and waterholes, but turn east instead of west and you'll discover a line of desert mountains just as beautiful but so often overlooked in the hurry west to see Standley Chasm/Angkerle Atwatye, Ormiston Gorge/Kwartatuma and company.

Stretching east for 150km (93 miles) from Alice Springs/Mparntwe, the East MacDonnell Ranges are the virtual mirror image of their western counterpart, only without the crowds. The nearest gorge and waterhole to Alice Springs/Mparntwe – Emily Gap – is in these ranges, as is the world's tallest ghost gum, a 33m (108ft) bone-white giant that dwarfs vehicles parked beneath it outside the mouth of Trephina Gorge.

In 2021, the Eastern Arrernte Traditional Owners made the largest-ever investment in infrastructure by a First Nations group in Central Australia, carving out the 8.2km (5-mile) Yeperenye Trail from Emily Gap to neighbouring Jessie Gap. Shared between walkers and mountain bikers, it provides views along the range and over the vast desert plains below, including to Alice Springs Airport's plane storage facility, with the tails of dozens of planes standing above the scrub.

A cultural highlight of the 'East Macs' is Irlwentye, or N'Dhala Gorge Nature Park.

Emily Gap passes through the ranges

Though just 11km (6.8 miles) off Ross Highway, it's accessible only by 4WD and contains around 6000 rock carvings as old as 10,000 years, many seen along a 1.5km (0.9-mile) walking track into the gorge. As anywhere, please respect the sites and don't touch or photograph the carvings.

◉ nt.gov.au/parks/find-a-park/ndhala-gorge-nature-park

Top **The imposing Kings Canyon**
Bottom **Taking a break to enjoy the view**

THE KING OF CANYONS

◉ WATARRKA NATIONAL PARK, NT
LURITJA & MULTITJARRA COUNTRY

The Garden of Eden has an unlikely setting in the parched landscape of central Australia, but delve deep into Kings Canyon and there it grows, a ring of green flourishing in the damp banks of a hidden waterhole (no swimming allowed). Ancient MacDonnell Ranges cycads, a plant that was here when the dinosaurs roamed the planet, add to the primeval image of this biblically named place.

Kings Canyon is a natural hatchet cut more than 1km (0.6 miles) in length and over 100m (328ft) in depth through the western end of the remote George Gill Range in Luritja and Multitjarra Country. The deep-red chasm is one of the Red Centre's most striking natural features, with a beauty that might be even more celebrated were it not hidden behind the back of Uluru.

One of Australia's best day walks makes a 6km (3.7-mile) loop around the clifftops, dipping into the Garden of Eden as it goes. This rim trail begins at the canyon's mouth, setting out immediately up a rock staircase of 400 steps that's known locally as Heart Attack Hill. On days over 36°C (96°F), you're not permitted to start this walk after 9am.

Other walks head inside the canyon along Kings Creek, while there's a sealed, wheelchair-accessible 2.4km (1.5-mile) trail (return) into Kathleen Springs, a waterhole inside Kathleen Gorge, 20km (12.4 miles) east of Kings Canyon.

Another highlight of a Kings Canyon visit is Karrke, a cultural tour run by Luritja woman Christine Breaden and Western Arrernte man Peter Abbott from their home at the edge of Watarrka National Park. A short walk through a series of stations, it's a compact circuit focused on culture and desert survival.

◉ nt.gov.au/parks/find-a-park/watarrka-national-park; karrke.com.au

Top **Umpherston Sinkhole/Balumbul**
Bottom **Blue Lake/Warwar turns a bright shade of blue in summer**

BEYOND THE BLUE

◉ **MOUNT GAMBIER, SA**
BOANDIK COUNTRY

South Australia's second-largest city, Mount Gambier, is famed for its Blue Lake/Warwar, a volcanic crater lake that turns as blue as a peacock every summer, but it's far from the only lake of note in the area. Draw a circle 20km (12 miles) around the city and it encompasses around 95 per cent of Australia's sinkholes.

Created by the erosion of water through the region's porous limestone, these sinkholes are reminiscent of the *cenotes* that dot Mexico's Yucatan Peninsula, which people travel the world to snorkel and dive. Similarly, you can snorkel and dive (the latter requires certification from the Cave Divers Association of Australia) at several sinkholes around Mount Gambier.

Prime among them is Kilsby Sinkhole, hole-punched into a multigenerational family farm 15 minutes drive from the city. Guided snorkelling or diving tours spend an hour in the 27m (89ft) subterranean pool, with its water as clear as gin – appropriate since the Kilsby family also distils its Sinkhole Gin from this water.

Further south, the rainwater that's been trapped within the limestone for thousands of years squeezes back to the surface at Picaninnie Ponds and Ewens Ponds, another pair of magnificent snorkelling sites. At Ewens Ponds, three deep dolines (depressions in the ground) are connected by clear channels. Entering the stream at the first doline, the gentle current carries you through the channels to the final pond.

Prefer to explore a sinkhole on foot? Descend the steps into garden-filled Umpherston Sinkhole/Balumbul and Cave Garden/Thugi, both within Mount Gambier's city limits. And if you just want a swim, do as the locals do and head out of town to Little Blue Lake, another crater lake 17km (10.6 miles) out of town that all but doubles as the city public pool on hot days.

◉ kilsbysinkhole.com; parks.sa.gov.au/parks/ewens-ponds-conservation-park

COAST OF FIRE AND WATER

BAY OF FIRES CONSERVATION AREA, TASMANIA
PALAWA COUNTRY

Take one look at the Bay of Fires beaches along Tasmania's north-east coast and it seems certain that they were named for the fiery blazes of orange lichen smeared across their headlands and boulders. But they weren't. This dazzling stretch of white beaches and azure seas was named by British explorer Tobias Furneaux for the number of palawa (Tasmanian Aboriginal) fires burning along the coast as he sailed past in 1773.

Running in an arc from Binalong Bay to larapuna/Eddystone Point, the Bay of Fires is a seamless progression of bays, beaches and granite headlands. Stretching behind it, providing easy access, is the C848, a quiet minor road from Binalong Bay to the nearby holiday-shack town of The Gardens. Dotted along it are seven rudimentary – but absolute beachfront – campsites, all free of charge with million-dollar views.

Each beach is a variation on a theme of perfect sand and the orange lichen that so defines the Bay of Fires. At spots such as Cosy Corner, it creates a postcard combination of orange-dipped granite boulders against sheets of white sand.

It's easy to stroll from beach to beach, rock hopping and beachcombing, or step it up by joining one of a pair of four-day guided walks that run the length of the coastline: the palawa-run wukalina Walk (*see* p. 268) and the Bay of Fires Signature Walk (taswalkingco.com.au/bay-of-fires-lodge-walk), with nights spent in style in the walk's private lodge, set in isolation 40m (131ft) above the sea, with spa treatments available at the walking day's end.

parks.tas.gov.au/explore-our-parks/bay-of-fires-conservation-area

Distinctive orange boulders can be found along the Bay of Fires

ACCESSIBLE NATIONAL PARK TRAILS

VARIOUS LOCATIONS

Australian hiking trails are on a fast track to accessibility, with more and more paths designed with wheelchair users and other people living with disability in mind. Here's a state-by-state guide to some of our favourites – all spectacular guaranteed.

ACT

Lake Burley Griffin
Canberra's central lake is lapped by 32km (20 miles) of accessible trails. Pick a section, any section.

Sanctuary Loop
A loop of 2.1km (1.3 miles) of trails and boardwalks link ponds in a wetland in Tidbinbilla Nature Reserve. Keep an eye out for platypuses. A TrailRider can be hired for free at the park visitor centre.

NSW

Three Sisters
An 800m (0.5-mile) return trail to the most famous viewpoint in the Blue Mountains.

Sawn Rocks
A 1.5km (0.9-mile) return trail to the base of cliffs resembling a wall of organ pipes in Mount Kaputar National Park.

All-terrain TrailRider and Hippocampe mobility chairs are available for free hire at Royal, Morton and Kosciuszko National Parks (book ahead).

Accessible trail through Daintree Rainforest

Queensland

Nurim Circuit
Elevated 500m (0.3-mile) walkway jutting out 25m (82ft) from the slopes of Mount Archer with views over the Fitzroy River and Rockhampton.

Daintree Rainforest
Feel the forest on any of three accessible trails near Cape Tribulation: the Majda (1.2km/0.75-mile), Dubuji (1.2km/0.75-mile) and Kulki (600m/0.4-mile) boardwalks. Kulki has views of Cape Tribulation.

NT

Uluru Base Walk
The 10km (6.2-mile) lap around Uluru is on compacted paths suitable to wheelchairs.

Ormiston Gorge
The paved 300m (0.2-mile) Waterhole Walk leads from the car park to the banks of a large waterhole pooled in a bend of the Tjoritja/West MacDonnell gorge.

Tasmania

Russell Falls
The base of Tasmania's signature waterfall (it appeared on one of Australia's first postage stamps) is reached on a sealed, accessible 1.4km/0.9-mile (return) trail through the forest.

Cape Tourville
Sneak a glimpse into Wineglass Bay along this 600m (0.4-mile) boardwalk that wraps around a lighthouse-topped cape. Whale sightings can be a winter bonus.

TrailRider chairs are available for free hire (book at least seven days ahead) at Cradle Mountain, Freycinet and Mount Field National Parks.

Victoria

Stevensons Falls
Off the Great Ocean Road, this 1.5km (0.9-mile) path rolls through towering sequoias to the base of a lovely waterfall.

MacKenzie Falls Lookout
The Grampians/Gariwerd's most impressive waterfall has a 1.9km/1.2-mile (return) accessible trail to Bluff Lookout, with views over the falls and gorge.

TrailRider chairs are available in a number of parks, with motorised TrailRiders in the Grampians, Dandenong Ranges and Wilsons Promontory National Parks.

WA

Natural Bridge to Island Rock
On the 1.8km (1.1-mile) loop trail atop Kalbarri National Park's red cliffs, watch for whales between June and November.

John George Trail
Explore Perth's lifeblood waterway on this 5.5km (3.4-mile) path along the Swan River, with views to the vineyards on the opposite bank.

SA

Robe Coastal Walk
Point-to-point track (6.3km/3.9 miles) wrapping around Robe's foreshore, past its obelisk, up to the edge of its lighthouse.

Remarkable Rocks
These scoured, surreal rocks – one of the symbols of SA – are reached on an accessible 1km/0.6-mile (return) boardwalk, though it stops at the edge of the rocks.

A TrailRider chair is available for free hire (for up to three days) in Deep Creek Conservation Park.

AUSTRALIA'S LARGEST NATIONAL PARK

◉ MUNGA-THIRRI–SIMPSON DESERT NATIONAL PARK, SA, QUEENSLAND & NT
WANGKANGURRU YARLUYANDI COUNTRY

For many years, Kakadu (*see* p. 90) was literally the biggest thing in Australian national parks, but in 2021 it was surpassed by the newly created Munga-Thirri–Simpson Desert National Park. At 36,000 sq km (13900 sq miles), this park along South Australia's northern border, spilling over into Queensland and the Northern Territory, is almost twice the size of Kakadu (and almost half the size of Tasmania).

Draped across its namesake desert, it covers one of the world's longest parallel dune systems and is a revered destination for 4WDers. There are several 4WD tracks – all serious missions – across the desert, the most popular of which is the combination of the French Line and QAA Line. Best driven from west to east (due to steeper faces on the eastern side of dunes), this drive crosses more than 1100 dunes, including the famed Big Red, a 30m (100ft) dune near Birdsville.

Note that the park is closed from 1 December to 15 March each year, and a Desert Parks Pass is required to travel and camp in the park.

◉ parks.sa.gov.au/parks/munga-thirri-simpson-desert-national-park

Munga-Thirri–Simpson Desert National Park
Opposite **The pink Hutt Lagoon**

THINK PINK

VARIOUS LOCATIONS

Australia's outback colours go from earthy to Barbie when you arrive at the shores of one of its smattering of pink lakes. The colour of these fairy-floss lakes comes from algae in the water that produces beta-carotene, the red pigment found in the likes of tomatoes and carrots. The lakes' colours are typically at their best on bright, clear days.

Think pink with a visit to one of the following:

Hutt Lagoon, WA

Stretching along the Indian Ocean coast, around six hours drive north of Perth, this 70-sq-km (230-sq-mile) lagoon glows brightest in the morning and at sunset, with many roadside pullouts along the road to Port Gregory on its shores.

Lake Hillier, WA

Perhaps the brightest of all, Lake Hillier is pooled on Middle Island, offshore from Cape Arid near Esperance. There's no way onto the island, but scenic flights from Esperance with Goldfields Air Services (goldfieldsairservices.com) can whisk you over the bubble-gum-pink beauty spot.

Murray-Sunset National Park, Victoria

This national park, tucked into the corner of Victoria's border with NSW and South Australia, has not just one pink lake but a sprinkling of four lakes. The two-hour Kline Loop Nature Walk weaves through the quartet.

Lake Bumbunga, SA

The most accessible of the pink lakes is less than two hours drive from Adelaide, outside the town of Lochiel, near the Clare Valley wine region. Look for the Loch-Eel Monster, a sculpture of a Loch Ness Monster–like creature rising from the pink sheet of water.

Lake Macdonnell, SA

Crossing Lake MacDonnell on the road to surfer-favourite Cactus Beach at the Nullarbor's edge is like driving through a paint chart. To one side is a green lake, then a blue lake, with the candy colours of the pink lake on the opposite side forming a vibrant contrast.

If you're on South Australia's Yorke Peninsula, you can tour an entire Salt Lake Trail (yorkepeninsula.com.au/yorke-peninsula-salt-lake-trail) for a day out in pink.

SENSATIONAL SWIMS OF LITCHFIELD

◉ LITCHFIELD NATIONAL PARK, NT
WERAT, KOONGURRUKUN, WARAY & MAK MAK MARRANUNGGU COUNTRY

Competing for attention with Kakadu National Park (*see* p. 90) is no easy challenge, but Litchfield National Park ably holds its own. An hour drive south of Darwin, on the country of the Werat, Koongurrukun, Waray and Mak Mak Marranunggu People, Litchfield is a land where sandstone pillars rise into the so-called Lost City, where some termite mounds tower as high as 8m (26ft) and others align themselves with magnetic perfection to the sun. Yet for all that, it's the waterfalls and swimming holes that unquestionably define this Top End park.

At the park's heart is the sandstone Tabletop Range, with its slopes falling away into cliffs. Over these cliffs pour an assortment of waterfalls, lining the base of the range with cool pools.

Wangi Falls

These are the most popular falls, pouring down either side of a cliff into a large waterhole. You can swim across to the falls or take the 3km (1.9-mile) walking loop to the top. Keep an eye out for signs in the wet season (October to March), when the falls are often closed to swimming for safety reasons.

Florence Falls

It's a short stroll from the car park to a lookout over Florence Falls, though you'll need to descend the stairs to take the plunge into its inviting pool, encased in monsoon forest.

Buley Rockhole

It's pools more than falls at popular Buley, on the road to Florence Falls. Here, several streams cascade through a collection of rock holes of different sizes and depths. If you're craving a spa effect, this is the spot for a bit of therapeutic lounging. A 3.2km (2-mile) walking trail connects Buley to Florence Falls.

Tjaetaba Falls

These falls are reached along the 2.7km (1.7-mile) Greenant Creek Walk. The Traditional Owners request that visitors swim only above the falls, where there are excellent rock holes.

Tjaynera Falls

Accessible only by 4WD, these are one of the least visited of Litchfield's waterfalls. It's a 1.4km (0.9-mile) walk into the falls, which rewards with a lovely pool at the base of one of Litchfield's taller falls.

Cascades

Want a spot you might have to yourself? Take the rugged 3.3km (2-mile) loop trail to the little-known Cascades, with its two swimming sites: Upper Cascades has shallow, spa-like pools; Lower Cascades has deeper plunge pools.

Walker Creek

This is a personal favourite. Dotted along the creek on a 3.5km (2.2-mile) return walk are eight individual campsites – book a site ahead, hike in with your gear and spend a blissful night beside a private plunge pool.

Tolmer Falls

These are the park's most spectacular cascades, pouring step-like over two sets of cliffs, but swimming isn't permitted.

Linking several of the falls and pools is the Tabletop Track, a 39km (24-mile), three- to five-day hike that loops around the Tabletop Range plateau, with link trails to Florence Falls, Wangi Falls, Tjaetaba Falls and Walker Creek. Hikers must book ahead through the park website, and the track is closed in the wet season.

Campers are spoiled for choice, with the park containing six campgrounds, including at Wangi and Florence Falls.

nt.gov.au/parks/find-a-park/litchfield-national-park

Top **Florence Falls**
Bottom **The pools of Litchfield National Park**

THE NATURE OF CITIES

◉ **VARIOUS LOCATIONS**

Australia has more national parks than any other country on Earth – more than 600 parcels of protected land – and many of them (including the world's second-oldest national park) are on the very doorstep of the states' capital cities. Think of the following as urban backyards.

Royal National Park, Sydney/Warrane

Proclaimed in 1879, just seven years after Yellowstone in the USA, the world's second-oldest national park skirts Sydney's southern edge. Known affectionately as 'Nasho', it's a place of high sandstone cliffs that break open into some of Sydney/Warrane's most beautiful beaches. The most absorbing way to experience the park is by hiking the two-day Royal Coast Track, traversing the park's length along the coastal cliffs.

◉ nationalparks.nsw.gov.au/visit-a-park/parks/royal-national-park

Dandenong Ranges National Park, Melbourne/Naarm

Melbourne's eastern suburbs reach an abrupt stop at the forest-coated Dandenong Ranges, which rise to 633m (2077ft) above sea level and are capped by this meandering park. One of Melbourne's most popular walking trails, the 1000 Steps or Kododa Memorial Walk, is here, adopted by veterans of the WWII Kokoda campaign because of its similarity to the first 100m (328ft) of Papua New Guinea's Kokoda Track. Seek out also Olinda Falls and Sherbrooke Falls, especially after recent rain.

◉ parks.vic.gov.au/places-to-see/parks/dandenong-ranges-national-park

Morialta Conservation Park, Adelaide/Tandanya

Picture parched Adelaide/Tandanya and it's typically not waterfalls that come to mind, at least until you step into Morialta. Spilling down the slopes of the Adelaide Hills to hit the very edge of Adelaide's eastern suburbs, this conservation park is split by Fourth Creek and a trio of waterfalls. A 1.6km (1-mile) return walk ascends to First Falls, while a 7.3km (4.5-mile) loop continues up the slopes to Second and Third Falls – all of the falls are at their best in winter. Morialta is also SA's most popular rock-climbing area.

◉ parks.sa.gov.au/find-a-park/Browse_by_region/Adelaide_Hills/morialta-conservation-park

D'Aguilar National Park, Brisbane/Meanjin

Only 12km (7.5 miles) from Brisbane's city centre, yet split by gorges and topped with rainforest, D'Aiguilar combines nature with play – take a cooling dip in the rockpools through Rocky Hole, ride a mountain bike skills course and visit the Walkabout Creek Discovery Centre, a park-run wildlife centre that's home to tree kangaroos, wombats and pythons, among other creatures. Despite its urban proximity, the park has seven remote bush camps.

◉ parks.des.qld.gov.au/parks/daguilar

Wellington Park, Hobart/nipaluna

The slopes of Hobart/nipaluna's hulking kunanyi/Mount Wellington all but tumble into the city. Summit lookouts peer across half the state, and the slopes are scribbled with walking and mountain-biking trails. Don't fall for the notion that this is a single peak – venture beyond to find trails to other summits such as Cathedral Rock, Collins Cap and Trestle Mountain.

◉ wellingtonpark.org.au

John Forrest National Park, Perth/Boorloo

Little more than 20km (12.4 miles) from Perth's city centre, WA's oldest national park is a spring spectacular, lighting up bright with wildflowers each year. The park, created in 1898, is a favourite among Perth walkers, with a wildflower trail, lookouts over the Perth plains, a pair of waterfalls and the chance to walk through the state's oldest railway tunnel, the 340m (1115ft) Swan View Tunnel, built in 1894.

◉ exploreparks.dbca.wa.gov.au/park/john-forrest

Dandenong Ranges National Park is a popular daytrip from Melbourne/Naarm

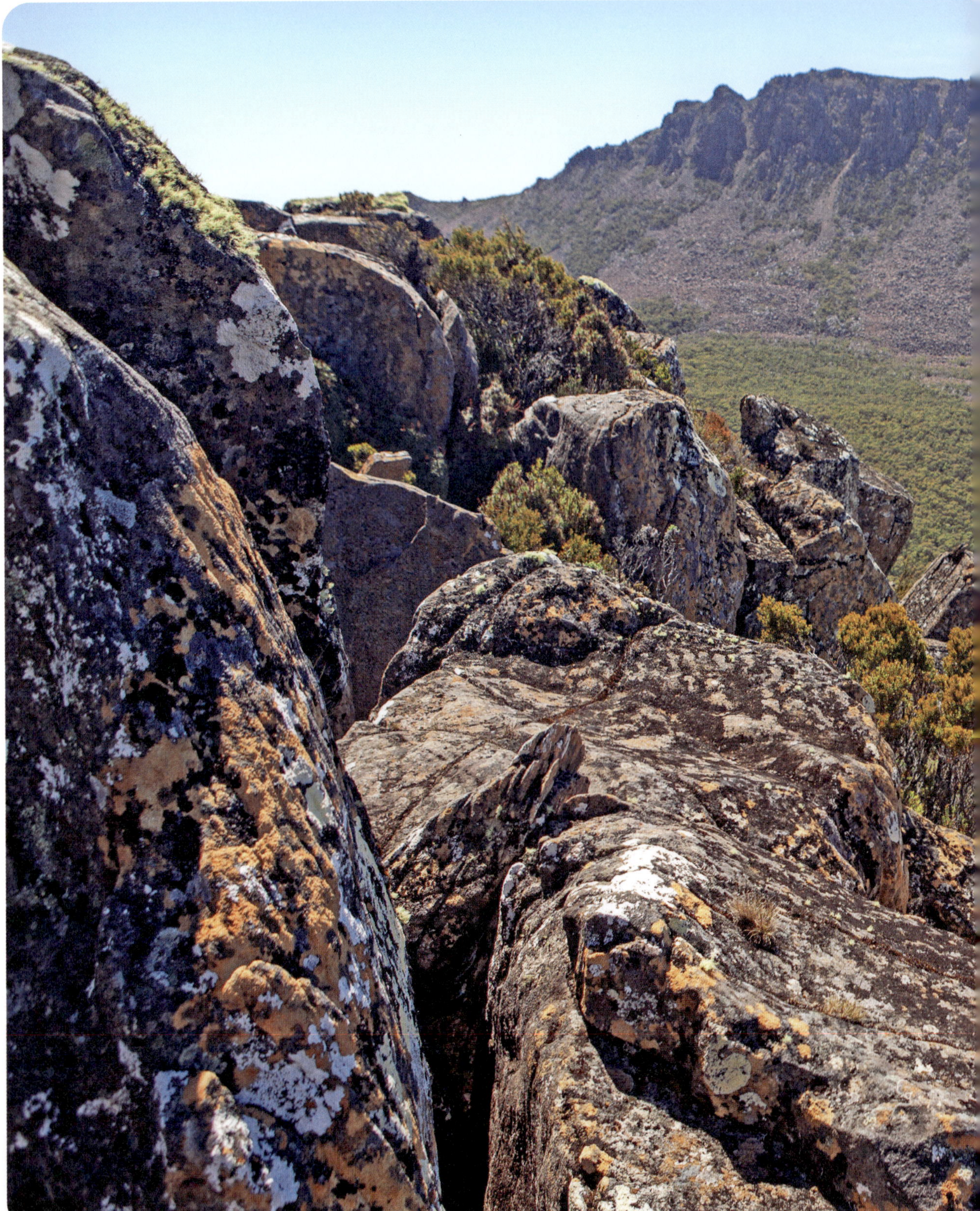

Collins Bonnet in Wellington Park

An impressive paddle through Cobbold Gorge

SUP THROUGH THE OUTBACK

◉ COBBOLD GORGE, QUEENSLAND
EWAMIAN COUNTRY

In the fractured sandstone country of north Queensland's savannah, six hours drive inland from Cairns, there's a gorge so well hidden in the literal cracks that it took local station owners almost 100 years to detect its presence (though it had long been known to the Ewamian Traditional Owners).

Little more than three decades later, Queensland's youngest gorge, formed 12,000 to 14,000 years ago, is one of the most welcome oases in the state's outback. Australia's first fully glass bridge was built across the gorge in 2019, and combined boat and walking tours delve into its depths, cruising among resident freshwater crocodiles and peering down at the cliff-shaded waters 17m (56ft) below.

The most intriguing experience in the elusive gorge, however, is stand-up paddleboarding (SUP) – have you ever imagined paddling through the outback?

Like all activities in the gorge, the experience is only available as a guided tour. Trips set out in the early morning and late afternoon, squeezing between 30m (100ft) cliffs on a waterway so narrow it's like a paper cut in 320-sq-km (150-sq-mile) Howlong Station.

At first, the gorge is wide as the tours head upstream, passing rock outcrops and platforms that are favourite sunbaking spots for the dozen or so freshwater crocodiles found in the gorge. As you glide beneath the glass bridge, the walls begin to close in, until they're almost in touching distance on either side of the board.

The gorge is navigable for about 850m (2790ft), at which point you turn the boards around (a trick in itself in this tight space) and paddle back through this sandstone spectacular.

◉ cobboldgorge.com.au

GREAT HIKING EXPECTATIONS

VARIOUS LOCATIONS, QUEENSLAND

Looking for a great walk in Queensland? It's hard to look past the actual Great Walks, the state's highlights reel of hiking trails, each one of the 10 dotted with walkers' camps – book them ahead at qpws.usedirect.com/qpws.

Gold Coast Hinterland

Three-day, 54km (33-mile) trail through World Heritage–listed Lamington and Springbrook national parks, hiking among ancient Antarctic beech trees, with a finish beside 100m (328ft) Purling Brook Falls – a celebratory swim, anyone?

Sunshine Coast Hinterland

Four-day, 58.8km (36.5-mile) walk across the Blackall Range, immediately inland from the Sunshine Coast. Warm hiking days are sated by waterfalls, rock holes, Obi Obi Gorge and some very cool lookouts to the coast as you pass through Kondalilla, Mapleton Falls and Mapleton national parks.

Whitsunday Ngaro Sea Trail

The Great Walk that isn't a walk, the Ngaro Sea Trail is a kayaking journey through the wondrous Whitsunday Islands (see p. 58), hopping from South Molle Island to Whitsunday and Hook islands. The walking comes when you glide ashore on each island, with climbs to lookouts, strolls on celebrated Whitehaven Beach and a respectful wander into the Ngaro Cultural Site with rock art from the Ngaro People.

Conondale Range

Head even deeper inland from the Sunshine Coast to find this four-day, 56km (34.7-mile) walk that dips into a range of landscapes – rainforest, dry forest, gorges, waterfalls and open country with expansive views – in Conondale National Park.

Cooloola

Sand blows, rainforest, beaches and the slow-moving Noosa River – there's plenty to like about this five-day, 102km (63.4-mile) journey through Great Sandy National Park. And the start is just 20km (12.4 miles) from Noosa Heads.

K'gari

One of the headline Great Walks, this 90km (56-mile), six- to eight-day hike wriggles past so many of the finest features on K'gari (formerly Fraser Island), the world's largest sand island. Ponder swims in clear-as-air lakes and wander beneath towering trees that are rooted in nothing but sand. All while walking on sand that's firm but still soft enough to cushion your steps.

Mackay Highlands

Roll across the top of the Great Dividing Range in Eungella and Homevale national parks on this 56km (34.7-mile), four-day hike, peering down into the cane fields of the Pioneer Valley and pausing to watch platypuses in Broken River.

Carnarvon

Probably the single-most spectacular day on a Great Walk comes as this trail squeezes through Carnarvon Gorge, beneath sandstone cliffs up to 200m (656ft) high, passing two First Nations rock-art galleries. Beyond this, the six-day, 87km (54-mile) walk climbs to a dry plateau and loops back to its start.

Goldfields Trail

Short and definitely sweet, this 19.5km (12.1-mile) trail ascends from the Goldsbourgh Valley to cross a saddle between Queensland's two highest peaks (Mount Bartle Frere and Mount Bellenden Ker), with the most welcome of finish lines at the clear green waters of the Babinda Boulders – it might be the best swimhole you've ever seen.

Wet Tropics

One walk, two options. The 20.6km (12.8-mile), two-day Jambal walk sets out from 90m (295ft) Blencoe Falls, squeezing into the Herbert River Gorge before turning back on itself at Blanket Creek walkers' camp. The more challenging (and suited only to experienced hikers) 43.5km (27-mile), four- to six-day Juwun walk continues through the untracked gorge, following the Herbert River downstream to the Yamanie pick-up point.

The impressive Whitsunday Ngaro Sea Trail

THE TURNING OF THE FAGUS

⊙ MOUNT FIELD NATIONAL PARK & CRADLE MOUNTAIN-LAKE ST CLAIR NATIONAL PARK, TASMANIA
PALAWA COUNTRY

In Australia, nature doesn't typically indulge in showy displays of colour ... unless you're in the mountains of Tasmania. In the island state, the so-called 'turning of the fagus' sees Australia's only winter deciduous tree paint entire slopes in shades of gold, orange and russet. For Tasmanians, it's a virtual annual pilgrimage to head to the mountains to witness the colourful conversion.

Fagus, or *Nothofagus gunnii*, is a small beech tree that grows at altitudes above 800m (2624ft). While it spreads its wiry limbs throughout the mountains of the Central Highlands, there are two locations that primarily draw visitors to its dazzling display.

In the north, fagus brightens the slopes above Dove Lake in Cradle Mountain-Lake St Clair National Park (*see p. 298*). With Tasmania's most famous peak, Cradle Mountain, rising directly out of the lake, it's a combination of colour and crags that can be easily witnessed from the viewing shelter on Dove Lake's shores or by taking a day hike to the Twisted Lakes high above Dove Lake.

The flashiest display of fagus is along the Tarn Shelf in Mount Field National Park, in the state's south. Reached on foot from Lake Dobson, the shelf is a chain of small lakes pooled atop a narrow bench of land high in the mountains. They're spectacular at any time of year, but especially vivid when the fagus encircling the lakes gets its glow on.

Timing of the fagus's turning is dependent on seasonal conditions, but locals usually pin its peak time to Anzac Day (25 April).

Tarn Shelf in Mount Field National Park

SYDNEY/WARRANE'S SECRET GARDEN

◉ SYDNEY/WARRANE, NSW
GADIGAL COUNTRY

Hidden in plain sight of Sydney/Warrane's city centre and the Harbour Bridge, Wendy Whiteley's Secret Garden is a thin slice of urban forest with a tale of grief and growth. Created by Sydney artist Wendy Whiteley after the death of her famous artist husband Brett Whiteley in 1992, the garden was hacked out of a mess of lantana and sticky weed beside the couple's home in Lavender Bay at the northern end of the Sydney Harbour Bridge. Today, it's a lush sliver of greenery where the city feels momentarily on pause, even as the garden's trees frame the skyscrapers and the Harbour Bridge.

A walk of just a few minutes from Milsons Point railway station or the madcap grin of Luna Park, the garden – which is free to wander – is an urban oasis that steps down a slope between Lavender Bay's apartment towers and a railway line. Moreton Bay figs stand tall over the garden, which was almost entirely planted by Whiteley and is tended by two full-time gardeners and volunteers, and dotted with sculptures among the undergrowth. A small sandstone cliff rises in the garden, with paths winding up the slopes beside it, creating a green maze dotted with seats, tables, engraved stone tablets and sculptures. Brush turkeys scratch at the leaf litter, and only the occasional train disturbs the peace. And each time a break appears in the trees, the Harbour Bridge peeps through – this might well become your new favourite Sydney view.

◉ wendyssecretgarden.org.au

SOAK IN THE SNOW

◉ KOSCIUSZKO NATIONAL PARK, NSW
WALGALU & NGARIGO COUNTRY

Yarrangobilly Caves thermal pool in winter
Opposite **A secret garden in the heart of Sydney/Warrane**

Japan might have its onsens, but Australia has the Yarrangobilly Caves thermal pool. Set in a valley in the country's highest mountain range – the Snowy Mountains – its waters pour from a natural spring that flows out of the earth at 27°C (80.6°F) year-round. In summer, the surrounds are a typical Australian bush setting, but it's most evocative in winter, when the slopes around the pool are covered in snow and steam pours from the water – forget where you are in the world and you might half expect a Japanese snow monkey to appear.

Yarrangobilly Caves also has six show caves, open to visitors year-round. Jersey Cave has unusual black flowstones, while the small Jillabenan Cave has an elaborate collection of delicate stalagmites, stalactites, straws, shawls and cave corals.

🔗 nationalparks.nsw.gov.au/things-to-do/swimming-spots/yarrangobilly-caves-thermal-pool

A 'SUNDAY SESSION

◉ WHITSUNDAY ISLANDS, QUEENSLAND
NGARO COUNTRY

There are more than 900 islands along the Great Barrier Reef, with 74 of the most beautiful of them clustered into the Whitsunday group, offshore from the popular tourist town of Airlie Beach. A combination of national-park islands, swanky resorts, basic campgrounds and dazzling beaches, these islands are all things to all people.

Hamilton and Daydream islands can be reached by ferry, with day-tripping tour boats heading to other islands. Even better is to come by bareboat yacht or kayak, exploring at your own pace and whim.

Sailing & Kayaking

The quintessential Whitsunday experience is to hire a yacht and sail through the island group, mooring among its protected bays and snorkelling the islands' fringing reefs. A boating licence isn't required to sail in the Whitsundays, though you will need to demonstrate some nautical experience to charter a boat. There are more than 100 moorings around the islands and they're free to use – please do so rather than use an anchor.

A slower and more active way to get around the island group is by kayak on the Ngaro Sea Trail (see p. 52).

Resorts

Despite their tropical temptation, the Whitsundays are sprinkled rather than sprawled with resorts – only four of the islands have accommodation that's not your own tent. Hamilton Island is the most versatile resort island, with options ranging from self-catering homes to swanky, adult-only Qualia, with its private beach, day spa and a pair of top restaurants. The island also has an airport with direct flights from Brisbane/Meanjin, Sydney/Warrane and Melbourne/Naarm.

Skinny Daydream Island is open only to guests at the island's resort, while Long Island and Hayman Island are home to Palm Bay Resort and the luxe InterContinental Hayman Island Resort, respectively.

Camping

More than 30 of the islands are protected as national parks, turning them into the Robinson Crusoes of camping. There are 25 national park campgrounds dotted across 11 islands (Whitsunday, Hook and South Molle are among the most popular). Campgrounds at Sandy Bay (Long Island), Boat Port (Lindeman), Whitehaven Beach (Whitsunday) and South Molle Island have access to walking tracks, while Maureens Cove (Hook Island), Crayfish Beach (Hook Island), Cairn Beach (Whitsunday) and the two South Molle campgrounds have walk-up snorkelling sites.

Scamper (whitsundaycamping.com.au) runs a campers' ferry service to South Molle, Whitsunday, Hook and Henning islands, and hires out camping equipment. None of the campgrounds have drinking water, so it's recommended to bring at least 5L (1.3 gal) of water per person per day.

ISLAND GUIDE

- **Whitsunday Island** The group's largest island is headlined by Whitehaven Beach, a swirling mix of white sands and azure seas. Away from this beach beauty, there are view-rich walking tracks to Whitsunday Peak, Whitsunday Cairn and the new multiday Ngaro Track, traversing 32km (20 miles) of the island.

- **Hook Island** Protected Butterfly Bay and Manta Bay offer some of the Whitsundays' best snorkelling over fringing reefs, while the Ngaro Cultural Site, reached along a short walking track, features rock art from the Ngaro People.

- **Hamilton Island** Reasons to stay on 'Hamo' include the walking track up Passage Peak (the island's highest point), the white sands of Catseye Beach and a golf course.

- **South Molle Island** The closest island to Airlie Beach was once home to a resort, but now tempts walkers with 15km (9.3 miles) of island trails – for views, seek out Spion Kop and Mount Jeffreys, passing the acrobatic Balancing Rock.

The famous white sand beaches of the Whitsunday Islands

TALL FALLS

◉ VARIOUS LOCATIONS

Australia's low landscapes might not lend themselves to raging waterfalls (the tallest waterfall in the country is ranked as just the 484th highest on the planet, but they are plentiful and spectacular.

The highest of all the waterfalls is Wallaman Falls, which take a 268m (879ft) plunge an hour drive inland from Ingham in north Queensland's Girringun National Park. A lookout onto the falls can be accessed by road, while the 3.2km/2-mile (return) Djyinda walk sets out from near the lookout to the base of the falls.

Other cascades:

Wollomombi Falls

Sometimes claimed as Australia's tallest, with a 260m (853ft) drop in Oxley Wild Rivers National Park, along northern NSW's well-named Waterfall Way.

Dandongadale Falls

Victoria's highest waterfall (255m/837ft) pours off Mount Cobbler in Alpine National Park.

Morialta Conservation Park

Not the tallest falls in South Australia, but the most numerous, with a 7.3km (4.5-mile) walking trail passing a trio of waterfalls at otherwise-dry Adelaide/Tandanya's edge.

Montezuma Falls

Hike or cycle an old rail trail to a suspension bridge beside Tasmania's highest waterfall (104m/341ft) near the west-coast town of Rosebery.

Jim Jim Falls

Kakadu National Park's greatest water feature, making a 200m (656-ft) dive over the Arnhem Land escarpment. Accessible by 4WD or on tours. In the wet season, they're a powerhouse best seen from the air.

STONE SURF

◉ HYDEN, WA
NJAKI NJAKI COUNTRY

Not all of Australia's best waves are in the ocean. Head to Hyden, 340km (211 miles) east of Perth/Boorloo, and one of the country's many geological curiosities, Wave Rock, rises 15m (49ft) out of the earth, curling like a striped granite wave about to break on a beach … even if the nearest beach is a two-and-a-half-hour drive away.

At its essence, Wave Rock is a 110m (361ft) cliff eroded into a lip over hundreds of millions of years. It's a flat, easy walk of 325m (0.2 miles) from the car park to the rock.

Head 19km (12 miles) north and the hollowed-out boulder known as Mulka's Cave contains more than 450 First Nations handprints, paintings and stencils. You're free to enter the cave to look at the art, but please don't touch.

Hyden is on Njaki Njaki Country, which can be explored further with First Nations guides on tours (Friday, Saturday and Sunday) with Njaki Njaki Aboriginal Cultural Tours (njakinjaki.com.au/tours), based in nearby Merredin.

The appropriately named Wave Rock
Opposite **Jim Jim Falls in Kakadu National Park**

GORGING ON WALKS AND WATER

◎ NITMILUK NATIONAL PARK, NT
JAWOYN COUNTRY

The escarpment of the Arnhem Plateau is an imposing wall – think of the ice wall in *Game of Thrones* but carved in red sandstone – rising out of the vast Top End savannah. Few things breach it, and nothing more spectacularly than Nitmiluk/Katherine Gorge.

Carved by the Katherine River, Nitmiluk is a chain of 13 connecting gorges that burrow 12km (7.5 miles) into the plateau, creating a waterway set beneath 70m (230ft) cliffs and filled with active options for visitors.

The gorge is the centrepiece of Nitmiluk National Park, which was returned to the Jawoyn Traditional Owners in 1989 and is now jointly managed by the Jawoyn People and the Parks and Wildlife Commission of the Northern Territory. The most popular way to view the gorge is on boat tours run by Nitmiluk Tours, the Jawoyn-owned company that manages all commercial activities in the national park. Go a step (or a paddle) beyond, however, and it becomes an even more intimate river.

Nitmiluk is arguably Australia's best canoeing destination. Canoes can be hired for a half-day, full day or two days from Nitmiluk Tours, and they're collected at the end of the boat tour in the second gorge.

The half-day or full-day options might get you into the third or fourth gorges, while an overnight paddle will take you deep into the chasm – you can paddle as far as the distant ninth gorge, with the journey only slowed by often long and tiring portages over rock bars between each gorge.

There are campsites for canoeists on elevated beaches in the fourth, sixth and ninth gorges. The first of these camps looks out onto a towering sandstone buttress known as Smitt Rock, its cliffs so smooth they look planed, while the remote camp in the sixth gorge sits pressed between cliffs. If you're paddling for two days, pack minimally as the canoes have limited space.

Nitmiluk is also the starting point for the multiday, waterhole-hopping Jatbula Trail. This 62km (38.5-mile) hike begins with a shorter boat trip – a hop across the river from the visitor centre – and follows the line of the escarpment north over five or six days to Leliyn (Edith Falls). What defines the trail most is not the walking but its waterholes, with each camp set beside a pool or waterfall. Walking stages aren't long – the longest stretch between camps is 16.8km (10.4 miles) – making it possible (and my

Top **Nitmiluk/Katherine Gorge**
Bottom **Nitmiluk is a chain of 13 connecting gorges**

recommendation) to set out walking near dawn each day, making camp by lunchtime and whiling away the afternoons in the water. A few hours in the infinity-like pool at the head of 17 Mile Falls is outback magic.

About an hour before reaching 17 Mile Falls, there's another of the Jatbula Trail's highlights, with a short detour leading into the Amphitheatre, a small gorge with a pocket of monsoon rainforest and cliffs covered in Jawoyn rock art.

Canoeing and hiking the Jatbula Trail are only possible in the dry season (around June to September).

nt.gov.au/parks/find-a-park/nitmiluk-national-park

nitmiluktours.com.au

MUNGO MAGIC

◉ MUNGO NATIONAL PARK, NSW
PAAKANTJI, MUTTHI MUTTHI & NGYIMPAA COUNTRY

In Mungo National Park, a convoy of vehicles is crossing a lake. The smallest of the 12 World Heritage–listed Willandra Lakes, Lake Mungo hasn't held permanent water for 18,000 years, but it's still a 10km (6.2-mile) drive across its flat, dry bed, through a knee-high sea of saltbush.

At the head of the convoy is a ranger's ute, leading a tag-along tour towards the lake's most extraordinary feature – a 30km (18.6-mile) line of dunes along its eastern shores. Composed of sand and clay blown from the lake surface over millennia, this lunette of dunes is punctuated by hundreds of fluted clay pinnacles rising out of the sand. Known post-colonisation as the Walls of China – named by Chinese labourers who saw a resemblance to towers along the Great Wall of China – they are the national park's spectacular drawcard, though the most striking feature of these dunes is actually unseen.

Uncovered in the 1960s and '70s, the bones of two First Nations people – Mungo Lady and Mungo Man, an 18-year-old woman and a man in his fifties – have been dated to 40,000 to 42,000 years, making them the oldest human remains found in Australia. The burnt bones of Mungo Lady are also one of the world's oldest known evidences of human cremation. Though the bones were removed from the site, they were returned to Country in 1992 (Mungo Lady) and 2017 (Mungo Man) and reburied in 2022.

The road across the lake is part of a 70km (43.5-mile) driving loop around the dunes, with a first stop at a lookout platform at the base of the Walls of China. The only way beyond – onto the dunes – is to join the park's lunette tour, led by a First Nations ranger.

Galahs watch down from one of the rare trees as we step off the boardwalk and onto the dunes. With the prevailing winds blowing from the west, the dunes move east by about 1m (3ft) a year, with the shifting sands revealing the darkened patches of old First Nations fireplaces, middens of freshwater mussel shells and the skeletal remains of wombats.

'Near where you're standing, we found a fireplace that was dated to 45,000 years,' says our guide Lance. 'I've found the bones of Tasmania tigers up here as well.'

Slowly rising up the dunes, the tour makes four or five stops for stories of culture and natural history, but between stops you're free to wander among the formations alone. Nearing the top of the dunes, which rise to 30m (100ft) above the lakebed, the pinnacles disappear, replaced by classically wind-shaped sand hills.

Mungo is around 90 minutes drive north of Mildura, and four hours south of Broken Hill. The best time to visit is in the cooler winter period from around May to September – temperatures on the dunes can reach 50°C (122°F) in summer. There's a national park campground just inside the park entrance and another, set among mallee scrub, midway around the driving loop. There are also five rooms with accommodation in the old shearers' quarters beside the park visitor centre.

nationalparks.nsw.gov.au/visit-a-park/parks/mungo-national-park

Top **The sands of Mungo National Park**
Bottom **Sunset over Mungo's towering rock formations**

MADE IN AUSTRALIS

⊙ VARIOUS LOCATIONS, TASMANIA
PALAWA COUNTRY

When the aurora australis flares into life across night skies, Tasmania typically has a box seat on the Southern Hemisphere's most dazzling natural light show. Though fainter than the famed aurora borealis of Arctic regions, the aurora australis – or southern lights – regularly appears across southern horizons and, because of the island's proximity to the polar region and its sparsity of light pollution, Tasmania is considered one of the best places in the hemisphere (outside of Antarctica) to see them.

Coordinating a visit with the appearance of an aurora is not easy – these lights run to no schedule and can occur at any time of year. March and September are considered the most reliable months, though auroras are at their most visible in winter because of Tasmania's long nights. For some advance warning of their likelihood, keep an eye on the Australian Space Weather Forecasting Centre webpage (sws.bom.gov.au/Aurora) for aurora watch notices.

The further south you head in Tasmania, the greater the possibility of lights. Seek out a dark, cloud-free night and head somewhere with an unobstructed view to the south, such as a beach or hilltop. Favourite spots among Hobart/nipaluna aurora chasers include Cockle Creek (the most southerly road end in Australia), Bruny Island, South Arm Peninsula, Howden, Dodges Ferry and the summit of kunanyi/Mount Wellington.

High-intensity solar storms produce more colour – the greens and pinks of aurora dreams – but displays are generally more muted. Often they can be invisible to the naked eye or resemble a faint haze above the horizon, with camera and smartphone technology drawing out the colours and brightness.

GLOWING GHOST MUSHROOMS

◉ GLENCOE, SA
BOANDIK COUNTRY

In the pine forests of Glencoe, on the outskirts of Mount Gambier, there's an eerie luminous glow at the base of a tree. It appears otherworldly, but it's not the light of an alien and it's not military. It is a bioluminescent mushroom and it's native to Australia.

Known as ghost mushrooms, these fungi, which grow on decaying plant material such as the stumps of felled trees, use a chemical reaction to create their own light. They grow in sites around Australia, but in the working pine plantations of Glencoe they've become Australia's first bona fide site of fungi tourism.

Ghost Mushroom Lane opened in 2017, a year after the glowing ghosts were first detected. The vehicle lane runs for more than 2km (1.2 miles) through the plantation, with ever-changing (according to the location of mushroom colonies) walking trails branching off from the road. In photos, the mushrooms grow bright green, but to the naked eye they are an incandescent white and best observed on the darkest of nights – avoid nights around a full moon. The season only lasts for two months (May and June).

Most years the lane is open to visitors in their own vehicles, while on Friday and Saturday nights during May and June, Walk the Limestone Coast (walkthelimestonecoast.com.au) runs 30- to 45-minute tours among the fungi. In 2024, the lane could only be accessed on the guided tours (due to low numbers of mushrooms), so check ahead on the website before visiting.

◉ forestrysa.com.au/ghostmushrooms

Glowing ghost fungus
Opposite **Aurora australis across the Tasmanian sky**

ART AND NATURE

⊙ CARNARVON GORGE NATIONAL PARK, QUEENSLAND
BIDJARA, KARA KARA & KARINGBAL COUNTRY

The term 'landscape painting' has never been more fitting than along the cliffs of Carnarvon Gorge, where the sandstone walls of this 30km (18.6-mile) cleft in the earth are adorned by two culturally significant First Nations art sites.

Four hundred kilometres inland from Rockhampton, on the lands of the Bidjara and Karingbal People, Carnarvon is framed by cliffs up to 200m (656ft) high and sprinkled with side gorges. The best way to absorb the gorge is on the 19.4km (12-mile) return walk to Big Bend, passing a host of side gorges and the two rock-art sites as you hike along the floor of the gorge. My tip of the day is to set out early and hike directly to Big Bend in the cool of the day, breaking up the return walk with stops in the cooling side gorges.

The two rock-art sites (known by their recently adopted names) are towards the gorge's far end – near Big Bend – where Cathedral Cave is covered in paintings, stencils and engravings, some of them thousands of years old and others (such as a rifle showing early contact with Europeans) around 200 years of age. The simply titled Art Gallery, 4km (2.5 miles) further along the gorge, is a 62m (24ft) wall featuring more than 2000 paintings, ochre stencils and engravings.

Nature's own etchings come in the form of the side gorges, which are small salons of beauty along the walk. As its name suggests, Moss Garden is carpeted in moss, and Ward's Canyon contains a single 40m (131ft) stand of king ferns – it's the only place in Australia's interior where these plants grow. Again these names are recently adopted, comparative to First Nations presence. The most acrobatic detour is into the Amphitheatre, where you ascend ladders to squeeze through a narrow crack in the cliffs into a 60m (197ft) deep, open-topped sinkhole.

There's a national park campground outside the gorge and another camping area at Big Bend if you want to spend a night inside the gorge.

🌐 parks.desi.qld.gov.au/parks/carnarvon-gorge

ROCK ART PHOTOS

Rock art holds profound significance in First Nations cultures across Australia. Creation stories, deities, totems, significant events, people and animals depicted on rock surfaces all possess deeply embedded spiritual and cultural meaning that provide a continuous thread across generations. As a result, not all rock art can be photographed. It is extremely special that these sites are observable in locations across the country, and serve as a physical representation of Australia's First Peoples' enduring connection to Country and culture.

By Jamil Tye

Top **The sandstone walls of Carnarvon Gorge**
Bottom **Moss Garden covered in greenery**

Red blossoms at Stirling Range National Park

BLOOMING GOOD

VARIOUS LOCATIONS, WA

Australia's greatest flower show is a natural one, blanketing Western Australia in blooms each spring. There are more than 12,000 wildflower species in this one state alone, 60 per cent of which are endemic, making it one of the world's biggest and brightest natural floral displays. The further north you head, the earlier the wildflower season begins – around June in the Pilbara compared to October around Margaret River in the south. Start at any of the following for a flower-filled immersion.

Fitzgerald River National Park

So noted for its flowers – roughly 1800 species – that it's been named as a UNESCO biosphere. Orchids are plentiful.

Wildflower Way

A 309km (192-mile) flower-lined driving route from Dalwallinu to Geraldton, with 21 interpretative sites along the way.

wildflowercountry.com.au

Kings Park and Botanic Garden

Why even leave Perth/Boorloo when one of the world's largest inner-city parks has such a colourful display of wildflowers? Look for everlastings and black kangaroo paw among the 3000 flowering plant species of the WA Botanic Garden. The Everlasting Kings Park Festival is held here each September.

bgpa.wa.gov.au/kings-park

Lesueur National Park

Around 10 per cent of the state's plant species are found in this coastal park in the sandy lands north of Perth/Boorloo, including many that flower profusely.

Stirling Range National Park

Climb southern WA's highest peak, Bluff Knoll, to wander among 1000 species of flowering plants, including around 80 that are endemic to the range. Mountain bells are the highlight, along with plenty of orchids.

IN THE FLOW ON THE FRANKLIN

◉ FRANKLIN-GORDON WILD RIVERS NATIONAL PARK, TASMANIA
PALAWA COUNTRY

It's no great stretch of the imagination to suggest that Tasmania's Franklin River changes lives. Just ask Bob Brown.

In 1976 the then Launceston GP and his companion Paul Smith were the first people to raft the 129km (80-mile) river (18 years after it was first canoed), naming many of its natural features and rapids as they went. Such was the river's emotional impact that Bob would famously become leader of a blockade in the early 1980s to prevent the Franklin from being dammed. More than 1200 protestors were arrested, and a Federal election swung in favour of the blockade. Dam construction was prevented, the Tasmanian Wilderness World Heritage Area was created and Bob would go on to become a senator and leader of the Australian Greens political party for 20 years.

Bob's life was never the same after those two weeks of solitude and wilderness on the river, and now, as rafts continue to navigate its often-furious flows, he says the river is just as affecting for many of those who follow his pioneering journey.

'I get letters almost every year from people saying that's the most profound experience of my life,' he says.

Such is the reverence for the Franklin that leading US adventure magazine *Outside* once named it the world's best white-water-rafting trip. I've rafted the river twice, and it remains my favourite single journey in Australia. Ask Bob the reasons for this transformative connection and he suggests the supreme wildness of the place, a rare feature for a river little more than 100km (62 miles) from a capital city.

'It's certainly not anywhere near being one of the big, roaring, wild rivers of the world, but it's that wildness that's so important,' he says. 'That's being eradicated right around the world – every day we wake up, there's less wildness.

'So far you can't check your devices when you're down there, so the river is bringing us back to a normal relationship with the world rather than the abnormal relationship we've now got in the age of cyberspace.'

The Franklin is no place for inexperienced paddlers on their own, but commercial rafting trips make it accessible. Trips typically take around eight days, launching on the Collingwood River (a tributary of the Franklin) and heading downstream through sections of river that range from the mirror-still waters of the deep Irenabyss gorge to the furious rapids of the Great Ravine – a concertina of white water that requires complicated and time-consuming portages. Nights are spent sleeping on the ground under tarps (or in caves notched into the cliffs on a night above Newland Cascades), with all waste – including

The reflecting waters of Franklin River

human waste – carried out on the rafts. It's a policy that Bob says has had the rare effect of making the river journey cleaner now than it was even in the late 1970s when the first rafting parties followed behind him down the river.

'The commercial operators are doing a great job, I think, of keeping the river in good order,' he says.

- franklinriver.com
- franklinriverrafting.com
- tasmanianexpeditions.com.au
- wildjourneys.com.au

Top and bottom **Perth/Boorloo's Cottesloe Beach**

CAPITAL BEACHES

◉ VARIOUS LOCATIONS

Soak up sun, surf and sand at these local-favourite beaches around Australia's state capitals.

Sydney/Warrane

Depending on which side of the harbour you hail from, Bondi and Manly tussle for the title of Sydney/Warrane's favourite strand. Bondi is Australia's most famous beach, complete with a 50m (164-ft) ocean pool (*see* p. 195) and a cluster of cafes, restaurants and hotels. Folks from the northern side of the harbour will happily pit the 3km (1.8-mile), promenade-lined Manly Beach against Bondi … and you can get there by ferry from the city.

Melbourne/Naarm

Wrapped around a protected bay, Melbourne/Naarm doesn't get the beach kudos of other capital cities, but St Kilda Beach heads the pack. Behind its sands, you'll also find some of the city's favourite weekend restaurants such as the Stokehouse and rooftop Captain Baxter. The breakwater gets a different kind of visitor – little penguins – at dusk.

Adelaide/Tandanya

Ride Adelaide/Tandanya's signature tram to its terminus and you arrive at Glenelg Beach – wide, sandy and lined with Norfolk pines, pubs and restaurants. Everything a good Aussie beach should be, and all for just a tram fare.

Perth/Boorloo

Think Perth/Boorloo, think Cottesloe. The western city's most famous beach, with its 1929 Brighton-like pavilion, is generous in its offerings – it's a place to swim, snorkel or even surf. Facing west, it has brilliant sunsets – a rarity on Australian beaches – and in March it hosts the annual outdoor Sculpture by the Sea exhibition.

Brisbane/Meanjin

Why head to the coast when there's a beach directly across the river from the city centre? Streets Beach is an artificial strand in the popular South Bank Parklands, complete with lifesavers and a lovely swimming lagoon.

Hobart/nipaluna

You might think that far-southern weather would put beach thoughts on ice, but get even a hint of spring or summer sun and Sandy Bay's Long Beach and its pontoon quickly fill like a lifeboat. Come winter, it's the setting for Dark Mofo's frosty midwinter nude swim (*see* p. 162).

THE GREEN BEHIND THE GOLD

◉ GOLD COAST HINTERLAND, QUEENSLAND
YUGAMBEH COUNTRY

All that glitters on the Gold Coast isn't gold. Peer behind the beaches, into the hilly hinterland, and the dominant colour quickly becomes green. Blanketing the hills and parcelled into two outstanding national parks – Lamington and Springbrook – is a swathe of temperate rainforest forming part of the Gondwana Rainforests of Australia World Heritage Area.

Walkers are drawn to lush Lamington, where the two main trailheads just happen to be park resorts (and campgrounds): Binna Burra Lodge (binnaburralodge.com.au) at the eastern end and O'Reilly's Rainforest Retreat (oreillys.com.au), known as Green Mountains, at the western end. Connecting the two is the 21.4km (13.3-mile) Border Track. Set out early if leaving a vehicle at both ends for the day walk, or build in a stay at one of the lodges and return on foot to your starting point the next day. The stars of this track are the region's Antarctic beech trees, insulated in moss and cut straight from the pages of a fairy tale. Up to 2000 years of age, these gnarled giants provide a connection all the way back to prehistory, when Australia was part of the supercontinent Gondwana more than 100 million years ago.

Shorter peeps into the Lamington forest include Binna Burra's rainforest circuit (1.2km/0.7 miles), Tullawallal circuit (5km/3.1 miles), Green Mountains' rainforest track (1.4km/0.9 miles) and Moran Falls track (4.4km/2.7 miles). The Border Track is also part of the longer Gold Coast Hinterland Great Walk (see p. 52), which connects the two national parks.

Adjoining Springbrook National Park adds waterfalls to the hinterland equation. Natural Bridge is the star feature, with its waterfall pouring into a cave. Come at night and the cave glitters with glow-worms. Natural Bridge is reached on a family-friendly 1km (0.6-mile) circuit track. The 4km (2.5-mile) Twin Falls circuit takes you not only to a pair of waterfalls, but behind them.

Outside the national parks, the hinterland is dotted with relaxed mountain towns, primarily around the extinct volcano of Tamborine Mountain. There are short walks to town's-edge waterfalls, such as Curtis Falls and Witches Falls, and the Tamborine Rainforest Skywalk that climbs 30m (98ft) into the forest canopy, but not all walks here are into the wilds.

Tamborine Mountain's Gallery Walk links around 60 craft and gift stores in town, while a wine tasting at Cedar Creek Estate can include a walk into the vineyard's purpose-built glow-worm cave. Other cellar doors around the mountain include Witches Falls Winery and Hampton Estate Wines (complete with a whisky bar).

Stay on the trail of Tamborine tastes with a visit to Witches Chase Cheese and Fortitude Brewing (both on the Gallery Walk), as well as long-running and inventive Tamborine Mountain Distillery, producing spirits as varied as a limoncello made with yuzu, a quandong and gentian bitters liqueur and a ginger-and-rhubarb gin.

- escapetotamborinemountain.com.au
- parks.desi.qld.gov.au/parks/lamington
- parks.desi.qld.gov.au/parks/springbrook

Top **Natural Bridge in Springbrook National Park**
Bottom **Hiking through Lamington National Park**

TALL TIMBER

⊙ VARIOUS LOCATIONS, TASMANIA & WA

Australia's tallest trees have few global rivals – only the mighty sequoias of California stand taller. Edging towards 100m (328ft) in height, the ramrod-straight mountain ash (*Eucalyptus regnans*) is the world's largest flowering plant and the second-tallest tree on the planet. Growing in Tasmania and Victoria, these natural skyscrapers reach as high as 30-storey buildings.

The tallest tree of all – Centurion, growing at the edge of the Huon Valley south of Hobart/nipaluna – was scorched in bushfires in 2019 that claimed more than a dozen other giants, but survived. The best place, however, to seek out an audience with Tasmania's literal royalty – 'regnans' means 'ruling' – is the Styx Valley, outside the town of Maydena, 90km (56 miles) west of Hobart/nipaluna. The Wilderness Society produces a definitive guide (wilderness.org.au/images/resources/StyxValleyGuide.pdf) to getting among trees such as 84m (276-ft) Gandalf's Staff and the 86m (282-ft) Big Tree.

Another way into Tasmania's trees is on the Tahune AirWalk (tahuneadventures.com.au), an elevated 620m (0.4-mile) metal walkway through the canopy of the southern forests, near where Centurion grows.

Across the country, in southern WA, it's karri trees that have star status. Another of the world's tallest tree species, karris grow up to 80m (262ft) in height, elevating them above the forest to the extent that, in the 1930s and 1940s, eight of the tallest karris were used as fire lookout trees, with metal pegs hammered into their trunks and lookout platforms installed in their canopies. Several were later converted in 'climbing trees' for visitors. They're now all closed for climbing, but you can ascend into the canopy on the well-named Valley of the Giants Tree Top Walk (treetopwalk.com.au), a 600m (0.4-mile) elevated walkway, or you can admire them in national parks such as Warren, Gloucester and Walpole-Nornalup and the westernmost stands of karri in the Boranup Forest near Margaret River.

Tahune AirWalk
Opposite **Mossman Gorge, part of the world's oldest tropical rainforest**

THE GIVING GORGE

◉ MOSSMAN GORGE, QUEENSLAND
KUKU YALANJI COUNTRY

In the beautifully clear waters of Mossman Gorge, 22km (13.7 miles) west of Port Douglas on the Traditional Lands of the Kuku Yalanji People, time has a whole new perspective. Here, the world's oldest tropical rainforest, the Daintree, is home to the world's oldest living cultures, which is shared in the Mossman Gorge Cultural Centre and tours run by Kuku Yalanji guides.

'The natural environment here is so spectacular,' says the centre's general manager Rachael Hodges, a descendant of the Goreng/Girramay/Gunggandji groups of Queensland and the Kuareg People of the Torres Strait. 'And the cultural connection to the environment is also what makes it special. You don't see these underlying connections to the place until you're actually here – feeling it, living it and breathing it with the local mob, the Kuku Yalanji.'

For safety reasons, the centre recommends that visitors don't swim in the gorge, but a series of walking tracks explore the gorge and its blanket of forest. Among these tracks is Baral Marrjanga, a 270m (885-ft), wheelchair-accessible boardwalk that heads through the rainforest to the main lookout over the gorge.

A stronger way to connect to the gorge is through the Ngadiku Dreamtime Walks, led by a Kuku Yalanji guide – more than half the centre's 70-or-so staff are Kuku Yalanji People. These 90-minute walks, which depart five times a day, begin with a smoking ceremony to let the ancestors know the guides are bringing people onto their Country and they're here with good intentions, and to ward off bad spirits and protect visitors while they're on the walk. Then the walks explore the rainforest, explaining how the Kuku Yalanji used plants for food and medicine.

'As Roy Gibson (a well-respected Kuku Yalanji Elder who helped set up, and still works at the centre) said to me, "We want to be able to sit down, share, talk. Yarn with our non-Indigenous brothers and sisters",' Rachael says.

'And that's key for me. This business has the ability to make reconciliation happen.'

◉ mossmangorge.com.au

NEXT DOOR TO ULURU

ULURU-KATA TJUTA NATIONAL PARK, NT
ANANGU COUNTRY

The rock domes of Kata Tjuta
Opposite **The Pinnacles in Nambung National Park**

In Australia's beating red heart, Uluru isn't the only rockstar. Head less than 50km (31 miles) down the road and the smooth rock domes of Kata Tjuta are equally impressive, rising almost 500m (1640ft) out of the desert sands – a full 150m (492ft) taller than Uluru.

Suitably, Kata Tjuta means 'many heads' in the Pitjantjatjara language, and trails here cut through and around the conglomerate domes rather than onto them. Stroll into Walpa Gorge (2.6km/1.6 miles return), squeezed between domes, or set out on the longer Valley of the Winds loop (7.4km/4.6 miles), weaving among them.

Kata Tjuta is a culturally significant men's site for the Anangu Traditional Owners, who ask that photos of the rock formations are not taken on the Valley of the Winds walk (close-up photos of flora and fauna are fine), and that photos of Walpa Gorge include both sides of the gorge in frame.

parksaustralia.gov.au/uluru/discover/highlights/kata-tjuta

THE PINNACLE OF LANDSCAPES

◉ NAMBUNG NATIONAL PARK, WA
YUED COUNTRY

Drive north from Perth/Boorloo and the low scrub intermittently breaks open into bald patches of sand and dunes. A massive field of dunes rises behind the seaside town of Lancelin – a favourite spot for sandboarding – but keep driving and you soon come to the most remarkable of all the patches.

Officially named Nambung National Park, on the Traditional Lands of the Yued People, it's a place that is today known by many as the Pinnacles – a desert landscape bristling with thousands of limestone formations spearing out of the sand to form one of WA's most recognisable natural scenes.

Winding through this otherworldly landscape is a 4.5km (2.8-mile) loop road dotted with parking bays. The 'road' is sand, but it's firm and easily covered in a 2WD vehicle. Pull over in the parking bays and set out on foot through the pillars – some as tall as 3.5m (11.5ft), some capped like mushrooms – and climb to the lookout platform in the middle of the loop for views over the Pinnacles and away to the nearby Indian Ocean coast.

⊙ exploreparks.dbca.wa.gov.au/park/nambung-national-park

POUNDS AND CRATERS

◉ VARIOUS LOCATIONS

A curious feature of the Australian outback is its collection of pounds (round amphitheatres of mountains) and impact craters (from meteorites) – 30 of the world's 176 meteorite craters are found in Australia alone. Connect the dots with a visit to the following rounds and pounds that sprinkle the landscape like beauty spots.

Wilpena Pound/Ikara, SA

The most famous pound of all is the centrepiece of the Flinders Ranges on Adnyamathanha Country 440km (273 miles) north of Adelaide/Tandanya. Walking tracks head into the pound – Wilpena Pound Resort (with campground) sits just outside the only break in the ring of peaks – and up to summits such as Mount Ohlssen Bagge. The geometry of the pound comes into full effect on a scenic flight with Wrightsair, while the resort runs a series of Adnyamathanha cultural tours, including a guided walk into Sacred Canyon, which is carved with ancient Adnyamathanha engravings. The canyon is accessible only to visitors on this tour.

◉ parks.sa.gov.au/parks/ikara-flinders-ranges-national-park; wilpenapound.com.au

Ormiston Pound, NT

Drive from Alice Springs/Mparntwe almost to the end of the Tjoritja/West MacDonnell Ranges and you come to ever-popular Ormiston Gorge. Behind the gorge's back, and often overlooked by visitors, is Ormiston Pound, set inside a circle of mountains and funnelling into the gorge at one end. An 8.5km (3.3-mile) loop walk heads from the main car park into the pound before burrowing through the gorge to its main waterhole and a cooling swim to finish.

◉ nt.gov.au/parks/find-a-park/tjoritja-west-macdonnell-national-park

Gosses Bluff/Tnorala, NT

Just 75km (47 miles) from Ormiston Gorge, Gosses Bluff/Tnorala looks almost Uluru-like from a distance. A sacred place to the Western Arrernte People, it stands alone, isolated from the area's other mountains, and was imprinted here by a 600m (0.4-mile) meteorite that smashed into the Earth around 140 million years ago – the force produced one million times more energy than the atomic bomb dropped on Hiroshima.

Tnorala's entrance road (the final 6km/3.7 miles is 4WD-only) burrows through a break in the mountains and into the 5km (3.1-mile) crater, where a 750m (0.5-mile) walking trail loops around the valley floor, with a short side trail climbing a rocky outcrop for an elevated view.

◉ nt.gov.au/parks/find-a-park/tnorala-gosse-bluff-conservation-reserve

The path to Ormiston Gorge

Wolfe Creek/Kandimalal, WA

The world's second-largest meteorite crater (behind the Vredefort Crater in South Africa) forms a near-perfect, 880m (0.5-mile) circle in the desert 150km (93 miles) south of the Kimberley town of Halls Creek. Formed by the collision of a 50,000-tonne (55,116-ton) meteorite some 300,000 years ago (give or take a day or two), the crater has long been known to the Jaru Traditional Custodians, who have several stories relating to its creation, but was 'discovered' by European settlers only in 1947. There's a short, steep climb to the top of the crater, or you can walk around it in about an hour. From Halls Creek, the crater can be reached by 2WD during the dry season (around May to October).

🌐 exploreparks.dbca.wa.gov.au/park/wolfe-creek-meteorite-crater-national-park

THE LORD OF ISLANDS

◉ LORD HOWE ISLAND, NSW

A flight to Lord Howe Island is a prized ticket. With only 400 tourist beds on the World Heritage–listed island, 600km (373 miles) off the NSW coast, visitor numbers are capped to match, keeping it free of crowds and full of space.

It's an island where visitors tootle about on bikes – Lord Howe is only 11km (6.8 miles) in length, with 14km (8.7 miles) of sealed roads, so nothing is far – pausing at beaches and sliding into the crystalline waters of the island's lagoon.

Few people know this lagoon, which is protected by the world's southernmost barrier reef, quite as well as Anthony Riddle. A sixth-generation islander, Anthony has been running snorkelling and glass-bottom boat trips in the lagoon since he began the tour company Marine Adventures in 2002.

'There's over 500 different fish species and over 100 coral species – they're finding and identifying new ones all the time – and probably about 15 per cent are endemic to the area,' says Anthony, whose ancestor, Nathan Chase Thompson, settled on the island in 1853. 'The reef is unique in that it's a growing reef – we're seeing development in the coral – and since I started doing turtle tours, I've seen an increase in the turtle numbers. Every time I go out, I basically see something new and exciting.'

Notched around the island, lining the lagoon and elsewhere, is a series of beaches. The airport runway almost runs out onto the sands of Blinky Beach, which Anthony describes as 'having probably the clearest water of anywhere I've seen in the world'. Ned's Beach is fringed with a coral reef, making for colourful snorkelling directly off the beach.

For all the leisure possibilities, there's also Mount Gower, rising 875m (2870ft) out of the Pacific Ocean at Lord Howe's southern end and sometimes described as one of Australia's toughest day walks. The unmarked ascent involves rope climbs and steep, exposed sections and can only be done with a licensed guide, but it's a journey into a remarkable world of mist forest and providence petrels, a bird species that's known to nest in only one place on Earth: Lord Howe Island.

'You can literally yell at the sky and they drop at your feet,' Anthony says of the petrels. 'If you're standing between two trees and you put your arms out, they'll walk across the back of your arms to go to the other tree.'

All this and still there's a happy sense of subtropical isolation, shared with just the 400 other visitors and the 380 island residents. 'It's not like other island resorts, where the resort is owned by one person,' Anthony says. 'Everyone feels invested in the island because it's so small, so it's got a better community feel than any other island I've been to.'

- lordhoweisland.info
- marineadventureslordhowe.com

The remarkable Lord Howe Island

THE BEEHIVE BUNGLES

⊙ PURNULULU NATIONAL PARK, WA
KARJAGANUJARU COUNTRY

Even in Australia's pantheon of fantasy landscapes, the Bungle Bungle Range has few peers. This cluster of sandstone peaks, inside World Heritage–listed Purnululu National Park, rises up to 250m (820ft) out of the Kimberley plains. Each one is shaped a bit like a beehive and striped in layers of rock. Seen from above, it's a little like looking into a stone egg carton.

Located 300km (186 miles) south of Kununurra, with the final 53km (33 miles) accessible only by 4WD, it's a place so remote that it was known only to the area's Karjaganujaru Traditional Custodians until 1983, when it was spotted from a helicopter by a documentary film crew.

For many visitors, an interaction with the Bungle Bungles is a literal flying glimpse, with scenic flights operating out of Kununurra with Kimberley Air Tours (kimberleyairtours.com.au) and Aviair (aviair.com.au). Helicopter flights with HeliSpirit (helispirit.com.au) depart from the Bellburn airstrip inside the national park. As spectacular as it is from the air, however, the best things here happen on the ground. Short walking trails (2km/1.2 miles return each) squeeze into Echidna Chasm with its 200m/656-ft-high walls and the amphitheatre of Cathedral Gorge. Most immersive is the two- or three-day unmarked hike around Piccaninny Gorge (a holdover racist name from colonisation). A personal locator beacon (PLB) must be carried on the Piccaninny Gorge hike; they can be hired from the park visitor centre.

Purnululu National Park is only open from April to November (the dry season). There are two campgrounds inside the park – Walardi and Kurrajong – and glamping and lodge accommodation at Bungle Bungle Wilderness Lodge (aptouring.com.au/experiences/wilderness-lodges/bungle-bungle) and Bungle Bungles Savannah Lodge (bunglebunglesavannahlodge.com.au).

⊙ exploreparks.dbca.wa.gov.au/park/purnululu-national-park

CATCHING THE TUBE

UNDARA VOLCANIC NATIONAL PARK, QUEENSLAND
EWAMIAN COUNTRY

It's been a tranquil 5000 years since the last volcano erupted in Australia (an event not about to be repeated since the country now has no active volcanoes), but ample evidence of their molten tempers remains. Western Victoria is one of the largest volcanic plains on Earth, dotted with around 400 volcanoes, and craggy peaks such as Queensland's Glass House Mountains and Tasmania's The Nut are the eroded remnants of volcanic lava plugs.

Arguably the most impressive volcanic relic is the Undara Lava Tubes on the Traditional Lands of the Ewamian outside of Mount Surprise, four hours drive inland from Cairns. Resulting from an eruption 190,000 years ago, the tubes formed when the outer edge of a 160km (99-mile) lava flow solidified but the lava within continued to flow, leaving behind one of the longest cave systems on the planet.

Tours into the tubes are run by Discovery Resorts – Undara (the caravan park inside the national park). The Archway Explorer tour (which runs from March to October) pokes its nose into the caves, providing an easy and family-friendly look at the rounded tubes, which are up to 11m (36ft) high. The Wind Tunnel Explorer (Easter to September) delves deeper, though it involves some scrambling over rocks.

As dusk approaches, the Wildlife at Sunset tour ventures back to the mouth of Barkers Cave to witness (among other critters) thousands of microbats exiting the cave. In the warmer months, there's the possibility of sighting pythons and tree snakes hanging from branches to pick off bat snacks as the animals fly past.

- parks.des.qld.gov.au/parks/undara-volcanic
- discoveryholidayparks.com.au/undara

Top See an impressive volcano relic up close
Opposite Sandstone peaks of the Bungle Bungle Range

90	**Crocs, Culture and Art**
92	**Turtle Time**
94	**Sandy Roos**
95	**Urban Dolphins**
96	**The Devils' Island**
98	**The Great Cuttlefish Migration**
99	**A Croc of Rainforest**
100	**Shark Patrol**
103	**Bird is the Word**
104	**Crabs for Christmas**
107	**In Pursuit of Platypus**
108	**Reef Peeps**

"It's an event Sir David Attenborough has described as one of his 10 greatest TV moments"

WILDLIFE

CROCS, CULTURE AND ART

KAKADU NATIONAL PARK, NT
BININJ/MUNGGUY COUNTRY

In Kakadu National Park, nature and culture combine like few places on Earth. Around 10 per cent of the NT's crocodiles cruise Kakadu's waterways and floodplains, and one-third of Australia's bird species have been recorded here. But the country's second-largest national park isn't just about birds, beasts and beauty; it's also home to one of the world's greatest concentrations of rock-art sites and remains a thriving cultural landscape that's now jointly managed between the Bininj/Mungguy Traditional Owners and Parks Australia. Little wonder it's one of only 39 places in the world inscribed on UNESCO's World Heritage list for dual cultural and natural values.

This is a park not to be hurried – it saves its biggest rewards for those who take the time to absorb and learn from the land and its custodians.

Art and Culture

The most visible legacy of the 65,000-plus years of First Nations existence around Kakadu is the park's rock art, best seen at two major sites: Ubirr and Burrungkuy (Nourlangie).

Ubirr is at the park's northern end and is a favourite sunset-viewing spot for visitors. Before reaching Ubirr's summit to watch the sun sink behind the surrounding wetlands, take the 1km (0.6-mile) loop walk that passes the art sites, many in the X-ray style depicting food from the area such as fish, wallabies and goannas. Look for the example of contact art, with a 'white fella' standing with his hands in his pockets (believed to be a 19th-century buffalo hunter), and a painting of a thylacine (Tasmanian tiger), an animal that also roamed the Australian mainland until about 2000 years ago.

The main Anbangbang gallery at Burrungkuy (Nourlangie), reached on a two-hour return walk, was a traditional camping site, and its rock art shows a stunning image of Namarrkon (lightning man), European sailing ships and X-ray art of animals and fish.

In Jabiru, Kakadu's main town, there's contemporary First Nations art at the Marrawuddi Arts and Culture gallery (marrawuddi.com.au). The First Nations-owned Guluyambi Cultural Cruise (kakaduculturaltours.com.au/index.php/tours/guluyambi) motors upstream on the East Alligator River – crocs aplenty – that forms Kakadu's border with Arnhem Land. First Nations guides provide insight into culture and bush tucker, while a stop on the Arnhem Land riverbank also brings a display (and use by the guides) of hunting weapons and tools.

Chances are you'll spot a croc in Kakadu

Wildlife

Ten thousand crocodiles and 280 bird species can't be wrong – Kakadu is prime wildlife country. The best and safest way to see crocodiles is from the water on a pair of boat trips. The East Alligator River has one of the highest croc concentrations of any river in Australia, and the Guluyambi Cultural Cruise (above) typically provides plenty of sightings.

The First Nations-owned Yellow Water Cruise (kakadutoursandtravel.com.au/cruise/yellow-water-cruise) has a particular wildlife focus, drifting through the Yellow Water (Ngurrungurrudjba) wetlands that form part of the South Alligator River floodplain. It's a portal into a water world of crocodiles, buffaloes and iconic Top End bird species such as the jabiru and brolga. The sunrise and sunset sailings, when wildlife is most active and visible, are particularly popular, so book ahead.

Walks

If there's any one anecdote that amplifies the fact that Kakadu is best explored on foot, it's the tale of a tin miner who, in the 1940s, attempted to be the first person to drive his truck into one of Kakadu's southern valleys. A creek thwarted his attempt and even today the only way to reach the waterfall named for that miner's folly – Motor Car Falls – is by hiking.

Motor Car Falls is one of Kakadu's quietest trails, even though amply rewarded by classic Top End scenes of cliffs, a waterfall and a deep-green pool surrounded by monsoon forest. But it's also just one of around 40 marked day walks in the park. Personal favourites include the 2km (1.2-mile) return walk to Maguk waterfall and waterhole; the 12km (7.5-mile) Barrk Sandstone Walk, which rises up and over the sandstone outlier of Burrungkuy (Nourlangie), weaving through a virtual lost city of sandstone stacks and pillars atop the plateau and passing two rock-art sites (including Anbangbang); and the Yurmikmik walks into Motor Car Falls and beyond to Kurrundie Falls (a permit is needed to continue past Motor Car Falls to Kurrundie).

Note that the trail to the popular natural infinity pool atop Gunlom Falls has been closed at the request of the Traditional Owners since 2019, so check the park website for updates on its status.

🌐 parksaustralia.gov.au/kakadu

TURTLE TIME

◉ MON REPOS, QUEENSLAND
TARIBELANG BUNDA, GOORENG GOORENG,
GURANG & BYELLEE COUNTRY

Every year from around the end of October, more than 350 turtles drag themselves ashore on the beach in Mon Repos, 15km (9.3 miles) east of Bundaberg, to lay their eggs in the sand. It's the largest concentration of nesting turtles on Australia's east coast, with around 50 per cent of the South Pacific's nesting loggerhead turtles coming to this one beach (along with a few flatback and green sea turtles) to lay clutches of up to 100 eggs. The success of hatchlings on this 1.5km (0.9 miles) of sand is critical to the survival of the endangered loggerheads.

From November to March, national park rangers at the Mon Repos Turtle Centre conduct nightly tours to observe the turtles and help raise awareness of on-going conservation efforts. Females lay eggs from November to January, with hatchlings emerging and scrambling for the water from January to March – you'll be silently cheering their slow journey in or out of the ocean. This is the only way to view the turtles, so book well ahead. Tours begin at 6.30pm, and you'll head to the beach once patrolling rangers and volunteers sight the night's first turtles – settle in; it can take a while.

The Turtle Centre is open year-round and is free to visit, with a couple of daytime tours available. The Turtle Tales Immersive Experience is a guided tour through the centre, while Turtle Tracks and Tales is a ranger-led walk out to the beach to see nesting sites and turtle tracks during sunlight hours. Note that there are no live captive turtles in the centre.

◉ parks.des.qld.gov.au/parks/mon-repos

A loggerhead turtle hatchling heads for the ocean
Opposite **Mon Repos Conservation Park**

SANDY ROOS

VARIOUS LOCATIONS

It's the quintessential Australian coastal scene: kangaroos lazing or bounding along a beach. It could almost be a collage, combining two of Australia's signature sights – roos and gleaming white beaches – except that it's real at the following beaches.

Lucky Bay, WA

Venture onto one of Australia's most beautiful beaches around dawn or dusk and you might find you're not the only species admiring the vivid Cape Le Grand National Park coastal colours (though the roos actually come to graze on seaweed). The beach is 5km (3.1 miles) in length, but the lucky thing about Lucky Bay, 45 minutes drive from Esperance, is that the kangaroos seem to like the section of beach directly in front of the campground.

Casuarina Beach, Queensland

This beach in Cape Hillsborough National Park is spectacular enough at sunrise even without all those kangaroos routinely adding evocative marsupial silhouettes to your photos. Cape Hillsborough is a 45-minute drive north of Mackay and there's a basic campground in the park at Smalleys Beach.

Pebbly Beach, NSW

Don't believe the myth about Murramarang National Park's surfing kangaroos, but do expect to find eastern grey kangaroos grazing the dunes and even venturing down to the water's edge at Pebbly Beach. The national park is pinched between Ulladulla and Batemans Bay on the South Coast, with a campground in roo central, right behind Pebbly Beach.

Diamond Head Beach, NSW

This Crowdy Bay National Park beach, 40 minutes drive south of Port Macquarie, has a population of wallabies that enjoys nothing more than a dawn beach stroll in the shadow of Split Rock. They'll probably also mow/graze the lawns of your campsite.

Wherever you might head to view beach-loving kangaroos, please don't feed or touch the animals.

URBAN DOLPHINS

⊙ PORT RIVER, SA
KAURNA COUNTRY

Adelaide Dolphin Sanctuary in Port River
Opposite **Roos on Diamond Head Beach**

Viewing wildlife often requires heading to remote locations, but not if you're in Adelaide/Tandanya, where wild dolphins have commandeered a space within South Australia's largest port.

Protected as the Adelaide Dolphin Sanctuary, the waters of the Port River around Garden Island, just a 20-minute drive from the city centre, are home to around 30 resident bottlenose dolphins, with hundreds more dolphins known to visit the area. The sanctuary, incorporating a 10,000-year-old mangrove forest on Kaurna Country, is also at the edge of the Adelaide International Bird Sanctuary – Winaityinaityi Pangkara, meaning 'a country for all birds and the country that surrounds these birds' in Kaurna language. It is the southern end of a migratory route (extending as far as Siberia and Alaska) flown by more than five million birds a year.

Dolphin-watching boat and kayak trips – the former departing from McLaren Wharf in Port Adelaide, the latter from Garden Island – also take in Australia's largest ship graveyard, where more than 25 ships have been scuttled.

⊙ parks.sa.gov.au/parks/adelaide-dolphin-sanctuary

THE DEVILS' ISLAND

◉ MARIA ISLAND NATIONAL PARK, TASMANIA
PALAWA COUNTRY

On the nibbled lawns below the Darlington convict penitentiary on Maria Island, a crowd gathers under the setting sun. Wombats bustle about, wallabies graze and Cape Barren geese dash here and there, honking like belligerent motorists.

Away to the south, where the lawns end over a rise, the island plunges into the sea at the Painted Cliffs with their ink-blot-like sandstone patterns. In the opposite direction, another remarkable set of cliffs – the Fossil Cliffs, composed of millions of ancient fossils laid down on the seabed some 300 million years ago – provides evidence that animal life of some sort has long existed here. It continues today, with Maria Island, one of the most assured places in Australia to view a range of wildlife, including Tasmania's emblematic Tasmanian devil.

In the 1960s and '70s, a host of endangered native animals were released on the island to protect them from extinction, a program that was so successful that the island became known as the Noah's Ark of Australia. Today, wombats, Forester kangaroos, wallabies and Cape Barren geese are readily sighted, most commonly on the Darlington lawns, just steps from the ferry that runs to the island from Triabunna. On a single day here with my kids, we once counted 132 wombats.

In 2012, the experiment was repeated, when the endangered Tasmanian devil was introduced to the island. Free of the facial cancer that has decimated the population on the Tasmanian mainland, the animal is thriving and the island is the surest place to see one in the wild. The campground at the foot of the Darlington lawns is among the best locations.

⌖ parks.tas.gov.au/explore-our-parks/maria-island-national-park

Top **Wombats are easy to spot on Maria Island**

Bottom left **The island was once a convict penitentiary**

Bottom right **The illusive Tasmanian devil**

THE GREAT CUTTLEFISH MIGRATION

◉ WHYALLA, SA
BARNGALA COUNTRY

Think of great animal migrations and it might be the likes of wildebeest, humpback whales and Monarch butterflies that spring to mind, but head to the waters of Whyalla from May to August and it's all about the giant Australian cuttlefish.

Known to many purely for the white cuttlebones that wash up across beaches, these cephalopods – relatives of octopus and squid – arrive in their tens of thousands to mate and lay eggs in a 10km (6.2-mile) stretch of shallow, rocky water between False Bay and Fitzgerald Bay on the country of the Barngala People. It's the largest such gathering of cuttlefish in the world and a kaleidoscopic treat for snorkellers and divers. The planet's largest species of cuttlefish, the Australian giant cuttlefish grows up to 60cm (24in) in length and weighs up to 5kg (11olb). They are the ocean's chameleons, with males constantly changing their colours and shape to impress potential mates.

To view this marine spectacle, you can simply don a snorkel and mask and swim out from the shores. Black Point and Stony Point, on the Point Lowly peninsula 35km (22 miles) north of Whyalla, are the best access sites – the latter has a waist-height chain running through the water, making it a particularly good option for families.

Whyalla Diving Services runs guided snorkelling tours that give you an hour in the water with the cuttlefish. It also operates diving tours, getting you in among the cuttlefish, for certified divers.

Prefer to stay dry? Set sail on Cuttys' (cuttys.au) 45-minute glass-bottom boat tours for a perspective from above.

Cuttlefish numbers peak in June and July and, like all wild animal encounters, be sure to look but don't touch.

◉ whyalla.com
◉ whyalladivingservices.com.au

A CROC OF RAINFOREST

◉ DAINTREE VILLAGE, QUEENSLAND
KUKU YALANJI COUNTRY

An estimated 70 crocs call the Daintree home
Opposite **The giant Australian cuttlefish**

In the 1950s and '60s, estuarine crocodiles were hunted to the brink of extinction in north Queensland. Numbers fell so low in the Daintree River, 120km (75 miles) north of Cairns, that at least one local safely took on the dare of swimming across the once-croc-filled river in the 1980s.

Today, with the world's largest reptile declared a protected species, there are an estimated 70 crocodiles living in the river, and they're now sought as sightings rather than souvenirs on cruises along the edge of the Daintree Rainforest.

There are half a dozen operators running cruises – typically lasting an hour – on the Daintree, with none of the gimmickry such as crocs leaping for chicken lunches on poles. The dry season (around April to September) is the best time for viewing, with the river level at its lowest and the potential of sighting crocs along the banks as well as in the water.

In addition to the animal with the strongest bite on Earth, there's plentiful birdlife, including kingfishers, ospreys and black-necked storks, and colourful tree snakes, while the encompassing rainforest itself is also a star of the show.

Dated at up to 180 million years, the 1200-sq-km (3937-sq-mile) Daintree – part of the Wet Tropics of Queensland World Heritage site – is the world's oldest tropical rainforest, home to 65 per cent of Australia's butterfly species and 40 per cent of its bird species. It's said that in one hectare alone, you can expect to find more than 100 species of tree.

Drive 10km (6.2 miles) north of the Daintree River, which is crossed by a vehicle ferry, and you can delve into this canopy in the 23m (75-ft) Canopy Tower at the Daintree Discovery Centre.

SHARK PATROL

◉ SHARK BAY, WA
NHANDA, MALGANA & YINGKARTA COUNTRY

Some places have names that are almost meaningless, but there are others with names as evocative and descriptive as literature. Such as Shark Bay. The World Heritage–listed bay at Australia's westernmost point is home to 28 of its namesake shark species, but they're not even the most famous creatures here.

With the planet's largest seagrass beds, Shark Bay is home to around 10,000 dugongs, or 10 per cent of the world's population. In addition, one of the oldest life forms on Earth, stromatolites, are found here, bottlenose dolphins make daily feeding visits to Monkey Mia and 70 per cent of the loggerhead turtles found in Western Australia lay their eggs in Shark Bay.

But on a beach lining Big Lagoon, a tidal lagoon running deep into Francois Peron National Park, it's the sharks that are making themselves known as Darren Capewell steps out of his kayak and onto a dune-lined beach. Harmless nervous sharks and a shovelnose shark patrol the shore, but Darren, a Nhanda man best known as 'Capes', is looking at the red dunes.

'This is where our ancestors camped for thousands of years,' he tells his group of kayakers. 'All along here are burial sites.'

Capes grew up on this Country, part of the Traditional Lands of the Nhanda, Malgana and Yingkarta Peoples, and his grandfather was

An overhead view of Shark Bay
Opposite **Thousands of dugongs reside in the bay**

one of the area's last traditional tribal men, living entirely off the land. In the 1990s, Capes moved away to Perth/Boorloo to play AFL football, but on returning home to Country, he started Wula Gura Nyinda Eco Cultural Adventures in 2004, leading kayaking tours (among other trips) through Shark Bay's aquarium-like waters.

The scenes around Big Lagoon are a colourful snapshot of the greater Shark Bay shores. The waters are clean and clear and ringed by dunes both red and white. Beside a campground at its eastern edge, Capes throws a handful of sand into the water as a sign of respect for the lagoon, and the group begins to paddle over water so clear the kayaks seem almost to levitate.

It's a 2km (1.2-mile) paddle – mostly over water little more than hip-deep – across the lagoon to the beach and dunes where Capes leads his group on foot to the top of the dunes. From this vantage point, the blue lagoon seems to almost wrap around the dunes. Asking each person to grab a handful of red sand, he leads them back down the dunes to the beach. Placing a hand on the white sand, they pour the red sand over it, creating an ephemeral hand stencil on the beach.

'Country was here before us and Country will be here long after we're gone,' he says. 'That's why we try to impress on people that we have to respect Country.'

Continuing around the shores, there will be time for a swim, a quick cast of a fishing line and a short walk into a hollow between dunes, where kangaroos have scratched a pit searching for fresh water. It's a perfect blend of Country, culture and kayaks.

'We don't just want people to fill up their eyes; we want them to feel it in here,' Capes says, tapping his stomach. 'To fill up their guts.'

- sharkbay.org
- wulagura.com.au

Top **Friarbird in Cairns**

Bottom **A pair of southern whitefaces in Capertee Valley**

BIRD IS THE WORD

◎ **VARIOUS LOCATIONS**

Mike Barrow describes birdwatching as a lifetime passion that became an obsession when he moved to Sydney/Warrane's northern beaches 15 years ago. In 2020 he formed Aussie Bird Tours, offering birding trips around Sydney/Warrane and beyond. We asked him for five of his favourite twitching locations across Australia.

Capertee Valley, NSW
It's the widest valley in the world – wider than the Grand Canyon – and it's home to more than 200 bird species. It's the breeding ground for the regent honeyeater, which is close to extinction – there are only about 200 pairs left in the world.

Cairns, Queensland
The Esplanade is excellent for its migrating shorebirds and waders – they roost at high tide, or you need a scope. The cemetery and Botanic Gardens are good for birds, and the Atherton Tablelands for upper-rainforest birds.

Bruny Island, Tasmania
Home to all 12 of Tasmania's endemic bird species. The most sought-after bird is the forty-spotted pardalote, and Bruny is a breeding ground for them. They're often seen near Inala and along the coastal road from near the ferry to Dennes Point.

Western Treatment Plant, Victoria
You might see up to 120 bird species in a day. There can be brolgas here and orange-bellied parrots when they migrate from Tasmania in winter – it's a good smelly day out.

Kakadu National Park, NT
More than 280 bird species have been spotted in Kakadu – that's about one-third of all the species in Australia. In three days in the park, you can tick off most of them.

◎ aussiebirdtours.com.au

CRABS FOR CHRISTMAS

CHRISTMAS ISLAND

When the first rains of the wet season hit Christmas Island, 1500km (932 miles) off the West Australian coast and just 350km (217 miles) off the Java coast in Indonesia, it's more than water that pours down the slopes. These October or November rains are also the trigger for one of the world's largest animal migrations, when tens of millions of endemic red crabs march from their burrows on the island's high slopes to the ocean to spawn.

It's an event Sir David Attenborough has described as one of his 10 greatest TV moments, and one that the 1700 residents of this external Australian territory must adjust their lives around every year. Roads close, construction can be stopped and daily life must work to the crabs' rhythms.

'The crabs move in the cool parts of the day – early morning and late afternoon – so what you try to do is not move around at that time,' says island resident Lisa Preston. 'If you get to four o'clock and you need milk or butter, or to get something for dinner, you get halfway along the road and realise there are crabs everywhere. You think, I'll wait till after dark when it slows down a bit, or you just park the car and walk the rest of the way. It's faster walking than trying to drive and avoid the crabs.

'We leave our sliding door open at home for the cat to pop in and out, and the crabs come in through that way. So you're lying in bed and you can hear crabs – tick, tick, tick – against the bedroom wall or under the bed.'

Lasting about one month – sometimes two – the migration sees the ocean turn black as millions of crabs shake loose their dark eggs (according to new research, each female crab might release up to 450,000 eggs) before climbing back to their high burrows, when the island settles back into its tropical normality.

It was in the middle of this migration, by coincidence rather than design, that Lisa arrived on Christmas Island on holiday in 1996. Within a year, she'd packed up her life in Perth/Boorloo and moved to the island, where her company, Indian Ocean Experiences, now runs nature tours, including crab spawning tours.

The crabs are just one component of Christmas Island's natural pedigree. Around 70 per cent of the 134-sq-km (51.7-sq-mile) island is protected as Christmas Island National Park, and it's one of Australia's best birdwatching locations – standout species include tropicbirds and the world's rarest booby and frigatebird.

Diving is also spectacular, with good coral reefs around the island and the little-heralded

One of the world's largest animal migrations

presence of whale sharks through the wet season.

'They think the whale sharks actually may come around for the crab spawn,' Lisa says. 'People have filmed the whale sharks filter feeding through the crab spawn. We don't have spotter planes like Exmouth, but we've got two proficient dive operators that are good at spotting them just from the vessel.

'Year on year it's different. Some years, sightings are a little bit sporadic; other times, there might be 13 different whale shark sightings on a dive.'

- christmas.net.au
- indianoceanexperiences.com.au

Top **A platypus on Lake Elizabeth**

Bottom **A platypus viewing platform in Eungella National Park**

IN PURSUIT OF PLATYPUS

◉ **VARIOUS LOCATIONS**

The most curious and confounding of Australia's native creatures is surely the platypus, the swimming monotreme that lays eggs, has a bill like a duck and a tail like a beaver. It's also one of the most elusive of the country's suite of emblematic mammals, but head to one of the following waterways around dawn or dusk and your luck might just be in.

Eungella National Park, Queensland

A viewing platform along Broken River provides a platypus vantage point with reliable sightings.

🌐 parks.desi.qld.gov.au/parks/eungella

Running River, Queensland

Evening tours from Hidden Valley Cabins, Australia's first 100 per cent carbon-neutral resort, will have you sitting quietly on the riverbank for near-guaranteed glimpses.

🌐 hiddenvalleycabins.com.au

Lake Elizabeth, Victoria

Join a dusk canoe trip, with your guide paddling you slowly among the drowned trees and platypuses of this lake formed by a landslide in 1952.

🌐 platypustours.net.au

Mersey River, Tasmania

Head to Warrawee Forest Reserve, just south of the town of Latrobe, where platypuses are commonly sighted in the Mersey River. If you luck out, there's always Latrobe's Big Platypus outside the Axeman's Hall of Fame – the stretch of river across the road is another platypus possibility.

Hobart Rivulet, Tasmania

The most unexpected sightings of all come in a city. Set out from the city centre, heading upstream along the rivulet and pause to scan the deeper pools where platypuses are often farming for food.

REEF PEEPS

GREAT BARRIER REEF, QUEENSLAND
NGARO–GURENG GURENG COUNTRY & ALL FIRST NATIONS IN BETWEEN

Michelle Barry is a Master Reef Guide, scuba instructor and passionate marine naturalist who has been diving and snorkelling on the Great Barrier Reef for more than 14 years. Here are five of her favourite snorkelling sites.

Cod Hole, Ribbon Reef #10

The Cod Hole, on the north-eastern edge of Ribbon Reef number 10, is a treasure trove steeped in conservation history. Its dynamic residents and powerful tidal flows create an unparalleled snorkelling experience. It's a favourite not only for the abundant hard coral and gin-clear water, but also for the resident potato cod, a fish species that can weigh up to 100kg (2.2lb) and measure nearly 2m (6.5ft). Intelligent and with their own individual personalities, these fish might cautiously observe or boldly approach snorkellers and divers, asserting their territorial presence.

Normanby/Mabel Island, Frankland Islands Group

I immediately fell in love with this quaint inshore island. Uniquely positioned with a gravitational current that predominantly moves northward most of the year, it's ideal for drift snorkelling along the reef crest. More than 80 giant clams adorn the sloping shelf, with numerous turtle-cleaning stations along the route. My favourite spot lies at Mabel Island's southern tip, in the Cabbage Patch, boasting incredible hard corals resembling thousands of bouquets of flowers. In May, manta rays gracefully glide around the island, utilising the cleaning stations, while lucky winter snorkellers might catch sight of humpback whales on their migration route.

Two Towers, Ribbon Reef #10

A tale of resilience and renewal, Two Towers has weathered countless hardships and emerged stronger than ever. Enduring predation by crown-of-thorns starfish, devastation from Cyclone Nathan (2015) and consecutive bleaching events, these isolated pinnacles now teem with rare wildlife such as orange-banded garden eels, dwarf minke whales (June–July), ornate ghost pipefish and so much more. While full recovery is still underway, the vibrant biodiversity and profound beauty in the site's top 8m (26ft) often move visitors to tears.

Moore Reef

Despite its status as the Great Barrier Reef's most visited site, Moore Reef remains spectacular. My favourite snorkel wall, accessible only from the Reef Magic pontoon, descends 25m (82ft) straight down and features deep canyons and swim-throughs that are a paradise for free divers and advanced snorkellers. Hard and soft corals in every colour of the rainbow adorn the reef's entire length, creating a mesmerising underwater landscape.

Ribbon Reef #9 1/3

Nestled in the south-western corner of this expansive reef, perched atop an ancient paleo river channel, is the reef that could arguably be deemed the most exquisite on our planet. Known by various names, the site stands out as an anomaly amid neighbouring reefs ravaged by cyclones, predation and bleaching events. These coral gardens appear untouched by time, boasting unmatched species diversity and colony sizes. With branching corals thicker than human arms and boulder corals resembling small homes, it's truly a visual feast. Colours and shapes intertwine to craft mesmerising forms, all meticulously created and sustained by tiny, pin-sized coral polyps.

Top **Scuba diving at Moore Reef**
Bottom **The Great Barrier Reef from above**

113	Sharing Hot Springs
114	From Private Wilderness Sanctuary to World Heritage Site?
116	Farm Fresh
117	A Great Ocean Road Wonder
119	Turning Wine into Water
120	Reef Recovery: Citizen Science Programs
123	Float Your Boat in the Huon Valley
126	Southern Hemishpere's Largest Island Research Centre

"The region was so geologically unique that it needed to be protected"

RESPONSIBLE TRAVEL

Top **Overhead Talaroo Hot Springs**
Bottom **The boardwalk allows access to the hot springs**

SHARING HOT SPRINGS

◉ TALAROO, QUEENSLAND
EWAMIAN COUNTRY

Talaroo Hot Springs in north-west Queensland's Gulf Savannah reach a scorching 68°C (154°F). They were formed over millions of years and are recognised as a rare ecosystem of extreme conservation value, one of only a handful of mound springs (natural outlets for the Great Artesian Basin) in Australia.

The springs are a significant cultural site for the Ewamian People, located on Talaroo Indigenous Protected Area (IPA). Talaroo IPA is managed for its conservation and cultural values and is rich in Dreaming stories centred on the healing waters of the hot springs.

During European expansion, Ewamian people were removed from Country, so returning here is critical, connecting them back to the land, their culture, language and story places. In 2013, Ewamian People received a native title determination over 29,000 sq km (11,200 sq miles) of their traditional Country and Talaroo is at the heart of it. Ewamian Rangers play a key role at Talaroo, protecting nature and culture by combining traditional knowledge and Western science. This includes protecting biodiversity, as well as fire, weed and feral animal management.

Ewamian Rangers also assist in managing Talaroo Hot Springs, which were opened to the public in 2021 and is now a leading cultural tourism business in the Etheridge Shire (you can visit from April to September). Talaroo Hot Springs offers daily guided cultural tours, soak pools, a bike trail and access to the Einasleigh River. A caravan park with over 40 powered and unpowered campsites, a communal camp kitchen and four eco-tents with private bathing combine to make the perfect visit for a unique experience.

The Ewamian Rangers are one of more than 50 ranger groups nationally that are part of Country Needs People's network, an independent not-for-profit organisation working alongside frontline Indigenous partners to grow, support and advocate for Indigenous Rangers Australia-wide. Over 25 per cent of Australia is now held in Indigenous ownership – that's more than 170 million hectares (420 million acres).

- talaroo.com.au
- countryneedspeople.org.au

Sharon Prior

FROM PRIVATE WILDERNESS SANCTUARY TO WORLD HERITAGE SITE?

◉ ARKAROOLA WILDERNESS SANCTUARY, SA
ADNYAMATHANHA COUNTRY

On a field trip to the northern Flinders Ranges in the late 1930s, Australia's most famous geologist, Sir Douglas Mawson, commented to a student that the region was so geologically unique that it needed to be protected. Thirty years later, after years of unsuccessfully petitioning the South Australian Government to preserve the area, that very student – Reg Sprigg – purchased the land and created the Arkaroola Wilderness Sanctuary.

'Dad went to the government on each occasion the property came up for sale, because it really wasn't a viable station,' says Reg's son Doug. 'Eventually, when it came on the market in 1967, someone from government said, "if you feel so strongly about it, do it yourself". So Dad bought the lease, and I think Mum found out about three months later when she looked at the bank balance.'

He wanted to run it along the lines of a national park and what he thought national parks should do – really be a place for future generations. But it had to generate its own funds through tourism.'

Named after Mawson, Doug is now the director of Arkaroola, a remote and mountainous 610-sq-km (236-sq-mi) private sanctuary on Adnyamathanha Country, eight hours drive north of Adelaide. Across more than five decades of protection, he's watched the landscape transform.

'My memory is fallible, but photographs are a good record, and I got out some photographs just recently of the Ridgetop area from about 1969, and it was desolate by comparison with now,' he says.

In the first 20 years of the sanctuary's existence, almost 100,000 feral goats were culled, which saw the native population of yellow-footed rock wallabies rebound. Where once they were barely sighted, they're now easily seen around Arkaroola Village and on the slopes of Griselda Hill beside the village.

'They bred up fantastically,' Doug says. 'So much so that when the first census of wallabies was done in 1982, the estimate was that over half the world's population was on Arkaroola.'

At the sanctuary's heart is Arkaroola Village, with motel-style accommodation, camping and a restaurant and bar. Among a host of 4WD tracks, most of which were built by uranium prospectors (there proved to be only enough uranium to hold their interest, not enough to be commercially viable), is the Ridgetop Track. This spectacularly precipitous road is open only to Arkaroola's safari-style tour vehicles, weaving across the mountains to Sillers Lookout, which peers out over the salt pan of Lake Frome, said to be one of the whitest spots on Earth (NASA uses it to calibrate satellites in much the way a camera takes a white balance). In 2023, a Ridgetop Sleepout was opened along the track, allowing visitors to stay the night in glamping-style swags atop a narrow ridge.

Arkaroola is now also part of an area through the Flinders Ranges that has been nominated for UNESCO World Heritage listing for its significant fossil deposits. These include Ediacaran fossils, which are some of the oldest known animal fossils in the world and were uncovered by Reg Sprigg in 1946. A decision from UNESCO on the listing is expected in 2026.

🜨 arkaroola.com.au

Top **Doug Sprigg, the director of Arkaroola**
Bottom **Arkaroola is a geological gem**

FARM FRESH

◉ BYRON BAY, NSW
BUNDJALUNG, ARAKWAL, MINJUNGBAL & WIDJABUL COUNTRY

The Three Blue Ducks restaurant

A day at the farm has never had so much possibility as a visit to The Farm near Byron Bay. This working 32-hectare (79-acre) farm, 6km (3.7 miles) inland from Byron Bay on Bundjalung, Arakwal, Minjungbal and Widjabul Country, houses a collection of complementary micro-businesses, creating a village-like setting fuelled by the farm's soil and produce.

The on-site Three Blue Ducks restaurant sources its meat and eggs from the property's heritage-breed pigs, Scottish Highland cattle and chickens (or grab a takeaway hamper in a hessian bag for a picnic on the property), and the Baylato gelateria uses milk from The Farm's cows. There's a florist, organic nursery, produce store and fermentary, all sourcing their produce (and flowers) from the property. It's food miles measured in footsteps.

For the kids, there's animal feeding daily at 10am, and guided farm tours run on Friday, Saturday and Sunday (bookings essential).

◉ thefarm.com.au

A GREAT OCEAN ROAD WONDER

◉ APOLLO BAY, VICTORIA
GADUBANUD COUNTRY

Among the many wonders of the Great Ocean Road, there's Wildlife Wonders. This social enterprise, 5km (3 miles) south of Apollo Bay on Gadubanud Country, is a private wildlife sanctuary, home to the likes of koalas, eastern grey kangaroos, bandicoots, sugar gliders and the carnivorous Otway black snail.

Created by Brian Massey, the art director on Peter Jackson's trilogy of Hobbit movies, the sanctuary conducts 75-minute, wheelchair-accessible guided tours through the property, which is ringed by a fox- and cat-proof fence.

All funds from the sanctuary go to the local Conservation Ecology Centre, which works to restore habitats and control feral fox and cat populations. The centre's research base is inside the sanctuary and is visited during the walks.

To see the wildlife at its most active, book ahead for the Dusk Discovery Wildlife Tour.

◉ wildlifewonders.org.au

Top **A New Holland honeyeater**
Bottom **Otway black snail**

Banrock Station wetlands

TURNING WINE INTO WATER

KINGSTON ON MURRAY, SA
NGARRINDJERI COUNTRY

The conversion of water into wine might be biblical, but the inverse – the conversion of a winery into a wetland – is no less a miracle. On the bank of the Murray River in South Australia's Riverland region, Banrock Station was, until 1994, a heavily worked sheep station. Purchased by a winery that year, the degraded land was destocked and vines were planted along the ridges. Most significantly, a remarkable wetland was planned inside a bend of the river.

Returning the land to cyclical periods of wet and dry, the 250-hectare/617-acre wetland has revitalised the land. In 2002, it was chosen as Australia's first privately owned Ramsar site, recognising it as a wetland of international importance. Almost 200 bird species – about 25 per cent of Australia's total species – have been recorded on the property.

Today, Banrock Station's rammed-earth cellar door doubles as a window onto the wetland, which is maintained by three full-time rangers. Walking trails set out from its doors to a boardwalk across the wetland – Banrock's most popular walk – and an 8km (5-mile) lap of the bird-hide-dotted wetland on a trail that's listed as one of South Australia's 40 Great Short Walks.

Along the shores of the wetland, it's easy to forget that this is one of the largest working wineries in the Riverland, though you can also order a picnic hamper of goodies, a bottle of wine and a rug to enjoy some creature comforts among the creatures.

banrockstation.com.au

REEF RECOVERY: CITIZEN SCIENCE PROGRAMS

GREAT BARRIER REEF, QUEENSLAND
NGARO–GURENG GURENG COUNTRY & ALL FIRST NATIONS IN BETWEEN

Commonly, a visit to the Great Barrier Reef prompts a wish to do something, however small, to help the preservation of the world's largest living structure, which faces multiple threats to its health and existence.

The reef is the primary focus of citizen science programs in Australia, giving visitors the chance to play a role as custodians and protectors. Projects recommended by Queensland's Department of Environment, Science and Innovation include the following.

Eye on the Reef

This app, created by the Great Barrier Reef Marine Park Authority (the reef's management body), asks visitors to record marine life sightings, reef activity and health reports on sections of the reef, creating an extensive database of reef life and activity for scientists and marine park managers.

www2.gbrmpa.gov.au/help/eye-on-the-reef

Great Reef Census

Each year, from October to December, divers and snorkellers take part in this census, submitting their photos of the reef for analysis. Starting in 2020, the census had, at the time of writing, compiled more than 110,000 images covering almost 20 per cent of the reefs that make up the Great Barrier Reef, creating an ongoing visual record of change.

greatreefcensus.org

CoralWatch

This University of Queensland program has been running for more than two decades. Participants apply for a Coral Health Chart from CoralWatch and then match the colours on the chart to the colours of the reef they visit, recording the coral type – boulder, branching, plate or soft – before submitting a data sheet to CoralWatch's database.

coralwatch.org

Reef Check Australia

To participate in this more committed program you need to complete an online theory training course followed by an in-water training session (which involves four to six dives or snorkels) in Brisbane/Meanjin, the Sunshine Coast or Gold Coast. Reef Check surveyors can then get involved in monitoring 40 sites across the reef, using globally standardised Reef Check surveys.

reefcheckaustralia.org

Visitors can lend a hand to protect the Great Barrier Reef

Top and bottom **Traditional wooden boat construction**

FLOAT YOUR BOAT IN THE HUON VALLEY

◎ FRANKLIN, TASMANIA
PALAWA COUNTRY

In a workshop on the bank of the Huon River in Franklin, 40 minutes drive south of Hobart/nipaluna, the air is rich with the scent of timber. On the floor, over days, a boat is being crafted from wood, its boards meticulously planed and sanded by knowing hands.

It is a typical project at the Wooden Boat Centre, Australia's only school devoted to traditional wooden boat construction, suitably situated in Tasmania, an island where almost one in every eight people possesses a boat licence. Participants at the Wooden Boat Centre can sign up for courses that range from half-day instruction on knotwork to multiday construction of sailing dinghies or canoes. Other options include the making of trout landing nets, shipwright stools and kayak and canoe paddles. There's even a year-long boat-building course.

Just want to see the work in action? Simply turn up at the workshop during opening hours, when volunteer guides lead 40-minute tours of the centre, detailing its history and the boats in construction.

The centre's work comes into particular focus during Hobart/nipaluna's biennial Australian Wooden Boat Festival, held over four days in February (odd-numbered years). Billed as the Southern Hemisphere's largest wooden boat festival, it fills the city's docks and estuary with a massive fleet of wooden boats, from tall ships and yachts to clinker dinghies.

◎ woodenboatcentre.com

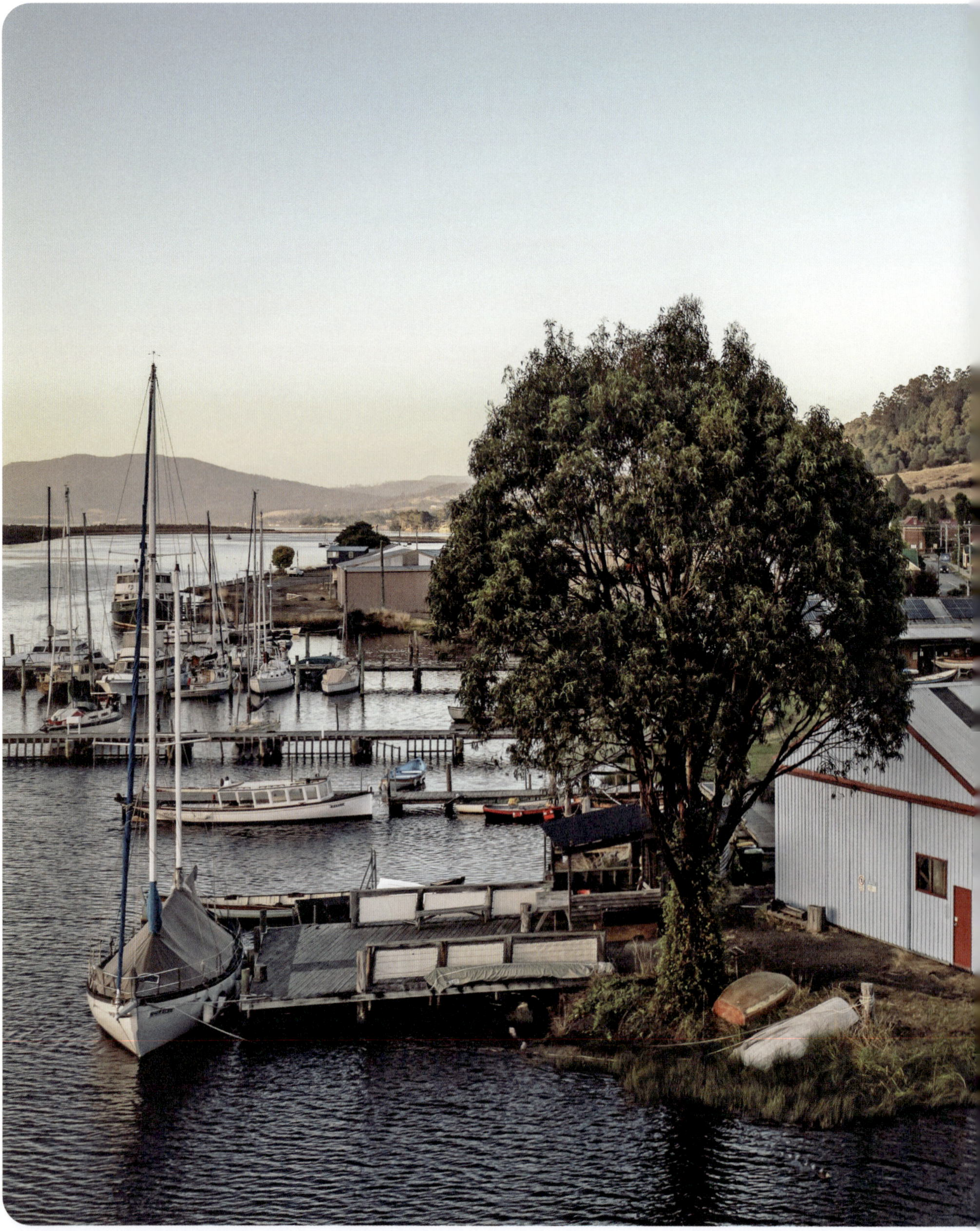

Wooden Boat Centre

SOUTHERN HEMISPHERE'S LARGEST ISLAND RESEARCH CENTRE

◉ HERON ISLAND, QUEENSLAND
GOORENG GOORENG, GURANG, BAILAI & TARIBELANG BUNDA COUNTRY

Less than 1km (0.6 miles) in length and bisected by the Tropic of Capricorn, the tiny coral cay of Heron Island is one of the Great Barrier Reef's southernmost islands, ensconced inside Heron Reef. From November to March, it's an important nesting site for green and loggerhead turtles (both threatened species), but the island's work on natural conservation stretches across the whole year.

The island, which is around 70km (43 miles) off the coast from Gladstone, has been home to the largest island-based research station in the Southern Hemisphere since the 1950s. Operated by the University of Queensland, the research and teaching facility runs researcher-led tours for guests at the surrounding Heron Island Resort (day visitors can't access the island). These tours provide insight into the centre's marine research through its wet and dry laboratories, its shark pool and its aquariums. Arrange research station tours through the resort reception.

If you're on the island during turtle nesting season, be sure to abide by a few simple rules. Lights can spook and confuse the turtles, so no flash photography; don't approach within 10m (33ft) of an animal; and avoid walking in the dunes so that you don't trample any nests. Hatchlings begin to emerge around early January.

◉ heronisland.com; uq.edu.au/heron-island-research-station

Top **The island is a crucial nesting site for local turtles**
Bottom **Heron Island**

130	**Bush Tucker Foraging**
132	**The Great Ocean Feed**
133	**Dining on Kangaroo (Island)**
134	**Straight to the Top: Urban Rooftop Bars**
136	**Wine and Trout**
137	**Wade for It**
138	**Margaret's Palate**
139	**Market Magic**
140	**Beyond Pub Grub**
142	**Bruny's Bounty**
144	**Fish Frenzy**
145	**Taste Your Birth Year at Seppeltsfield**
146	**Tasmania's Whisky Revolution**
149	**Australia's First City of Gastronomy**
150	**Australia's Top Cooking School**

"You could easily finish Australia's most famous road trip just as enamoured with the food"

FOOD & DRINK

BUSH TUCKER FORAGING

VARIOUS LOCATIONS

Growing up on Country in Western Australia's East Kimberley, Jaru woman Samantha Martin spent plenty of time with her mum and aunties learning about surviving off the land. It was an upbringing that seeded a passion for bush tucker – native Australian food – that has seen her dubbed the Bush Tukka Woman.

'First Nations people have been hunting large and small game animals, fresh and saltwater marine life and gathering fruit, nuts, seeds and roots from the abundant Australian bush for tens of thousands of years,' says the author of the *Bush Tukka Guide*.

'People treat bush tucker as a novelty, but it can be a lot more than that. I've explored this magnificent country by land and by sea, and have discovered some great possibilities and opportunities for people to explore. I'd like to introduce you to some hunting, gathering and foraging experiences that will enhance and enrich your love, respect and appreciation for not only our cultures but also our bush foods.'

palawa kipli

Tasmania's only Aboriginal food business, based at piyura kitina/Risdon Cove, a 15-minute drive from Hobart/nipaluna's CBD. On this Aboriginal returned land, palawa kipli offers an array of cultural food experiences, including a kipli takara bush tucker tour and catering with traditional Aboriginal food.

palawakipli.com

Southern Cross Cultural Tour

From Ardyaloon community in the West Kimberley, Bardi-Jawi man Bolo Angus and his family run half-day tours across diverse Kimberley landscapes to reach the coastline at the back of Lullumb. You'll learn hunting stories and techniques for catching mud crabs, and collect oysters and mud mussels out of the mangroves. It's all then prepared over a traditional cook-up at their bush camp. This tour, which runs from April to September, is also great for bird lovers.

facebook.com/southerncrosslullumb

Kimberley Dreaming

Tag-along tours operated by Ngarinyin (Wilinggin) and Jaru woman Sally Martin and partner Ben Smith. Guests on these three- to seven-day tours on traditional lands in East Kimberley experience camping with custodians and on Country near beautiful waterholes tucked away in rugged ranges. Stories are shared around the campfire and there's bush tucker such as freshwater *cherabins* (prawns), barramundi, even turtles if you're game, caught and cooked on the hot coals. It's the taste of the Kimberley.

kimberleydreaming.com.au

Kuku Yalanji Cultural Habitat Tours

Explore special north Queensland places and hunting grounds of the Kuku Yalanji Bamas, learning first-hand from proud traditional Kuku Yalanji brothers Linc and Brandon Walker. The pioneers of bush-food and hunting tours, they've been operating since 1999 and, in my humble opinion, bring a 100 per cent authentic traditional cultural experience in the ever-changing mudflats and tidal lagoons. These fullas don't just do this as a business; this is their way of life.

Following in the footsteps of their ancestors, you use traditional spears made and crafted by Brandon and Linc and their sons (after a crash course on how to use the spears). Everything you hunt and gather is taken back to their beach camp and cooked into a massive one-pot wonder using Brandon's secret chilli mud crab ingredients. You then feast on the beach under the trees, enjoying an educational lesson about ancient artefacts.

kycht.com.au

Bush Tukka Woman Samantha Martin

THE GREAT OCEAN FEED

📍 TWELVE APOSTLES FOOD ARTISAN TRAIL, VICTORIA
EASTERN MAAR, GUNDITJMARA, GADUBANUD & WADAWURRUNG COUNTRY

The scenery along the Great Ocean Road is delicious, but you could easily finish Australia's most famous road trip just as enamoured with the food. Centred on Timboon, inland from the iconic Twelve Apostles sea stacks on Eastern Maar, Gunditjmara, Gadubanud and Wadawurrung land, the 12 Apostles Food Artisan Trail bakes together more than a dozen gourmet food and drink stops along an 88km (55-mile) driving loop.

Turning off the Great Ocean Road at Princetown Rd, just 2km (1.25 miles) from the 12 Apostles, the trail begins sweetly, stopping for treats at Gorge Chocolates and Dairylicious Farm Fudge (both with cafes) then washing them down at Keyang Marr Vineyard, set on the fertile slopes of an extinct volcano outside Cobden.

The greatest concentration of producers is in and around food-focussed Timboon, where the options include Timboon Fine Ice Cream (complete with its 'Sundae School' if you want a primer on the ice-cream-making process) and the Timboon Railway Shed Distillery, claiming the country's largest collection of Australian-made spirits (in addition to its own single malts). Completing the triumvirate of vigneron, distiller and brewer is the Sow and Piglets Brewery, with its English- and German-style beers as the trail returns to the Great Ocean Road in Port Campbell sated and ready to digest more of the drive's celebrated seascapes.

🌐 12apostlesfoodartisans.com.au

Timboon Fine Ice Cream
Opposite **A Kangaroo Island Spirits cocktail**

DINING ON KANGAROO (ISLAND)

KANGAROO ISLAND, SA
RAMINDJERI, NGARRINDJERI, KAURNA & BARNGALLA COUNTRY

Best known for its natural menagerie of koalas, fur seals, sea lions and eponymous roos, Kangaroo Island has an equally impressive collection of food and drink experiences. Symbolic of the island's preserving isolation is its honey, produced by Ligurian bees that were first brought to 'KI' in the 1880s and are now considered the world's purest strain of Ligurian bees.

Touring the island, you'll find a trio of honey producers – Clifford's Honey Farm, Kangaroo Island Living Honey and Island Beehive – offering everything from tastings to tours and beekeeping experiences. Other farm gates include a lavender farm, eucalyptus distillery and the Oyster Farm Shop.

KI is also making a splash among drinkers, with half a dozen winery cellar doors and the farm-based Kangaroo Island Brewery with its taproom cobbled together from parts of old shearing sheds, wharves and locally quarried stone. Kangaroo Island Spirits, a five-minute drive away, was Australia's first dedicated gin distillery. Almost 20 years on, it's crafting a range of gins (and vodkas) using botanicals from its distillery garden as well as running cocktail masterclasses and blend-your-own-gin sessions.

Shading all experiences – literally – is the Enchanted Fig Tree, a living outdoor restaurant among the limbs and leaves of a 120-year-old fig tree. Open from November to early April (the warmest months on the island), meals focus on island produce – marron, island meats, honey, native boobialla – and begin with canapes in a surprise location before shifting to dining tables hidden within the sprawling branches of the tree.

- tourkangarooisland.com.au
- gastronomodining.com.au

STRAIGHT TO THE TOP: URBAN ROOFTOP BARS

◉ VARIOUS LOCATIONS

In the warm Australian climate, the best place to be with a drink in hand is often on the roof. Capital cities (and beyond) abound in rooftop bars, providing experiences and views the equal of any cocktail you might order.

Sydney/Warrane
Blu Bar on 36 stares directly down onto the punk hairdo of the Opera House and the arch of the Harbour Bridge from the 36th floor of the Shangri-La Sydney hotel.
Others: Zephyr Bar, The Glenmore, Smoke

Melbourne/Naarm
Atop five-storey, 120-year-old Pacific House, HER ROOFTOP's open-air city views and natural wines are just the beginning. Descend one floor to find the excellent BKK Thai restaurant, and another floor to enter the Music Room, a tiny 'listening bar' with a collection of 3000 vinyl records.
Others: Naked in the Sky, Runner Up, Johnny's Green Room

Brisbane/Meanjin
Look one way to see the city, look the other way to peer into the Gabba stadium right beside you at the well-named Sunsets atop a Kangaroo Point apartment block.
Others: Fiume, Valley Hops Brewing

Adelaide/Tandanya
2KW popularised rooftop revelling in the South Australian capital. Balanced atop the historic Bank of NSW building, it's a festive spot with ripping views over the Festival Centre and Adelaide Oval.
Others: Nineteen Ten, Hennessy

Perth/Boorloo
Less about the views and more about the buzz, the small Mechanics' Institute Bar might only be two levels off the street, but that places it among the historic rooftops of Northbridge.
Others: AGWA Rooftop, Prince Lane

Hobart/nipaluna
Braving the southern outdoor climes is 12th-floor AURA, with the triumvirate of Hobart/nipaluna views – mountain, city and water – plus the refined touch of Saturday High Tea.
Others: Telegraph Hotel

Darwin/Garramilla
Take in sunset over the water, or watch tropical storms roll in, from Zen Rooftop Lounge atop the Ramada Suites.
Other: Smith St Social

Top **Mechanics' Institute Bar** in Perth/Boorloo
Bottom **HER ROOFTOP** in Melbourne/Naarm

WINE AND TROUT

ORANGE, NSW
WIRADJURI COUNTRY

At Printhie Wines' cool-climate vineyard, the question isn't so much which wine you'd like with your fish as which fish you'd like with your wine. At this winery in Orange, four hours drive west of Sydney/Warrane, cellar door visits can be combined with a lesson in fly-fishing in the vineyard's lake.

Under the watch of a private instructor for two hours, you'll learn to rig the rod, cast and reel in a rainbow trout, aided by a glass or two of a Printhie sparkling. When the fishing is done, the visit continues with a private wine tasting inside the cellar door and the option to move onto the wine bar – awarded a chef hat in the respected 2024 *Good Food Guide* – for oysters fresh from Printhie's oyster tank.

The cellar door is open Thursday to Sunday, and fishing experiences must be booked ahead.

printhiewines.com.au

WADE FOR IT

📍 COFFIN BAY, SA
NAUO COUNTRY

Play a game of word association with any Australian and the name 'Coffin Bay' is almost always going to match with 'oysters'. Revered like an appellation, these oysters are farmed off the southern Eyre Peninsula, on the Traditional Lands of the Nauo People.

Tours at the Coffin Bay Oyster Farm are highly interactive, with visitors donning waders and walking through the translucent shallows to a semi-submersible 'Salt Water Pavilion' set among the oyster racks. Sitting in the sea at the pavilion, there's a shucking lesson from farmer Ben Catterall and then the real reason you're here – tastings.

When you leave the leases at tour's end, you don't necessarily have to leave the oysters. Along Coffin Bay's Esplanade, oysters continue to hold pride of place. Waterfront Oyster HQ serves up oysters 14 different ways, and it's a short stroll on to the sea-view deck at 1802 Oyster Bar for another briny fix.

Coffin Bay's famed oysters
Opposite **Wine and dining at Printhie Wines**

MARGARET'S PALATE

⊙ MARGARET RIVER, WA
WADANDI & PIBLEMAN BOODJA COUNTRY

Since its first commercial vines were planted at Vasse Felix in 1967, Margaret River, on Wadandi and Pibleman Boodja Country, has risen to become one of Australia's largest wine regions, with more than 200 vineyards producing around 25 per cent of the country's premium wine.

This is a place where the food is so good that even a local burger van (Normal Van Main Street) made the list of state's top 100 restaurants in the 2024 West Australian *Good Food Guide*, along with six winery-based restaurants. Check them out at the Cullen Biodynamic Wine Room, Vasse Felix, Leeuwin Estate, Wills Domain, Voyager Estate and Cherubino.

To this, add some very distinctive winery experiences. Tour the vines (and taste the forthcoming vintage) in a solar-powered EV buggy at Fraser Gallop Estate. Grab a picnic rug from the cellar door at organic Stormflower and piece together a platter from the offerings of salumi, cheeses, olives, obatzda and the house-made grape chutney. Most curiously, drop in at farm-based Glenarty Road, which uses the seabed as a cellar for its sparkling wine, placing crates into the sea and using ocean currents to stir the bottles as they mature.

There are no less than four chocolate makers in the region, from the original Margaret River Chocolate Company to the choc concoctions of Cowaramup-based Temper Temper – ever had salted caramel, cauliflower and chilli, or honeycomb and dukkah chocolate?

⊙ margaretriver.com

Vasse Felix vineyard
Opposite **Fresh fruit at the Adelaide Central Market**

MARKET MAGIC

◉ ADELAIDE/TANDANYA, SA
KAURNA COUNTRY

Started in 1869 as a trading post for a handful of farmers, the Adelaide Central Market is Australia's oldest surviving market and still one of its most enticing. It remains a marketplace for fresh fruit, vegetables and meat, but a world of flavours now fills its five undercover avenues, be it Algerian paella, authentic Turkish delight, a mozzarella bar or Adelaide/Tandanya's oldest pizzeria.

The best way to introduce yourself to the market is to be guided through its avenues and 70 stalls by the *Adelaide Central Market Audio Tour* podcast (available on all podcast apps), which delivers morsels of information on a 48-minute walking tour. Narrated by Katie Spain, author of *Adelaide Central Market: Stories and People*, and Adelaide celebrity chef Adam Liaw, it spins together history, tastes and tales on a journey through nuts, Portuguese custard tarts, Sarawak laksa, French terrine, oh-so-Adelaide metwurst and a 50-year-old mushroom stall run by a trader allergic to porcini.

Stalls to seek out as you wander include Blackebys Old Sweet Shop for yesteryear treats for the kids, the local flavours of Barossa Fine Foods and the Kangaroo Island Stall, and the bush tucker and open-range game meats – think kangaroo, emu, finger limes, bush apples and Kakadu plums – at First Nations–owned Something Wild. Its gin bar is the perfect place to try a locally made green ant gin or native yam vodka.

◉ adelaidecentralmarket.com.au

BEYOND PUB GRUB

◉ VARIOUS LOCATIONS

There's a soothing familiarity to Aussie pub grub – good old chicken parmi, reef 'n' beef and hot chips served with any and every meal – but a few country pubs have taken the ordinary and turned it into the extraordinary.

Royal Mail Hotel, Dunkeld

At the southern foot of Victoria's Grampians/Gariwerd, the Royal Mail's Wickens restaurant works from Australia's largest kitchen garden (garden tours available) to produce ever-changing five- and eight-course degustation menus with wine pairings from a cellar that holds 30,000 bottles, including the Southern Hemisphere's largest collection of Burgundy and Bordeaux wines.

◉ royalmail.com.au

Prairie Hotel, Parachilna

Feral food, in the finest of ways. This Flinders Ranges pub specialises in introduced species such as camel, goat and wild boar, along with native ingredients like kangaroo, emu and saltbush. It's also the home of South Australia's most remote brewery.

◉ prairiehotel.com.au

Craig's Royal Hotel, Ballarat

A grand gold-rush relic, Craig's Royal has played host to Prince Albert and Mark Twain (with Dame Nellie Melba once singing from its balcony) and now serves up the likes of Wagyu steak or banana prawns and blue swimmer crab pappardelle, along with Sunday high tea.

◉ craigsroyal.com.au

Mapleton Public House, Mapleton

Purchased by the owner of nearby Falls Farm in 2022, this Sunshine Coast hinterland pub focusses its menu on organic produce from the farm, just 3km (1.9 miles) down the road – it's food miles at their minimum.

◉ mapleton.pub

Settlers Tavern, Margaret River

'The Tav' sports a laid-back 1970s surf vibe, but there's also a bistro brimming with local Southwest produce and an encyclopaedic wine list – more than 600 wines – that was named the best in regional Australia at the Australian Wine List of the Year Awards in 2022.

◉ settlerstavern.com

Top left **Outdoor dining at Settlers Tavern**
Top right **Craig's Royal Hotel**
Bottom **Prairie Hotel**

BRUNY'S BOUNTY

◉ BRUNY ISLAND, TASMANIA
PALAWA COUNTRY

Across much of elongated Bruny Island, there's only one road (suitably and simply named Bruny Island Main Road) and it's akin to a drive through an aisle of a gourmet grocer.

Alight from the vehicle ferry at Roberts Point and it's just 3km (1.9 miles) to the Bruny Island House of Whisky – save it for later and keep driving another 11km (7 miles) to Get Shucked, a working oyster farm with a licensed oyster bar. The bar's deck peers out onto the leases, and if you're in a hurry there's always the world's first drive-through oyster window.

It's just a couple of buildings on to Bruny Island Cheese Co and its companion, Bruny Island Beer Co. Book ahead for a combined tasting of cheeses (tell the lovely Otto cheese we send our regards) and beer, or sit out under the gum trees for a platter and a pint.

Things get sweet around the Neck – the thread-thin, penguin-central isthmus that holds dumbbell-shaped Bruny together – with Bruny Island Honey on one side and Bruny Island Chocolate on the other, before the road meanders on to Bruny Island Premium Wines, Australia's southernmost vineyard, set among bush near Lunawanna. A menu of local produce (Bruny oysters, cheeses, wallaby, olives) complements the pinot noirs and chardonnays.

Backtracking (it's your only option on Bruny), you'll pass the Hotel Bruny, curiously the only place on the island open for dinner – it also brews its own cider – before returning to the House of Whisky at a more civilised whisky hour. It features one of the state's most comprehensive collections of Tasmanian single malts, including its own exclusive Bruny Island Single Malt Whisky, made in collaboration with some of Tasmania's best distilleries.

◉ brunyisland.org.au

Top **Gourmet spread at Bruny Island Cheese Co**

Bottom **The Neck joins north and south Bruny Island**

FISH FRENZY

SYDNEY/WARRANE, NSW
GADIGAL COUNTRY

Think Australian cuisine and it's likely that seafood sits front of mind. It's an industry worth about $3 billion a year, and nowhere can you get an insight into its journey from boat to fishmonger to plate as completely as the Sydney Fish Market.

Behind-the-scenes tours of Australia's premier seafood market run every weekday, providing an experience as raw as sashimi. At 6.40am, before the market has opened to the public, tours begin in the midst of the action – the trading floor – joining the wholesalers, fishmongers and restaurateurs as they bid on the crates and catches from across Australia and New Zealand that cover the warehouse space. (If you think you've had an early start, the buyers have been here since about 4am.)

After some time in the buyers' stand, tours descend to the market floor, wandering among an ocean of seafood – the likes of mud crabs, lobster, tuna, kingfish, snapper, flathead and the by-catch of rays, Balmain bugs, mantis shrimp, scorpion fish and other creatures that are also auctioned – as the buyers' agents scurry around you, wheeling their purchases out to waiting vans.

Beyond the auction house, the Fish Market has seafood for sale, restaurants, a sushi bar and even a baker, greengrocer and wine store, but its other great treasure is the Sydney Seafood School, which has a regular roster of cooking classes, from instruction in seafood basics to masterclasses with some of Australia's top chefs. Get schooled, get cooking and get eating.

sydneyfishmarket.com.au

TASTE YOUR BIRTH YEAR AT SEPPELTSFIELD

◉ BAROSSA VALLEY, SA
NGADJURI, PERAMANGK & KAURNA COUNTRY

Seppeltsfield is the perfect stop for wine lovers
Opposite top **Fresh catch at the Sydney Fish Market**
Opposite bottom **Outdoor seafood dining**

Beneath the heritage-listed buildings of Seppeltsfield Barossa, there's a stone cellar that's as much a museum as a wine store. Built in 1878, it houses a single barrel of tawny port created in every year since the cellar's opening – a treasury of barrels that now dates back almost 150 years. This Centennial Collection is the world's longest unbroken line of vintage fortified wine, and each year Seppeltsfield releases a prized 100-year-old tawny from the collection.

You don't necessarily need the $1650 required to purchase a 100mL (3.4oz) bottle of the Para Centenary Tawny to experience the remarkable collection. Seppeltsfield's Taste Your Birth Year tour delves into the Centennial Cellar, wandering among the storied barrels before giving you the opportunity to taste the tawny from the barrel that was filled in the year in which you were born.

◈ seppeltsfield.com.au/taste-your-birth-year-tour

TASMANIA'S WHISKY REVOLUTION

⊙ VARIOUS LOCATIONS, TASMANIA
PALAWA COUNTRY

When a young Hobart/nipaluna surveyor named Bill Lark decided he wanted to make whisky in the early 1990s, he faced a rather sizeable impediment. Distilling had been outlawed in Tasmania for more than 150 years, ever since Governor John Franklin enacted a law in 1839 to assuage Lady Jane Franklin's frustration with the drunken behaviour of Hobart/nipaluna's early settlers.

In lobbying to overturn the law, Lark inadvertently set in motion one of the state's most successful modern industries. Little more than 30 years on, Tasmania boasts more than 70 distilleries and a string of international awards – including world's best single malt (won by Cambridge distiller Sullivans Cove in 2014) and gold at the World Whiskies Awards for a small batch single malt (won by Waubs Harbour Distillery in 2024). They place the island state among the world greats of whisky.

'If you'd said to me 30 years ago that there'd be that many distilleries, I'd have said you're mad,' says Bill. 'I always thought nobody else would be silly enough to do what we did, but it wasn't long before people started coming to me saying they'd like to set up a distillery.'

Bill, who has been dubbed the 'Godfather of Australian Whisky', has mentored and guided many of the distilleries that have followed him into the industry, even as his own Lark Distillery has progressed from a 5L (1.3 gallon) still on his kitchen table to a publicly listed company occupying a grand 1820s estate 30 minutes drive north of Hobart/nipaluna.

Billed as 'Tasmania's only working whisky village', Lark Distillery is a distinctive setting for a distillery tour or tastings, but it's not alone, with many of Tasmania's whisky producers providing experiences as rich and varied as their tipples.

Belgrove Distillery

Twenty minutes drive north of Lark, farm-based Belgrove Distillery is a paddock-to-bottle producer growing its own grains. Australia's first rye distillery, it distils in a hand-built, biodiesel-powered still, fired by used cooking oil from a neighbouring roadhouse. Completing the eco-circle, water for the whisky is trapped from the roofs of Belgrove's farm sheds, and the mash is fed to the property's sheep.

Callington Mill Distillery

Opened in 2022 in the Midlands town of Oatlands, this distillery sits in the grounds of Australia's third-oldest windmill (which was suitably used to illegally distil in the late 1830s). Alongside tastings and meals, it runs a 'Serendipity Experience', with participants creating their own single-malt whisky.

Launceston Distillery

There's more history in a bottle at Launceston Distillery, inside the oldest commercial aviation building in Tasmania, beside the runways of Launceston airport. Look for the photo of Queen Elizabeth II outside the hangar on her 1954 royal visit to Tasmania.

Waubs Harbour Distillery

Commanding a setting with a difference, this distillery occupies the sheds of a former oyster hatchery at the ocean's edge in Bicheno.

Spring Bay Distillery

Further down the east coast, Spring Bay's 'Smooth as Velvet' tasting experience takes you into its modest tin shed, which has been transformed into a salon featuring the velvet lounge suite from co-owner Suzy Brett's childhood home in Ireland.

Top **The 'Godfather of Australian Whisky', Bill Lark**
Bottom **Launceston Distillery**

Central Bendigo, gastronomic capital

AUSTRALIA'S FIRST CITY OF GASTRONOMY

BENDIGO, VICTORIA
DJA DJA WURRUNG COUNTRY

In 2019, an Australian city became the first in the nation to be designated as a City of Gastronomy by UNESCO, joining a select collection of (at the time) 36 world cities deemed worthy of the tasty title. It wasn't Sydney/Warrane and it wasn't Melbourne/Naarm. It was the Victorian gold-rush town of Bendigo.

The designation recognises cities with vibrant dining scenes and cuisine characteristics of the region (among other criteria), making it clear that Bendigo is a gourmet destination of the highest order. The city's gift-wrapping is its wine region, with more than 60 cellar doors noted for their bold shirazes and cabernet sauvignons. Set among them in Heathcote is Chauncy (chauncy.com.au), with its French chef producing a changing *menu du jour* for its lunchtime-only openings.

In town – indeed in Bendigo's coolest street, Chancery Lane – the Dispensary (dispensarybendigo.com) is a long-time favourite restaurant, focussing on regional produce with an encyclopaedic drinks list that's equal to the menu. Each month it also hosts a Gin Experience (second Saturday of the month) and a Whisky Experience (fourth Saturday), with tastings and a study of the nuances of Australian spirits.

Other Bendigo classics include Ms Batterhams (mackenziequarters.com/ms-batterhams), in the basement of a former school, and ever-so-refined Masons of Bendigo (masonsofbendigo.com.au). History is on the menu at the Goldmines Hotel (goldmineshotel.com), built in 1872 at the height of Bendigo's golden heyday, and now serving up pub grub a cut above the norm.

In 2021, Bendigo was joined by a second Australian City of Gastronomy: Tasmania's second city of Launceston.

bendigogastronomy.com.au

AUSTRALIA'S TOP COOKING SCHOOL

◉ NEW NORFOLK, TASMANIA
PALAWA COUNTRY

Inside the thick concrete walls of an old prison yard, a group of people wander among one of Australia's largest kitchen gardens, stripping off beans, cutting greens and filling baskets with a range of other garden produce. They're not prisoners preparing the mess; they're guests gathering the ingredients for a day at the country's leading cooking school.

'A very large proportion of what we use – 90-plus per cent – comes from this garden,' says Agrarian Kitchen founder and owner Rodney Dunn, looking over the acre of no-till vegetables, spices and berries.

The garden, school and attached Agrarian Kitchen Eatery, which was named *Gourmet Traveller*'s best restaurant in Australia in 2024, sit inside a former ward and the prison yard of Willow Court, Australia's oldest continually run asylum until its closure in 2000.

The Agrarian Kitchen began its classes in 2008 in Rodney and wife Severine's nearby home in Lachlan, seemingly opening its doors just as Tasmania began its meteoric rise as a food destination. Once known by the singular moniker of the Apple Isle, Tasmania has rapidly developed a reputation for arguably Australia's finest and freshest produce and food, ranging from berries and seafood to the country's first black truffles and even avocadoes, saffron and kimchi.

'When we started, there was this genesis of something that was going to be amazing, but even the people in Tasmania didn't realise it was special,' Rodney says. 'But there were these little glimpses of it – I remember seeing this menu that had a recipe from Chris Jackman [founder of Hobart/nipaluna's popular Jackman and McRoss bakeries] for Lloyd George raspberry vacherin, and I was like, "wow, imagine being able to put raspberries on your menu that are a varietal", it blew my mind. And that was just the start of my foray into how special Tasmania was in terms of food and varietals and people growing things.

'Back then, people would go to France and Italy for food, but in Australia I felt that Tasmania had a real opportunity to explore that.'

Dunn, who apprenticed at Sydney/Warrane's celebrated Tetsuya's Restaurant, guides the school, which has more than a dozen class options, from natural cheesemaking to fermentation and learning to cut and use a whole pig – nose to tail. In the weekly Agrarian Experience, three courses are prepared from recipes created for their seasonality, with each participant preparing individual details from one of the 12 kitchen workstations for a lunch (with paired wines) that will last long into the afternoon. Noted chefs are also regular guest tutors, from Quay executive chef Peter Gilmore to Tasmanian chef, forager and TV presenter Analiese Gregory.

'It's giving people that I admire the run of my garden and seeing what they come up with, and having them share their knowledge with a group of people who may be fans,' Rodney says. 'It's creating a lovely intimate cooking experience with some of the best chefs in the country.'

🌀 theagrariankitchen.com

Top and bottom The kitchen gardens at The Agrarian Kitchen are filled with a variety of fresh produce

155	Dancing Up a Barunga Storm
156	Happy Mardi Gras
158	Dog Days in Casterton
159	Australia's Biggest Flower Show
160	A Genre for Everyone
162	Embrace the Winter Night at Dark Mofo
163	Heads Up at the Beanie Festival
164	Elvis Has NOT Left the Building
166	Sydney/Warrane at Its Most Vivid
167	Ute Beaut
168	Garma Festival
170	Darwin's Largest Market
171	Desert Mob
173	A Flight of Festivals
174	Sydney Lunar Festival
175	Let There Be Light
177	Found in Translation

"The Garma Festival is not an experience easily bundled into a glossy travel brochure"

FESTIVALS & EVENTS

Top **Barunga Festival is a celebration of culture, music, art and sport**
Bottom left **Yidakis** (didgeridoos)
Bottom right **Cooking damper**

DANCING UP A BARUNGA STORM

◉ BARUNGA, NT
BAGALA COUNTRY

In the savannah lands of Barunga, a First Nations community 80km (50 miles) east of Katherine, the sun is setting and the red soil is being kicked into clouds by the stamping and dancing of feet. It's the nightly bunggul – traditional dances from First Nations performers across the Top End – a spectacular transition from the daytime activities to the nightly dance and music programs at the annual Barunga Festival.

First held in 1985, and the brainchild of Peter Apaak Jupurrula Miller, vocalist for popular First Nations band Blekbala Mujik, the Barunga Festival is an encompassing celebration of culture, music, art and sport. It was here in 1988 that Australian Prime Minister Bob Hawke was handed the Barunga Statement calling for a treaty between the Australian nation and First Nations people.

As much an invitation into community life – it's about joining the community rather than confecting a show – the four-day festival swells Barunga's population tenfold each King's Birthday long weekend (early June). The packed program includes workshops on First Nations artforms such as weaving, painting and didgeridoo making, and more than 40 teams from First Nations communities take part in fiercely contested AFL, basketball, softball and rugby sevens competitions.

Evening is when the festival really fires to life, with dances from the likes of Numbulwar's famous Red Flag dancers and Barunga's own dance troupe, and music from top First Nations bands from around Numbulwar, Maningrida, Groote Eylandt and Arnhem Land.

One of the festival's neatest touches is the Barunga Junior Guides – community kids who run town tours and bush tucker walks across the days.

The road from Katherine to Barunga is fully sealed, making for easy access, and there's camping on-site for tents, caravans and campervans during the festival. Otherwise, there are accommodation options in Katherine.

🌐 barungafestival.com.au

HAPPY MARDI GRAS

◉ SYDNEY/WARRANE, NSW
GADIGAL COUNTRY

As the roar of motorbikes echoes up and down Sydney/Warrane's Oxford St, it's official. The Sydney Gay and Lesbian Mardi Gras parade has begun. What started as a parade that ended with arrests and brutal bashings by the police in 1978 has grown into one of the biggest celebrations of LGBTQIA+ communities in the world.

Since 1991 the Dykes on Bikes have led the parade, and the sound of their engines is the start of a night that, for many, will kick on until sunrise as they go from watching floats pass by to dancing the night away.

At the post-parade Mardi Gras Party, around 10,000 people bounce between more than 50 artists in six venues – past performers have included Cher, Kylie Minogue, Dua Lipa and George Michael. At midnight the Community Show of volunteer dancers is a highlight, as is the pure joy on dancers' faces as they fulfil their dream of dancing on the Mardi Gras stage before partying with their friends.

Over the years, the Sydney Gay and Lesbian Mardi Gras has grown into a festival with more than 100 events. The festivities traditionally begin at Fair Day, a free party in the park where more than 70,000 people head to Victoria Park to see bands, DJs and Doggywood competitions where dapper dogs strut with their owners. From there, it's a choose-your-own adventure with more than two weeks of LGBTQIA+ events, including theatre, comedy, film, talks and pool parties.

Mardi Gras runs from the second Thursday in February to the first Saturday in March.

🔗 mardigras.org.au

By Amanda Woods

Top left **One of Australia's most famous drag queens, Courtney Act**

Top right **The parade runs along Oxford Street in Sydney/Warrane**

Bottom **Confetti flies at the parade**

DOG DAYS IN CASTERTON

CASTERTON, VICTORIA
GUNDITJMARA COUNTRY

In 1871, a puppy was born at Warrock Homestead, 30km (18.6 miles) north of Victoria's Western District town of Casterton. Named Kelpie, the dog was the first of a breed that would become as Australian as Vegemite.

Held over the King's Birthday weekend each June, the Australian Kelpie Muster celebrates Casterton's claim as the birthplace of the nation's favourite working-dog breed. Events are many and varied across the weekend, from a Waggiest Tail contest to a Kelpie High Jump competition (with a current record of almost 3m/10ft) and the 50m (164ft) Kelpie Dash.

The more serious business begins on the Sunday at the Australian Premier Working Dog Auction, where farmers bid on prized kelpies – in 2021, a kelpie named Eulooka Hoover sold for a then-world record of $35,200.

At any other time of year, drop into Casterton to visit the Australian Kelpie Centre in Henty St.

castertonkelpieassociation.com.au

Kelpies are Australia's hardest-working dogs
Opposite **Floriade is a colourful spring celebration**

AUSTRALIA'S BIGGEST FLOWER SHOW

CANBERRA, ACT
NGUNNAWAL COUNTRY

Canberra has bought you flowers. Billed as 'Australia's biggest celebration of spring', Floriade is a month-long floral flurry, featuring more than one million flowers in bloom in Commonwealth Park on the northern shores of Lake Burley Griffin.

Held from mid-September to mid-October, it's Australia's largest flower show. Inspired by the Keukenhof garden in the Netherlands, Floriade, which has free entry, is unsurprisingly renowned for its tulips, but it's no one-petal show. In addition to the flowers, there's live music, gardening workshops, food and wine and market stalls.

The program and theme change year on year, but staple events include the four-day Nightfest, with live music, cabaret and light installations across the garden beds; Dogs' Day Out on Floriade's final Sunday, with activities targeted at pooches and owners; and the Great Big Bulb Dig, held the day after Floriade's closure, when you can dig up the bulbs for your own garden.

floriadeaustralia.com

A GENRE FOR EVERYONE

VARIOUS LOCATIONS

Australian music festivals have a depth and breadth to please every kind of fan. Whether your beats of choice are rock, jazz, blues, country or hip-hop, there's a festival or a few with your genre on it.

Tamworth Country Music Festival

Tamworth is Australia's capital of country music, with the Southern Hemisphere's largest country music festival to prove it – held across 10 days in January. Be sure to check out the Australian Country Music Hall of Fame while in town.

tcmf.com.au

Blues on Broadbeach

Things get smooth on the Gold Coast at this doyen of blues festivals, featuring local and international events – free and non-ticketed.

bluesonbroadbeach.com

Port Fairy Folk Festival

For nearly 50 years, the Victorian seaside town of Port Fairy has been staging this folk festival over a long weekend in March.

portfairyfolkfestival.com

Melbourne International Jazz Festival

Running since 1988, this is Australia's largest jazz festival, with 10 days of gigs at venues across the city in October.

melbournejazz.com

Juicy Fest

Touring hip-hop and R&B festival that pops up for a day in Melbourne/Naarm, Sydney/Warrane, Perth/Boorloo and Brisbane/Meanjin in January.

juicyfest.co

ROCK AND POP FESTIVALS

Things go long and loud at a world-class collection of rock and pop festivals. Some of the biggest gatherings on the annual calendar include:

* **St Jerome's Laneway Festival** (Brisbane/Meanjin, Sydney/Warrane, Adelaide/Tandanya, Melbourne/Naarm, Perth/Boorloo, February)
  lanewayfestival.com
* **Splendour in the Grass** (Byron Bay, July)
  splendourinthegrass.com
* **Golden Plains** (Meredith, March)
  goldenplains.com.au
* **WOMADelaide** (Adelaide/Tandanya, March)
  womadelaide.com.au

Top **Taking the stage at WOMADelaide**
Bottom **Byron Bay Bluesfest is one of Australia's best blues and roots festivals**

EMBRACE THE WINTER NIGHT AT DARK MOFO

◉ HOBART/NIPALUNA, TASMANIA
PALAWA COUNTRY

There was a time, not so long ago, that Hobart/nipaluna all but hibernated through winter. Australia's southernmost city – next stop south, Antarctica – endured rather than embraced its dark season, with the sun above the horizon for just nine chilly hours a day. Then along came Dark Mofo in 2013, transforming the Tasmanian capital into the Cinderella of darkness.

Dark Mofo's nifty party trick was to take Hobart/nipluna's winter gloom and celebrate it in equally dark and often controversial ways – turning crosses upside down or burying an artist beneath one of Hobart/nipaluna's main roads for three days. Public art, international music acts and immersive theatre are esoteric, confronting and often downright weird and wonderful. In turn, they've transformed Hobart/nipaluna into Australia's coolest winter city, at least for the fortnight of its black salute.

Among the ever-changing events are two Dark Mofo staples – so popular that they continued even when the festival took a pause to refresh in 2024. The Winter Feast brings together many of Tasmania's best food and drink producers in a delightfully Gothic banquet on Hobart/nipaluna's docks, while the nude solstice swim does everything the name on the tin suggests. On the stroke of sunrise on 21 June – the winter solstice – more than 2000 people strip to their birthday suits and sprint into the sea, which at this time of year, this far south, is around 11°C (51.8°F). It's chilly willies (and other bits) as far as the eye can avert itself. It's also insanely popular, so book your free ticket well ahead.

◉ darkmofo.net.au

Dark Mofo celebrates Hobart's dreary winters
Opposite **Beanie tree**

HEADS UP AT THE BEANIE FESTIVAL

⊙ ALICE SPRINGS/MPARNTWE, NT
ARRERNTE COUNTRY

Winter nights in Alice Springs/Mparntwe can get pretty cold – the average minimum temperature is around 7°C (44.6°F) – which makes a beanie the streetwear of choice for heads around town. Celebrating these knitted noggin warmers is the Beanie Festival, held each June and filling the 'Beanie Central' market at the Araluen Arts Centre with more than 5000 beanies of all shapes, shades and sizes.

There are two ways to get involved in the Beanie Festival: visit Alice Springs/Mparntwe over the four-day event or get knitting, felting or crocheting to supply a beanie to the festival. Entry forms are available on the website, and up to two beanies can be entered per person – the more colourful and quirky the better. At least one of the beanies is required to be put up for sale at Beanie Central, where more than $200,000 of beanies are sold each festival. Entries also go into the National Beanie Competition, competing for awards that reflect the changing theme of each festival, plus the coveted People's Choice Prize.

The festival has been running since 1997 and has turned beanie-making into a Red Centre artform. The bulk of the profit each year goes into running beanie-making workshops in surrounding First Nations communities, which in turn sees community-made beanies feature as a key part of the festival. There are also demonstrations of First Nations' craft methods from communities such as Ernabella, the oldest First Nations arts centre in Australia and a long-time collaborator with the Beanie Festival.

🌐 beaniefest.org

ELVIS HAS NOT LEFT THE BUILDING

PARKES, NSW
WIRADJURI COUNTRY

In the early 1980s, Anne and Bob Steele opened a restaurant and convention centre in Parkes, 350km (217 miles) west of Sydney/Warrane. They named it Graceland, a lament from Anne – a lifelong Elvis Presley fan – at having missed out on visiting Elvis's home on a recent family holiday to the USA. When a regular patron planned a birthday celebration in 1993, the Steeles decided to theme it as an Elvis party. Almost 200 people attended and somehow the Parkes Elvis Festival was born.

More than 30 years on, this festival in NSW's Central West attracts an estimated 25,000 visitors to Parkes for five days of Elvis-related events and concerts. Put it to Anne that it's become one of Australia's greatest festivals and she's definitive in her reply.

'Never mind one of the greatest; it's the greatest one,' she laughs.

Anne and Bob remain at the forefront of the Parkes Elvis Festival, which is held in the second week of January to coincide with Elvis's birthday. Recalling its beginnings, they paint an unlikely picture of an event that would become a town-defining festival.

'Anne was the biggest fan (of Elvis),' Bob says. 'I just went along for the ride.'

'Bob learned to be a fan,' Anne adds quietly.

At that first festival in 1993, they had a single Elvis tribute artist – famed performer Eddie Youngblood – though Anne wasn't sold on the concept. She'd even decided she wasn't going to the concert; she'd just work in the restaurant that night.

'I thought, I don't like fake anything, so I'm not going to go to this,' she says. 'Then I heard an interview with Eddie on the radio and he said he's not an impersonator, he's a tribute artist and he sings Elvis his way. I thought, I like you, so I went to the concert with Bob, and Eddie was brilliant.

'A lot of the local men were brought along kicking and screaming that they didn't want to come, but when they left that night, they were the first ones to book for the next year.'

Today, Elvis tribute artists (or ETAs, as they're known) are the mainstay of the festival, with hundreds from around Australia and abroad performing each year. Alongside them is a street parade, look-a-like Elvis competitions and vehicle shows of Elvis-era cars. A Miss Priscilla competition keeps local hairdressers busy, with the winning Priscilla installed as the face of the festival. There's even a rugby match played between two local teams dressed in Elvis jumpsuits.

'The great thing about the festival is that everyone's in a good mood; they're all looking for a good time,' Bob says. 'It's probably what you'd call the Friendly Festival.'

parkeselvisfestival.com.au

Top **Parkes Elvis Festival**
Bottom **Attendees can board the Elvis Express Train to get to the festival**

SYDNEY/WARRANE AT ITS MOST VIVID

⊙ SYDNEY/WARRANE, NSW
GADIGAL COUNTRY

The Sydney Opera House and Harbour Bridge look good in any light, but never better or more colourful than under the literal spotlight of Vivid Sydney. The world's largest festival of light, music and ideas spreads across 23 days of May and June, painting Sydney/Warrane in a kaleidoscope of light projections and art installations. The 'sails' of the Opera House become canvasses for ephemeral artworks – typically works from First Nations artists – while the Harbour Bridge and myriad city structures are also lit with colour.

To get the most from the display, set out for an evening wander on the Vivid Sydney Light Walk, stretching 8km (5 miles) along the harbourfront from Circular Quay around Darling Harbour to the Goods Line in Ultimo.

Lights switch on at 6pm each night of the festival.

⊙ vividsydney.com

UTE BEAUT

📍 **DENILIQUIN, NSW**
WAMBA WAMBA & PERREPA PERREPA COUNTRY

The rustic entrance to Deni Ute Muster

Opposite **Vivid Sydney lights up the Sydney Opera House**

There's nothing more Australian on the road than a ute, and the ultimate celebration of these trayed vehicles is the annual Deni Ute Muster. Held in the Riverina town of Deniliquin, on Wamba Wamba and Perrepa Perrepa Country just north of the Murray River, the two-day muster began in 1999 to help alleviate the hardship of a drought and has grown into an event attracting around 20,000 visitors each October.

Things at the muster are as Aussie as they come, with events ranging from bush poets to monster truck rides, wood chopping, free camping, nightly concerts and lots and lots of utes – the record stands at 9736 utes.

Can you help break the record of 4136 blue singlets at a single event?

🌐 deniutemuster.com.au

GARMA FESTIVAL

◉ GULKULA, EAST ARNHEM LAND, NT
GUMATJ COUNTRY

In the dry-season stillness of morning, Joel Blanco is seated beside a smoking fire in the 'house of stories' (the Darwonimaka), an open-sided architectural wonder of arching stringybark and roped canvas. 'I've only ever danced barefoot with Bangara Dance Theatre, my foot coffin off,' Joel confides. 'It's the relationship with space that gives me power, dancing on country, feeling my feet in the skin of the earth.'

The skin of the earth here, on Gumatj Country, is about 40km (25 miles) from the town of Nhulunbuy in remote north-east Arnhem Land. It's one of the great strongholds of traditional Yolŋu culture but just a dot in the vast tract of First Nations land that measures almost 100,000 sq km (38,610 sq miles) across the Gove Peninsula in the Northern Territory.

What began as a small community barbecue in 1999 has evolved into the Garma Festival, Australia's largest First Nations gathering and a celebration of Yolŋu life and culture hosted by the Yothu Yindi Foundation. Taking place in early August each year, and showcasing traditional miny'tji (art), manikay (song), bunggul (dance) and storytelling, it's held on a primordial ceremonial site of the Yolŋu People, an escarpment that curls like the spine of a crocodile along the Gulf of Carpentaria. It takes 45 minutes by air from Darwin to Gove, then a 20-minute bus ride, to reach this sacred place.

Traditional welcome begins with the shifting tide of pulsating bodies moving to the beat of clapsticks. Red-flag-wielding Dilak elders and men and women of all ages draped in cloth and pelt, branded t-shirts and trucker's caps stomp the dust into clouds between dancing children.

This colourful, freewheeling frenzy is a practiced and curated invitation to the clans to join in the diplomacy of kinship. It's dance not just as entertainment, but as a continuation of story and a permit to engage unfettered over four days with the oldest living culture on Earth.

The Garma Festival is not an experience easily bundled into a glossy travel brochure. It's a gift to be unwrapped slowly, much like the snaking line for food served from bain-maries and the queue for the cold-water showers. It's loud like the bands that play till 11pm and the generators that snarl through the night. And basic, like the accommodation in tents packed, sardine style, at the edge of the ceremonial grounds.

The festival leads national discussion on issues of importance to all Australians. At the rim of the escarpment, in the Garrtjambal Auditorium, senior First Nations thinkers sit shoulder to shoulder with other policy makers. Pressing issues around life expectancy, education and justice are topics of important discussion.

Visitors who have completed a registration of interest, and been accepted, are granted a permit to attend from the Northern Land Council. Tickets include a tent and meals and a chance to join in with different aspects of Yolŋu culture through cultural walks and traditional healthcare and weaving workshops.

A pathway through bush leads to the Gapan Gallery, an outpost of the respected Yirrkala Art Centre, where limited-edition prints and etchings hang in a serene grove of stringybark trees. At the end of another track, there's a huge screen for evening films, flecked with birds and bats flitting like meteors across sightlines.

There's a sense of deep cultural significance to it all – time in which to ponder the shared beauty of a culture that continues to flourish in the gaze of the ancestral crocodile at the edge of the Arafura Sea.

yyf.com.au/garma-festival

By Anabel Dean

Garma Festival showcases traditional miny'tji (art), manikay (song), bunggul (dance) and storytelling

DARWIN'S LARGEST MARKET

◎ DARWIN/GARRAMILLA, NT
LARRAKIA COUNTRY

Dishing up sunset with a side serve of shopping, Mindil Beach Sunset Market is strung along Darwin/Garramilla's best beach each Thursday and Sunday evening (4pm to 9pm) during the dry season (late April to late October). The city's largest market, set on Larrakia Country, features more than 200 stalls that reflect Darwin/Gulumerrdgen's inimitable character – laid-back, multicultural, richly influenced by First Nations cultures.

Running for almost 40 years, the market's food vans range from Greek to Bangladeshi, Vietnamese, Turkish, Sri Lankan, Spanish and the humble Aussie spud, while other stalls bring together local First Nations artists, jewellery designers and a thong (sandal) maker. The star of the show is the sun, making a fiery finish to the day as it sets into the Timor Sea.

🌐 mindil.com.au

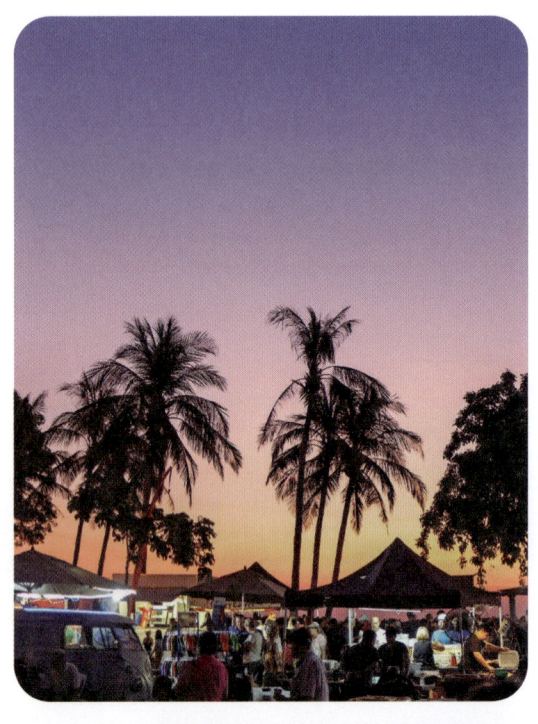

DESERT MOB

ALICE SPRINGS/MPARNTWE, NT
ARRERNTE COUNTRY

In the Araluen Arts Centre, even the Albert Namatjira paintings get packed away when the Desert Mob comes to town. Alice Springs/Mparntwe's largest gallery is home to one of the country's biggest collections of Namatjira works, but every year Desert Mob clears three of Araluen's four galleries for a six-week showcase of art from First Nations art centres in the NT, WA and SA.

First held in 1991, the event is an exhibition of work from more than 30 art centres, ranging from famous centres such as the Hermannsburg Potters and Tjanpi Desert Weavers to Australia's oldest art centre, Ernabella Arts.

Held in September/October, Desert Mob includes a one-day marketplace where visitors can buy works directly from the artists and a day-long symposium with artists talking about their works, family and Country.

desertmob.com

Araluen Arts Centre
Opposite **Mindil Beach Sunset Market**

Top left **Performers at Adelaide Fringe**
Top right **Music fans gather at WOMADelaide**
Bottom **Adelaide Fringe**

A FLIGHT OF FESTIVALS

ADELAIDE/TANDANYA, SA
KAURNA COUNTRY

South Australia is known as Australia's festival state for good reason, and nowhere more so than in its capital, Adelaide/Tandanya, with this city on Kaurna Country hosting a clutch of the nation's premier art and food events.

Adelaide Fringe

Top of the pops is this festival first held in 1960. The annual February/March extravaganza brings more than 6000 performers to 500-plus venues across the city, making it Australia's biggest arts festival and said to be the second largest in the world, behind only the Edinburgh Festival Fringe.

adelaidefringe.com.au

WOMADelaide

This March festival is a perpetual favourite with music fans. Billed as 'the world's festival', it celebrates the diversity of world music and dance across four days of open-air concerts in Botanic Park/Tainmuntilla. In 2024 alone, it featured artists from countries as wide-ranging as Ethiopia, Haiti, Lebanon, South Korea and Bosnia and Herzegovina.

womadelaide.com.au

Adelaide Festival

WOMADelaide falls under the broader blanket of this 17-day cultural colossus of arts, music, theatre, dance and the Adelaide Writers' Week, drawing big-name authors and poets into the swirl of Adelaide/Tandanya's festival season.

adelaidefestival.com.au

Tasting Australia

Hungry for more? As the other festivals wind down, Tasting Australia is cooking up another party. This week-long graze, held in May, is one of the country's longest-running food festivals and features a series of pop-up 'dining galleries' on central Victoria Square/Tarntanyangga, where themed feasts occur each day and night. It also spreads its festival wings with 'Tasting Australia Airlines' flights that take festival goers to regional dining and produce experiences, be it on Kangaroo Island, Eyre Peninsula or the wine-producing Limestone Coast.

tastingaustralia.com.au

SYDNEY LUNAR FESTIVAL

◉ SYDNEY/WARRANE, NSW
GADIGAL COUNTRY

Sydney/Warrane's feted New Year's Eve celebration is a global phenomenon, sending eight tonnes of fireworks into the sky and drawing more than one million people to vantage points around the city's shores. But it's not the only new year in town.

The Sydney Lunar Festival is one of the largest Lunar New Year celebrations outside of Asia. Dragon boats take to Darling Harbour in the Southern Hemisphere's biggest such event, lion dancers snake down a multitude of city streets and spaces and the 16-day festival opens with Sydney Lunar Streets, a Haymarket street party filled with market stalls, food trucks and live performers.

Festivities aren't limited to the city centre. Head to the western suburbs to find the Bankstown Lunar New Year Festival (held in Griffith Park and Olympic Parade), one of the year's biggest events for an area where almost 20 per cent of residents are of Chinese or Vietnamese descent.

◉ cityofsydney.nsw.gov.au/sydney-lunar-festival

LET THERE BE LIGHT

◉ **ALICE SPRINGS/MPARNTWE, NT**
ARRERNTE COUNTRY

Light installations have become a feature of Central Australian travel – Uluru's Wintjiri Wiru drone and light show, the Field of Light Uluru, Light Towers at Kings Canyon – but the outback comes to its brightest blaze at Parrtjima.

This free, 10-day festival of light is the only First Nations light festival in the world and uses the landscape of the Alice Springs Desert Park as its canvas and screen, projecting artworks from First Nations artists onto the desert and the framing mountains of the Tjoritja/West MacDonnell Ranges.

Each year the festival and its works run to a different theme, and featured artists are predominantly from art centres around Central Australia. The modern works for this ancient landscape are chosen by the Parrtjima Festival Reference Group of respected local Traditional Owners.

◉ parrtjimaaustralia.com.au

The Landing Kultcha installation lights up Parrtjima
Opposite top **Lanterns hang to celebrate Lunar New Year**
Opposite bottom **Lunar New Year celebrations on Dixon Street**

Top and bottom **Mikey Webb, Auslan interpreter**

FOUND IN TRANSLATION

PROFILE: MIKEY WEBB

On the edge of a festival stage in Hobart/nipaluna, Mikey Webb is rocking out to a punk tune. Arms wave, feet stamp and the beat seems to consume his body. It's hypnotic to watch, but these aren't random dance moves. Mikey is an Auslan interpreter, bringing song lyrics to deaf patrons in his inimitable style at concerts and festivals across Australia.

'I had someone say the other day, "so, what are you on?",' he says with a laugh. 'I'm actually not on anything. I just run on adrenaline.'

Growing up with deaf parents, grandparents and cousins, Mikey describes Auslan as his first language and he came to prominence in 2020 when a video was posted of him doing his dance of interpretation at Perth's Highway to Hell festival. Through the Covid pandemic, he was a regular on Australian TV screens, interpreting for Queensland's daily press-conference updates. But it's on festival stages, standing side by side with bands and artists, that he's found his greatest expression, rocking hard and interpreting in fluid combination, despite having no background in dance.

'Not even a little bit (of background),' he says. 'I'm just the guy on the dancefloor, dancing to the beat of his own drum. I very much feed off the crowd. If the crowd's having a ripper time, that gives me that bit of extra energy, that little extra kick.

'And when I see deaf people in that mainstream crowd having fun like everyone else, that's what gets me out of bed in the morning. This is what it should be – they're getting the atmosphere, they're getting the feel of the whole concert. All I'm doing is giving them the lyrics.'

One of more than 350 Auslan interpreters represented by Auslan Stage Left, Mikey has quickly become a celebrity in his own right, noted for his man bun and his manic moves. In what he describes as a 'surreal' 2023 alone, he worked on stage with the Red Hot Chili Peppers, Post Malone, Ed Sheeran, Mumford and Sons, Lizzo, Hilltop Hoods, Def Leppard, Motely Crue, Paul Kelly, Jamiroquai and Beck.

It's been a whirlwind few years of rubbing stage shoulders with the greats, but still Mikey says the ultimate satisfaction comes in the sense of change and inclusivity that the presence of Auslan interpreters has brought to music events.

'It's been amazing,' he says. 'People say to me, "they're deaf, what do they get from a concert?". I say to them, why do you go to a concert? You could just listen to it on a CD, or you could sit outside the stadium and listen. The same thing applies to a deaf person. They feel the beat, but it's about the atmosphere and the vibe and being with your peers.

'I do feel that pressure of if I'm shit, that's not fair on them. I still, to this day, sometimes do the power chuck before I go on because nerves get the better of me.'

181	The Other Great AFL Grand Final
182	Play the World's Longest Golf Course
183	Bloody Football
186	Get Wrecked
189	In the Flow at Blue Derby
190	Melbourne/Naarm's Sporting Passion
192	Noosa's Wild Side
195	Cool Pools
196	Canyon Country
197	The Great Surf Pilgrimage
198	No Barrier to This Dive and Snorkel Site
200	Wild Times Underground
201	Booting It Through Rotto
202	Snow Melt: Ski Resorts in Summer
204	Surf's Up

"Bells embodies the tale of Australian surf history"

ACTIVITIES & SPORTS

THE OTHER OTHER GREAT AFL GRAND FINAL

Footy fans rejoice, you can now get double the grand final fun on the same day. December 2023 saw the debut of the Tiwi Islands Football League Women's Premiership, following the inaugural season for the women's league. In August 2024, both grand finals were played back-to-back, making for an epic day of sport for fans.

Top and bottom **They take their footy seriously on the Tiwi Islands (photography by Wayne Quilliam)**

THE OTHER GREAT AFL GRAND FINAL

◉ TIWI ISLANDS, NT
TIWI COUNTRY

There's an allure to the Tiwi Islands/Yermalner. Anchored 80km (50 miles) off the coast of Darwin/Garramilla and comprised of Melville and Bathurst/Nguyu Islands (the second- and sixth-largest islands in Australia), they've been home to the Tiwi People for more than 20,000 years. They have a population of less than 3000 people, and yet they have revered status in one of Australia's national sports, the AFL – mention surnames such as Rioli and Long to any AFL fan and watch them smile in appreciation. It's said that 900 of the 3000 islanders play football, which is the highest participation rate in Australia.

Staying on the islands requires a permit from the Tiwi Land Council (apply at least 30 days ahead of a visit), but they're open to all visitors for one day in August when the Tiwi Islands Football League grand final is played in Wurrumiyanga, the islands' largest town. Typically an exhilarating, skilful and colourful match between the league's top two teams, it's the biggest day of the year on the islands, attended by most of the population and a host of visitors.

On the same day, just down the road, the equally compelling Tiwi Islands Art Sale is held, with the islands' four art centres – Tiwi Design (tiwidesigns.com), Ngaruwanajirri (ngaruwanajirri.org.au), Munupi Arts (munupiart.com) and Jilamara Arts (jilamara.com) – coming together to display and sell their works. Tiwi art has spread far across the globe, including to the Vatican Museums.

Wurrumiyanga is reached from Darwin by SeaLink ferry (2.5 hours; sealink.com.au/tiwi-islands) or a 30-minute flight with Fly Tiwi (flytiwi.com.au)

PLAY THE WORLD'S LONGEST GOLF COURSE

◉ NULLARBOR, SA & WA
MIRNING COUNTRY

Roos on the green
Opposite **Queenstown's** renowned gravel oval

Some golf courses are so long and challenging that they demand the use of a golf cart, but the Nullarbor Links might be the only course in the world that requires the use of a car and days of driving. The world's longest golf course has 18 holes (and many more wombat holes) dotted along the Eyre Hwy as it crosses the Nullarbor Plain. Each roadhouse and town along the 1365km (950-mile) journey from Ceduna to Kalgoorlie features a hole, consisting of a tee and artificial-turf green and natural 'fairways' carved through scrub – birdies here are just as likely to be emus.

Pick up a scorecard at the visitor centres in Ceduna, Kalgoorlie or Norseman, pay the $70 green fee and set out on the longest golf game of your life.

◉ nullarborlinks.com

BLOODY FOOTBALL

◉ QUEENSTOWN, TASMANIA
PALAWA COUNTRY

They breed them tough in mining towns, and there's no greater demonstration of this than a weekend footy (AFL) game in the barren lands of Queenstown on Tasmania's west coast. Infamously denuded by the poisons and tree-felling of its mining history, Queenstown has a classically bleak moonscape where little greenery grows – even grass fails to appear on the town oval.

Instead, the local Queenstown Crows play on Australia's only gravel oval, where falling to the ground – inevitable in an AFL match – is almost certain to skin knees, elbows and any other body parts that connect with the stones.

Catching a game is a unique sporting experience, with a 'bloody' good time guaranteed. Matches are played on Saturday afternoons during the April to August season, while an exhibition match is played for the Unconformity Cup during Queenstown's biennial Unconformity festival, held in October of odd-numbered years.

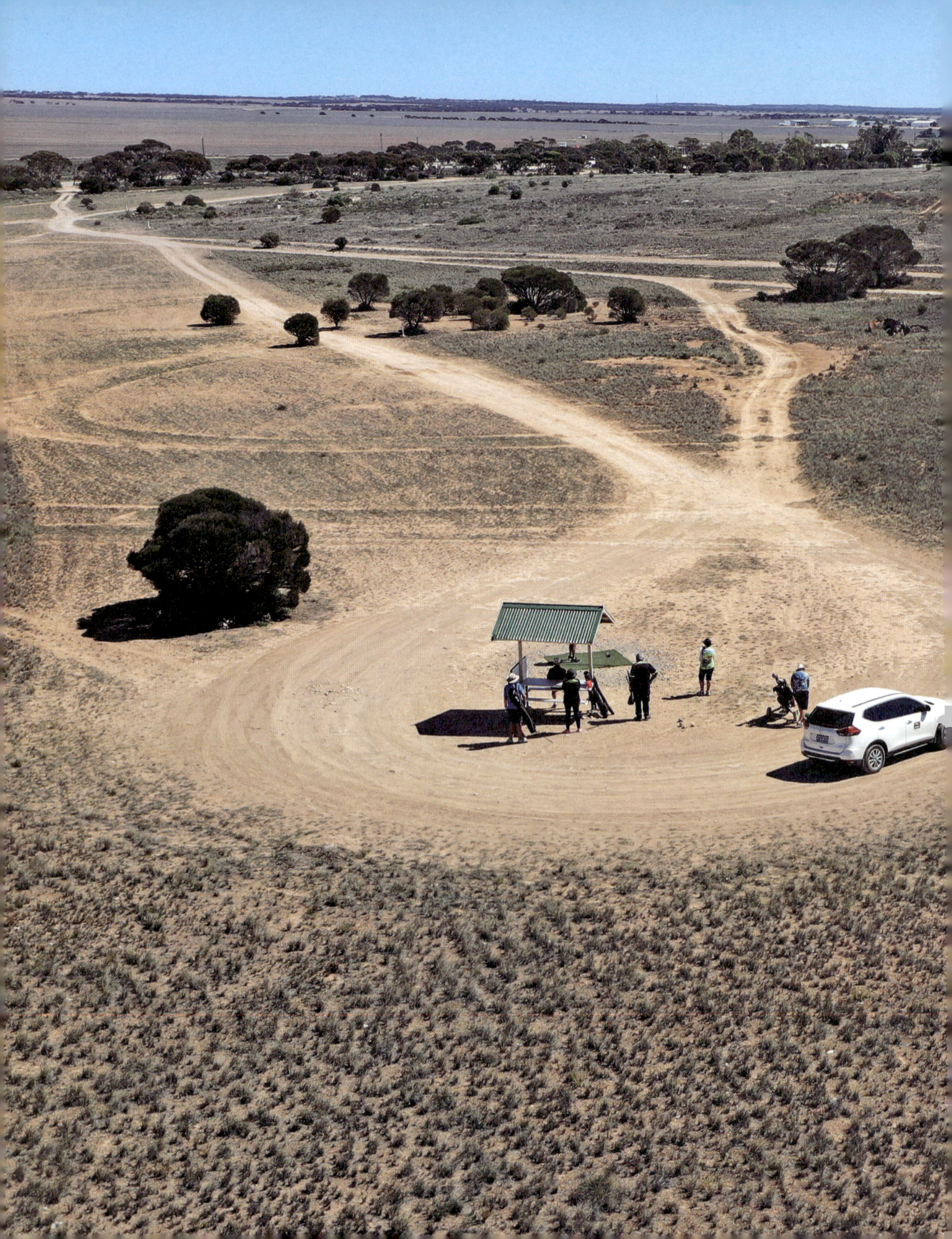

A quick round along the Nullarbor

GET WRECKED

◉ AYR, QUEENSLAND
JURU COUNTRY

Not all of the Great Barrier Reef's best dives are on reefs. Lying on the ocean floor, about 20km (12.4 miles) off the Queensland coast near Ayr, the SS *Yongala* sailed into a cyclone in 1911 and simply disappeared, with 122 lives lost. The remains of the ship weren't found until 1958, but now form Australia's most famous wreck dive.

The steam ship rests in 28m (92ft) of water, with the top of the vessel 14m (46ft) below the ocean's surface. Much of its surface is encrusted with coral, and the marine life that inhabits it is Nemo-worthy – giant groupers, barracuda, moray eels, Maori wrasse and marble rays, to name a few.

To dive the wreck, you need open water certification with six logged dives and deep-dive training.

◉ yongaladive.com.au

SHIPWRECK DIVES

Other dives among the 8000 registered shipwrecks around the Australian coast include:

- **SS *Nord*** A 1915 wreck in 42m (138ft) of water off the Tasman Peninsula, Tasmania.

- ***Batavia*** A 1628 wreck in 6m (20ft) of water in the Houtman Abrolhos Islands, WA.

- **HMAS *Adelaide*** Scuttled off Avoca, NSW, in 32m (105ft) of water in 2011.

- **RMS *Orizaba*** A 140m (460ft) steamer wrecked off the coast of Rockingham, WA, in 1905; it rests in 6m (20ft) to 10m (33ft) of water.

- ***Star of Greece*** A shore dive at Port Willunga, SA, the wreck is just 200m (656ft) from the beach and 4m (13ft) below the surface. The three-masted ship was wrecked in 1888 and can be snorkelled as well as dived.

Diver explores the SS *Yongala* wreck

Cycling Derby's impressive mountain bike trails

IN THE FLOW AT BLUE DERBY

DERBY, TASMANIA
PALAWA COUNTRY

Once upon a time, the north-east Tasmanian town of Derby was a forlorn and forgotten tin-mining town. A highway ran through it, but it seemed just a spirit or two short of vanishing into a ghost town.

In an unlikely reversal of fortune, Derby went from bust to boom in 2015 when a mountain bike trail network – Blue Derby – was laid out around the town. A round of the Enduro World Series was held at Blue Derby that very year, and Derby was soon revered as Australia's top trail network, largely kickstarting the country's love affair with mountain biking.

With 125km (78 miles) of flowing trails, the network now wraps around a lake at the town's edge, rises up the slopes of the heavily forested Blue Tier mountains and tumbles down their other side to the coast on the marathon-length Bay of Fires trail. The trails are as scenic as they are fun, winding through rainforest, crossing streams and breaking open to views over Derby. There are also rides for all abilities, from simple trundles such as Lake Derby and Valley Ponds to technical testers such as Trouty and Detonate – the latter was named the best trail of the entire Enduro World Series in 2017 and requires riders to squeeze through a chute between boulders that's millimetres wider than their handlebars.

The town itself has well and truly morphed into a mountain-biking service centre, filled with bike-hire stores, trailhead shuttle services and myriad accommodation options – pitch a tent by the Ringarooma River, book a plush B&B for a fireside finish to your riding days or join a luxury tour, staying in pods hidden within the trail network, with Blue Derby Pods Ride.

- ridebluederby.com.au
- bluederbypodsride.com.au

MELBOURNE/NAARM'S SPORTING PASSION

📍 MELBOURNE/NAARM, VICTORIA
WURUNDJERI COUNTRY

Few world cities can rival Melbourne/Naarm for sporting passion. Australia's second-largest city is a place where two public holidays are devoted to sporting events and stadiums fill with up to 100,000 people for a match.

Australian Rules Football (AFL) is the enduring passion for Melburnians, played across a March–September winter season. It's a near-nationwide competition played across 24 rounds (plus a finals series) between 18 teams (expanding to 19 teams in 2028 with the formation of a Tasmanian team) from Victoria, SA, WA, NSW and Queensland. Nine of those teams are based in Melbourne/Naarm.

Matches in Melbourne/Naarm are played at two stadiums: Marvel Stadium in the Docklands neighbourhood at the city centre's edge and the Melbourne Cricket Ground (MCG), which is the closest thing the city has to a secular cathedral.

The competition, which drew more than eight million fans to matches across the 2023 season, distils down to a single Saturday afternoon in late September (sometimes early October) when the Grand Final between the top two teams is played at the MCG. It's in this week that Melbourne/Naarm's footy fanaticism is at its most evident and colourful.

In the three days leading up to the match, a free Footy Festival is held in the grounds surrounding the MCG, culminating in a traditional Grand Final parade on the Friday. In this parade, players from the two competing teams are driven through the city in the back of utes, with the streets lined by up to 100,000 fans.

Come game day, there's another common tradition of grand final BBQs across the city, until finally the ball is bounced to signal the start of the game at 2.30pm to the spine-tingling roar of another 100,000 people (the record attendance at a Grand Final is 121,696 in 1970, still short of the stadium's highest-ever crowd of more than 130,000 at a Billy Graham evangelical appearance in 1959).

Despite such a massive attendance, purchasing a ticket to the Grand Final is a difficult task, with club members and corporate ticket holders securing most seats. If you can't get inside, another crowd forms in Federation Square, 1km (0.6 miles) away, where a big screen is set up to broadcast the match. Pubs across the city also echo to the sounds of the broadcast.

Visiting the city at another time of year? Tours of the MCG run most days of the year, taking you onto the playing surface and into the player changerooms and the famous Long Room. The stadium is also home to the Australian Sports Museum.

🔗 afl.com.au
🔗 mcg.org.au

A crowded MCG on AFL Grand Final day

A SPORTING CALENDAR

Across the rest of the year, Melbourne/Naarm's sporting focus switches to a host of changing national and international events:

* **Australian Open** (January) One of the world's four Grand Slam tennis tournaments. ausopen.com

* **Formula One Australian Grand Prix** (March) The world's fastest cars buzzing around Albert Park lake. grandprix.com.au

* **Australian Motorcycle Grand Prix** (October) Head out of town to Phillip Island for the Australian round of the MotoGP, the world's top motorcycle racing competition. motogp.com.au

NOOSA'S WILD SIDE

NOOSA, QUEENSLAND
KABI KALI COUNTRY

Noosa might consider itself the Paris end of the Sunshine Coast, celebrated for its refined charms of gourmet dining, chichi shopping and luxury resorts, but peel back its layers and it reveals a wild side, of the most natural kind.

Noosa National Park

Where the town ends, Noosa's namesake national park begins, blanketing the Noosa Headland that rises to the east. The park is just a 1km (0.6 miles) walk from central Hastings St and is laced with short hiking trails. The most enticing of these is the Coastal Walk, a 5.4km (3.3-mile) route (one-way) that takes in the park's entire coastline, stretching from Noosa around the headland into Sunshine Beach. Wildlife is a key feature of the walk, with koalas likely in the trees overhead, and dolphins, turtles and humpback whales (June to November) in the seas. Beaches such as Tea Tree Bay, Granite Bay and long Alexandria Bay offer sandy stops.

- parks.des.qld.gov.au/parks/noosa

Surfing

When you're on the Coastal Walk, expect to encounter plenty of surfboards tucked under arms. Due to the quelling presence of the Great Barrier Reef to the north, Noosa is Australia's northernmost surf location and one of only 11 World Surfing Reserves, chosen for its revered point breaks, proximity to the national park and the town's long surfing history and culture. There's surfing as near as Noosa Main Beach, which is known for its clean waves protected by the headland, making it also the focus of the town's surf schools. Noosa is best known, however, for its five right-hand point breaks – First Point, Little Cove, Boiling Pot, Tea Tree Bay, Granite Bay – racked along the northern end of the national park. First Point is the closest to town and a favourite with longboarders, while Tea Tree is the local favourite, as the crowded line-up can often attest.

- noosabeachsurfhire.com.au
- gorideawave.com.au

Kayaking

North of town, the Noosa River flows almost entirely through Great Sandy National Park, only leaving the reserve to wash out into the sea through a chain of lakes. At the river's heart are the Noosa Everglades, an ecosystem of submerged marshlands found only here and in Florida. Conditions through the everglades are typically so still that the waterway has earned itself the moniker 'River of Mirrors' and make it one of the most spectacular flat-water kayaking rivers in the country. Hire a kayak or join a tour at shallow

Lake Cootharaba, paddling 5km (3.1 miles) upstream to enter the well-named Narrows through Fig Tree Lake. It's in the Narrows that the celebrated reflections are found. You can paddle into the Narrows and back to Lake Cootharaba in a day, but the river is also lined with 10 campsites, making an overnight trip a welcome Noosa escape into nature. The longest gap between campsites along the 21km (13-mile) stretch of river is 3.5km (2.2 miles), providing a wealth of options to break the journey.

 parks.des.qld.gov.au/parks/cooloola/journeys/upper-noosa-river-waterway

Top **Noosa's waves makes it a popular destination for surfers**
Bottom **Kayaking on the Noosa River**

Bondi Icebergs Pool at Bondi Beach

COOL POOLS

SYDNEY/WARRANE, NSW
GADIGAL COUNTRY

For an experience as Sydney/Warrane as the Opera House or Harbour Bridge, make for the chain of ocean pools that line the city's shores. Uncommon in other parts of the country, these pools carved into rock platforms arose in the late 19th century to provide safe swimming at a time when beach-going first gained popularity. Of the 150 known ocean pools around the world, more than 30 are found in Sydney/Warrane (with another 40 along the NSW coast), so get into the swim at one of the following.

Bondi Icebergs Pool

Australia's most famous pool sits at the southern end of Bondi Beach and features two concrete pools with lane markings and waves often breaking against its rock wall. It's the world's only licensed swimming club and also features a sauna and gym.

icebergs.com.au

Mahon Pool

Cut from a smaller natural pool as part of a Depression-era employment scheme, Maroubra's Mahon Pool is a low-tide favourite (it's best avoided at high tide when it can be swamped by waves) complete with a small library of books for a spot of poolside reading.

McIver's Ladies Baths

Since 1922, this Coogee pool has been reserved exclusively for women and children – the only such seawater pool in Australia. Almost 34m (111ft) in length, it's accessed on steep steps and while it shares a rock platform with popular Wylie's Baths (open to all), its sense of privacy is delightful.

mciversladiesbaths.com.au

South Curl Curl Rock Pool

Standing strong against South Curl Curl's rough swell, this pool on Sydney/Warrane's Northern Beaches is divided into two – a 50m (164-ft) lap pool and a 25m (82-ft) wading pool – making it a good option for families.

Shelly Beach Pool

This Cronulla pool has a small beach and calm water conditions and is ideal for families. A ramp provides access into the pool for wheelchair users.

CANYON COUNTRY

◉ BLUE MOUNTAINS NATIONAL PARK, NSW
DHARUG, GUNDUNGURRA, WANARUAH, WIRADJURI, DARKINJUNG & DHARAWAL COUNTRY

Many of the best things in the Blue Mountains at Sydney/Warrane's western edge are hidden in the cracks. More than 900 canyons fracture the cliffs of the World Heritage–listed mountains, and each one is an underworld marvel.

With such a wealth of canyons, the 'Blueys' are unsurprisingly the heartland of Australian canyoning, an activity that involves scrambling, swimming, leaping, wading and abseiling to navigate your way through the slot. Local favourites include Claustral Canyon, Butterbox Canyon, Twister Canyon and Rocky Creek Canyon, but newcomers to canyoning or the Blue Mountains will find the best introduction in a guided canyoning trip through Empress Canyon.

Unlike many laborious approaches to Blue Mountains canyons, it's a short walk to the entrance of Empress Canyon and it's one of the few canyons you can complete in half a day. Slipping on a wetsuit, harness and helmet, you enter the 500m (1640ft) chasm and begin to puzzle your way through its narrow passage. There are jumps up to 3m (10ft) in height into cool pools, interspersed with sections of canyon that are mere strolls beneath towering cliffs.

Empress's most exciting and spectacular moment comes on its dismount, with the canyon ending at 30m (98ft) Empress Falls. To exit, you abseil beside (and in) the waterfall, all but skating down the mossy, slippery cliffs and finishing with a dunk in the pool below.

Tour operators running guided trips through Empress and other canyons include Blue Mountains Adventure Company and the Australian School of Mountaineering.

◉ bmac.com.au; climbingadventures.com.au

Climbing the slippery Empress Falls

THE GREAT SURF PILGRIMAGE

◎ TORQUAY, VICTORIA
WADAWURRUNG COUNTRY

Bells Beach at sunrise

Australia's greatest surfing legend doesn't ride a board. It's a cliff-lined beach at the eastern end of the Great Ocean Road named Bells Beach, and when this bell tolls, there are few more wild patches of ocean in the world.

Famously the place where Patrick Swayze disappeared into the ocean, never to return, in search of a once-in-a-lifetime wave in the movie *Point Break* (though, to burst a bubble, the scene wasn't filmed at Bells Beach, or even in Australia for that matter), Bells embodies the tale of Australian surf history.

It's been the scene of the world's longest continuously running surf competition, the Rip Curl Pro, since 1962. Global surf brands Rip Curl and Quiksilver were born out of its surf scene, and the town of Torquay, 10km (6.2 miles) to the east, is the keeper of the world's largest surfing museum, the Australian National Surfing Museum (australiannationalsurfingmuseum.com.au), complete with the Australian Surfing Hall of Fame. Waves are literally the heartbeat of this slice of shore known as the Surf Coast.

Bells has two main right-hander reef breaks – Rincon and the Bowl – but this is no place for a beginner. If you're new to a board, head to the likes of Cosy Corner in Torquay or seek out a surf school in Torquay or Anglesea. The Bells waves, and those riding them, are always on display from a lookout by the beach car park and along clifftop trails such as the 3km (1.9-mile) Bells Track, stretching from nearby Jan Juc to Bells, with views of the surf-dotted all the way along.

NO BARRIER TO THIS DIVE AND SNORKEL SITE

◎ MORETON ISLAND/MULGUMPIN, QUEENSLAND
QUANDAMOOKA COUNTRY

One of Queensland's best reef dives isn't on the Great Barrier Reef. For many, it's far closer to home – just a 90-minute ferry ride from Brisbane/Meanjin to the world's third-largest sand island, Moreton Island/Mulgumpin.

Immediately beside the Micat ferry dock on Tangalooma Beach is a tight line of 15 shipwrecks, scuttled through the 1960s, '70s and '80s to provide shelter for mooring yachts. As a happy by-product, the rusting hulls of the wrecks have transformed into coral gardens that attract a wealth of marine life.

The deepest of the wrecks is 12m (40ft) below the surface, making the ships well suited even to novice divers, while many of the hulls reach to the surface, creating equally good snorkelling, which can be accessed simply by swimming out from the beach – aim to do so around an hour either side of low or high tide, when the current is at its gentlest. The Tangalooma Island Resort, 1km (0.6 miles) down the beach, also runs paddling tours in kayaks with transparent bottoms (which can also be hired for an independent paddle from a truck on the beach beside the wrecks).

The hulls of the ships form steel cliffs that are alive with coral and colourful clouds of fish, while you can also swim over the decks or into the hulls of some ships, particularly those at the southern end of the line, which provide the best snorkelling.

Stars of this sea show might include lionfish, harmless (if fearsome-looking) wobbegong sharks and green sea turtles – five of the world's seven turtle species are found around Moreton Bay.

◉ parks.des.qld.gov.au/parks/gheebulum-kunungai-moreton-island

◉ tangalooma.com

Shipwrecks on Tangalooma Beach

WILD TIMES UNDERGROUND

⦿ VARIOUS LOCATIONS

Australia has no shortage of caves that dazzle with their stalagmites, stalactites, flowstones and helictites. All told, there are said to be some 6500 caves pockmarking the country, with the likes of Jenolan Caves (NSW), Buchan Caves (Victoria), Hastings Caves (Tasmania), Jewel Cave (WA) and Kelly Hill Caves (SA) open as show caves to visitors.

A select few caves go beyond, offering the chance to experience adventure caving – crawling, squirming and squeezing through narrow chambers and darkness. Don some overalls and a headtorch and set out on a guided spelunk at any of the following.

Naracoorte Caves National Park, SA

Ranger-led adventure tours explore a trio of caves, though all cavers must begin in the introductory Stick-Tomato Cave and then progress (if you wish) to Starburst Chamber and Fox Cave. Starburst Chamber is reached through Victoria Fossil Cave, passing the fossil beds that have earned the Naracoorte Caves a World Heritage listing, and then crawling on your belly through a tiny tunnel to reach the chamber with its stalactites that sparkle like the starbursts of its name.

⦿ naracoortecaves.sa.gov.au

Mole Creek Karst National Park, Tasmania

Of the 300 caves inside this national park, Marakoopa and King Solomons are open for gentle ranger tours, but locally based Wild Cave Tours can have you burrowing into other, wilder caves, be it stepping over underground waterfalls in labyrinthine Honeycomb Cave or experiencing the calm of a glow-worm chamber and reflective pools in Sassafras Cave.

⦿ parks.tas.gov.au/explore-our-parks/mole-creek-karst-national-park; wildcavetours.com

Capricorn Caves, Queensland

Squirming through the likes of Jack's Beanstalk or the ominously named Entrapment slot at these caves outside of Rockhampton is like a subterranean game of Twister. On the Capricorn Adventurer tour, there are chutes to slide down and others to climb through, and you might even share the space with bent-wing bats, flickering in and out of your torchlight.

⦿ capricorncaves.com.au

BOOTING IT THROUGH ROTTO

ROTTNEST ISLAND/WADJEMUP, WA
WHADJUK NYOONGAR COUNTRY

Rottnest Island/Wadjemup is Perth/Boorloo's holiday playground, just 90 minutes by ferry from the city (or 30 minutes from Fremantle) and gift-wrapped in 63 beaches. With no motor vehicles other than the island bus allowed on its roads, 'Rotto' has traditionally been the domain of bikes, with visitors radiating across the island to the various beaches and reefs. But now it's also a place to explore on foot, with an interconnecting series of trails covering much of the island.

Known as Wadjemup Bidi ('bidi' is a Noongar word for trail), the network consists of five tracks that can be walked in isolation or combined into a 45km (28-mile) island loop, returning each night to your accommodation on the Island Explorer bus.

A clockwise loop from Thomson Bay (where the ferries from Perth/Boorloo and Fremantle dock) begins on the 10km (6.2-mile) Ngank Yira Bidi, hitting the south coast at Henrietta Rock – site of an exposed shipwreck – before climbing to meet the 9.8km (6-mile) Wardan Nara Bidi section atop Oliver Hill. One of the more spectacular sections, Wardan Nara Bidi passes a snorkelling trail at Little Salmon Bay, rises to the island's highest point (ok, it's only 45m/148ft above sea level) at Wadjemup Lighthouse before finishing beside Rotto's best surf at Strickland Bay. Ngank Wen Bidi (7.8km/4.8-mile loop) continues the journey to the island's wild western tip, where there's a natural arch and a fur seal colony.

Looping back, the walk follows the beach-dotted north coast on Karlinyah Bidi (5.7km/3.5 miles), returning to Thomson Bay (with another snorkelling stop at the hollowed-out reef at The Basin) on 9.5km (5.9-mile) Gabbi Karniny Bidi.

rottnestisland.com/see-do/wildlife-nature/Hiking-the-Wadjemup-Bidi

A friendly quokka
Opposite **Fossils on display at Naracoorte Caves**

SNOW MELT: SKI RESORTS IN SUMMER

VARIOUS LOCATIONS

Australian ski resorts no longer hibernate once the snow has melted from their slopes. The arrival of warmth and sun instead heralds a new breed of activity. Pack away the ski goggles and pop on the sunglasses at these mountain playgrounds.

Thredbo

Fringing Australia's highest mountain, Thredbo has been morphing into a mountain-bike park each summer for more than 30 years. Australia's only lift-accessed MTB park has more than 40km (25 miles) of trails and 600m (1969ft) of vertical elevation, or you can set out cross country on the 35km (22-mile) Thredbo Valley Trail, linking the resort village to the Gaden Trout Hatchery aquaculture farm near Jindabyne. This is also the time to hike to the top of Australia, Mount Kosciuszko (*see* p. 27), or set out for four days on foot on the new 55km (34-mile) Snowies Alpine Walk.

thredbo.com.au/summer

Falls Creek

Victoria's largest ski resort also has a mountain-biking habit, with another 40km (25 miles) of trails. Victoria's longest downhill gravity ride is here, with 535m (1755ft) of descent, but there are also 10km (6.2 miles) of trails aimed at novice riders. A weekend shuttle service (it runs daily during summer school holidays) eases the burden back to the top. Hiking trails venture across the plateau to historic High Country huts and Rocky Valley Lake, while the Falls to Hotham Alpine Crossing is a three-day, 37km (23-mile) hike connecting Falls Creek to the neighbouring ski resort on Mount Hotham.

fallscreek.com.au/summer

Mount Buller

Buller is similarly laced with mountain bike trails, including the Alpine Epic, Australia's first trail classified as an 'Epic' by the International Mountain Bicycling Association – prepare for 2000m (6562ft) of descent and 1200m (3937ft) of climb on a big day out on the 46km (29-mile) trail. New to Buller in 2024 was RockWire, Australia's first via ferrata, traversing the mountain's West Face on ladders, wire bridges and metal rungs, all while securely clipped to a metal cable.

mtbuller.com.au/summer

Top **Hiking Mount Buller**
Bottom **Chairlifts take mountain bikers to the top of Thredbo**

SURF'S UP

◉ BOGANGAR, NSW
BUNDJALUNG COUNTRY

Belén Alvarez Kimble has seen a lot of firsts for women in surfing. In the mid-1990s, in her Californian hometown of San Diego, she worked at the world's first all-woman surf shop, then as an instructor at the first all-woman surf school. After a long career as a professional longboard freesurfer, she moved to Australia and, in 2008, opened this country's first all-woman surf school, Salty Girls Surf School.

'I'm really lucky that where I grew up, it just happened to be kind of a hub of women's surfing,' Belén says, noting that surf culture in Australia has also evolved to become very welcoming of women.

'Australian surf culture for women is amazing now. Everything is catered for women to enter the water and safe spaces. The ocean here is so inviting and so are surfers.

'Australia was my favourite place to come to as a freesurfer and as a contest surfer. You have every kind of wave you could possibly want, from your elite style of surfing to your absolute beginner wave for children. It also offers a supportive culture in the water so long as you are respectful of the people in the water.'

More than 15 years on from the establishment of Salty Girls, all-woman surf schools and classes have proliferated across Australia. Belén says the surfers who come to learn at Salty Girls range from women who grew up in the '80s watching *Puberty Blues* and always wanting to surf to young women wanting a fun, supportive environment among women coaches.

'I don't think a female coach is better than a male coach, but I feel like a female coach can relate to a female more because we can understand the hormones, we can understand coming back from childbirth, we can understand the physical differences of breasts and hips and menopause and periods and all that kind of stuff,' she says. 'It's a really beautiful space where women can connect.'

Belén's chosen home of surfing is northern NSW's Tweed Coast, near the Queensland border on the land of the Bundjalung People, a place she describes as an ideal surfing environment for newcomers.

'We live in a beautiful spot, we've got perfect learning surf waves – very gentle, very safe – and the water's warm for the most part all year long,' she says. 'And we've got a community that's just so supportive of what we're doing.'

Beyond the Tweed, she says there are many great places to learn to surf in Australia. Three of her picks:

The Pass, Byron Bay (NSW)

'It's amazing. It's a rolling, gentle wave that gives you so much time to practice popping up and standing up – getting your feet in the right position. It's one of the longest waves we have in Australia, and it really gives you an opportunity to progress quite quickly because of the amount of time you're standing up and riding.'

Currumbin Alley (Queensland)

'It's a really long, rolling wave and there are a lot of learn-to-surf schools.'

Noosa (Queensland)

'It's quite gentle and rolling, with long rides. It's protected, so the waves are often quite small and the majority of the people surfing there are women.'

saltygirls.com.au

Surfing The Pass

208	Burrawa-ing Into Sydney/Warrane's History
210	Leading and Writing – Grampa Thomas Shadrach James and the Rise of Yorta Yorta Activism
212	Australia's First World Heritage Site for First Nations Cultural Value
214	Captive Sights: Australian Convict Sites World Heritage Area
216	Ghosted by History
217	Australia's Oldest European Building
218	The Great Aussie Pub
220	Eureka!
221	Casting Light on Dark Days
222	The Dog Fence
225	Australia's Favourite Bad Boy
226	The Fossils Fantastic
229	National Treasures

"It tells a totally different story to what they've been taught at school"

HISTORY

BURRAWA-ING INTO SYDNEY/WARRANE'S HISTORY

◉ SYDNEY/WARRANE, NSW
GADIGAL COUNTRY

The best views from the Sydney Harbour Bridge might well be deep into history. Stand atop the bridge, 134m (440ft) above the waters of Sydney Harbour, and the city towers stand like stakes and the plains stretch west to the hazy wall of the Blue Mountains, but on a Burrawa BridgeClimb, history overwrites every scene.

The newest tour offering on the famous BridgeClimb provides a First Nations perspective on the city and its past. Led by a First Nations guide, or 'storyteller', the twice-weekly tour (Wednesday and Saturday) ascends the bridge's famous arches, peering down onto the Opera House and the armadas of harbour and bridge traffic.

The real treasure of this climb is not so much the impressive views, but the story of First Nations' custodianship of these Gadigal lands. Each stop along the bridge delivers a new view of history, from the stream that flowed down what's now Pitt St (the stream remains beneath the street), where Gadigal People gathered to eat, drink and socialise (as modern city workers still do along the street) to the three-storey-high First Nations midden that the First Fleet observed near Bennelong Point (where the Opera House stands).

The stories span thousands of years, but it's the early years of contact with European settlers that dominate the narrative. They are stories about familiar, but underrepresented, First Nations figures such as Bennelong, Barangaroo and Pemulwuy, the Bidjigal warrior who spent 12 years fighting the invaders for his land and people.

The views are sublime, but this overlay of First Nations history is even better.

◉ bridgeclimb.com

Burrawa BridgeClimb guides climbers through the history of Gadigal Country

LEADING AND WRITING – GRAMPA THOMAS SHADRACH JAMES AND THE RISE OF YORTA YORTA ACTIVISM

⚲ MALOGA/CUMMERAGUNJA, NSW
YORTA YORTA COUNTRY

In the late 19th century, most Aboriginal children were taught only to the age of nine, and that education was designed to usher them into domestic or labouring positions. It certainly didn't encourage them toward independent thinking. Yet my community at Maloga and later Cummeragunja, both located in Yorta Yorta Country on the Murray River near Moama in NSW, received the very highest standard of education available anywhere, thanks to Thomas Shadrach James.

Born in Mauritius of Indian heritage in 1859, James arrived in Australia in 1879. He soon met the Maloga Revival Church Camp comprised of Yorta Yorta people from Maloga Mission at Brighton Beach. Mission founder Daniel Matthews invited him to teach at Maloga, and James gladly accepted. This would mark the beginning of a lifelong connection. James would later become known affectionately by our community as 'Grampa' after marrying Ada Cooper, a sister of one of his most accomplished pupils Uncle William Cooper.

Grampa James taught children by day and adults by candlelight at night at the 'Scholars Hut', equipping them with not only literacy and numeracy skills, but an understanding of global matters of importance relating to the uplift of other First Peoples and marginalised groups.

In his own words he taught them to 'lead and write'. He taught the power of advocacy by developing petitions and equipped his pupils with the skills to fight for their rights, conditions and futures. Grampa also knew the importance of Aboriginal self-determination, occasionally writing to newspapers or government bodies himself to draw attention to conditions or issues under a nom-de-plume – 'One Who Suffers' – to ensure

Thomas Shadrach James

SHARING STORIES

Yarn (unless you're knitting) has very little to do with wool; in Australia it generally refers to having a chat or telling a good story. But yarning circles are a long-observed First Nations Cultural practice that has deep significance, used formally and informally as a way of sharing knowledge, building relationships and passing on Culture.

the gravitas of the message was not lost by being delivered by a non-Aboriginal person.

Grampa's graduates include some of the best-known activists post-colonisation who, aside from Uncle William Cooper, included the likes of Uncle Doug Nicholls, Aunty Geraldine Briggs, Aunty Marg Tucker, Uncle Jack Patten and Uncle Bill Onus. Such was his impact that multiple attempts were made by the Aboriginal Protection Board to remove him from his post for inciting unrest, as so many of his pupils began to push for change.

Aside from teaching, he was also a herbalist, healer, coach and mentor. Grampa formed part of the fabric of Maloga and Cummeragunja and, for the first time since the brutal impacts of colonisation, he offered hope that a better future might be possible for our people. I am proud to be his descendant – we share the middle name Shadrach – and I am inspired by his work every day.

We continue to advocate for improved social, economic and health outcomes through rights such as Aboriginal self-determination, treaties and representation in parliament (though in a different form since the defeat of the 2023 referendum). It is important to reflect on those who have gone before us and the origins of activism in this country. Personally, I celebrate the likes of Grampa and am thankful for their courage and commitment – their work has ensured we have a foundation from which to 'lead and write'.

● For more information, read *Dharmalan Dana* by George and Robynne Nelson

● williamcooper.monash.edu/people/thomas-shadrach-james/

By Jamil Tye

AUSTRALIA'S FIRST WORLD HERITAGE SITE FOR FIRST NATIONS CULTURAL VALUE

◉ BUDJ BIM CULTURAL LANDSCAPE, VICTORIA
GUNDITJMARA COUNTRY

Budj Bim aquaculture system (photography by Wayne Quilliam)

Around 6600 years ago there was no Stonehenge and no Great Pyramid, and agriculture was in its infancy across the globe. But 6600 years ago there was Budj Bim, a cleverly designed and sustainable aquaculture network of channels and traps created in the shadow of a volcano by the Gunditjmara People of south-western Victoria. Using specific techniques to shape basalt rocks to divert waterways into channels cut by a lava flow, they laid down woven eel traps, creating a year-round source of food whilst living in permanent stone huts around the channels – dispelling the nomadic hunter-gatherer narrative around First Nations people circulated by Europeans post-colonisation.

'A volcano doesn't destroy the country, but it changes it completely,' says Joey Saunders, one of Budj Bim Cultural Landscape's tour coordinators. 'We used that to our advantage in a real sustainable way.'

In 2019 this remarkable place, four hours drive west of Melbourne, became the first Australian site inscribed on UNESCO's World Heritage list purely for its First Nations cultural value. Joey grew up learning the stories of Budj Bim, but he says that even now he marvels at the ingenuity of the traps and, with the stone huts, the way they've debunked myths about First Nations existence.

'It's a bit like truth-telling,' he says. 'People come here and see us as people that have had permanent settlements, and it blows their mind. It tells a totally different story to what they've been taught at school.

'We were permanently living on Country and manipulating Country to our purpose to live there all year. My father said this was like our supermarket – there was no need to go anywhere else.'

When Budj Bim's centrepiece, Lake Condah (Tae Rak), was returned to Gunditjmara People in 2008, a lake restoration program – long a dream of Gunditjmara Elders – also begun. Today, the lake's shores are home to the Tae Rak Aquaculture Centre, a charred-timber and red-gum building featuring a bush tucker cafe (give the eel tasting plate or the smoked eel arancini balls a try) and an eel holding tank.

'The centre blends into the country,' Joey says. 'As Gunditjmara People, we really wanted something that was sustainable and not an eyesore. We wanted it to be really low-key in the way that you can sit there and enjoy the view.'

Gunditjmara-led tours of Budj Bim operate out of the centre, ranging from two-hour glimpses to full-day tours taking in Budj Bim's three distinct sections: Budj Bim National Park, Kurtonitj and Tyrendarra. It's a chance to walk through Tae Rak's wetlands, hear the creation story of Budj Bim's (Mount Eccles) eruption and visit the eel channels and 'smoking trees' in which kooyang (eels) were traditionally cooked.

'We want to give visitors an understanding of who we are as people – being able to walk on Country with a Traditional Owner and get that understanding of what we did on Country and who we are,' Joey says.

Tae Rak Aquaculture Centre is open from Wednesday to Sunday. Tours run on the same days.

🌐 budjbim.com.au

CAPTIVE SIGHTS: AUSTRALIAN CONVICT SITES WORLD HERITAGE AREA

VARIOUS LOCATIONS

In the first century of Australia's colonial settlement, more than 160,000 convicts arrived from the United Kingdom, many for the pettiest of crimes. Penal sites and convict-built structures remain across the country, with 11 of them collectively inscribed on UNESCO's World Heritage list in 2010 as the Australian Convict Sites World Heritage Area.

Visit one or collect the set.

Port Arthur Historic Site, Tasmania

Australia's most (in)famous convict site, with a four-storey penitentiary and a seemingly inescapable location – the only way out was across a narrow isthmus guarded by savage dogs. Spectacular location, with a series of guided tours and boat trips available.

portarthur.org.au

Coal Mines Historic Site, Tasmania

Wander through the bush 30 minutes drive from Port Arthur to find Tasmania's first operational mine, worked by the so-called 'worst class' of Port Arthur's convicts. A 2km (1.2-mile) walking trail loops through the ruins where convicts were required to extract 25 tonnes (27 tons) of coal every shift.

coalmines.org.au

Cascades Female Factory, Tasmania

More than half the female convicts transported to Australia (or around 12,500 women) were sent to Tasmania, where they were imprisoned in 'female factories' in Launceston, Ross and Hobart/nipaluna. Traces of the female factory in Ross remain, but Cascades, high on the slopes above Hobart/nipaluna, is the most significant and chilling of the prisons. Three of its five courtyards remain, encased in the original perimeter wall. There are daily tours and a self-guided audio tour.

femalefactory.org.au

Darlington Probation Station, Tasmania

Established five years before Port Arthur, Maria Island's Darlington is Australia's most intact probation station. Ferries from Triabunna make the half-hour crossing to the island, where you can wander through the penitentiary surrounded by a host of grazing wombats and wallabies.

parks.tas.gov.au/explore-our-parks/maria-island-national-park

Brickendon and Woolmers Estates, Tasmania

Adjoining estates that were developed and farmed by a large contingent of convicts. Many convict-built structures remain, and the properties provide a glimpse into the lives of the myriad convicts who were assigned to landowners.

🔗 brickendon.com.au; woolmers.com.au

Hyde Park Barracks, NSW

Designed by a convict and inhabited by many convicts, the industrial-looking barracks in Sydney/Warrane's city centre is now a museum telling the story of the site as well as the harmful impact on Australia's First Nations people.

🔗 mhnsw.au/visit-us/hyde-park-barracks

Old Government House and Domain, NSW

The Parramatta country mansion of NSW's early governors, and Australia's oldest surviving public building, was built by convicts and maintained by convicts – labour never came so cheap.

🔗 nationaltrust.org.au/places/old-government-house

Cockatoo Island/Wareamah, NSW

Convict prison in the middle of Sydney Harbour with a reputation for brutality. Catch a ferry to wander the relics and a former naval dockyard, and stay the night in anything from your own tent to a glamping tent to harbour-view apartments.

🔗 cockatooisland.gov.au

Old Great North Road, NSW

This convict-built road once ran 250km (155 miles) from Sydney/Warrane to the Hunter Valley. Only 43km (27 miles) of the original remains, which can be walked or cycled. A shorter 9km World Heritage Walk passes the road's quarry (complete with convict graffiti) along with 9m (30ft) road buttresses and other original features.

🔗 nationalparks.nsw.gov.au/things-to-do/walking-tracks/old-great-north-road-world-heritage-walk

Fremantle Prison, WA

Built by convicts for use as their own barracks (and used as a prison until 1991), the so-called 'Establishment' processed around 10,000 convicts. Offers a range of tours, including into tunnels and submerged pathways cut beneath the prison by convicts.

🔗 fremantleprison.com.au

Kingston and Arthur's Vale Historic Area, Norfolk Island

Established just five weeks after the First Fleet landed in Sydney/Warrane in 1788, this much-feared penal station is Australia's second-oldest European settlement. The well-preserved site includes the remains of two convict gaols and standing military and government buildings. It might also be the planet's only World Heritage Site with a golf course.

🔗 kingston.norfolkisland.gov.au

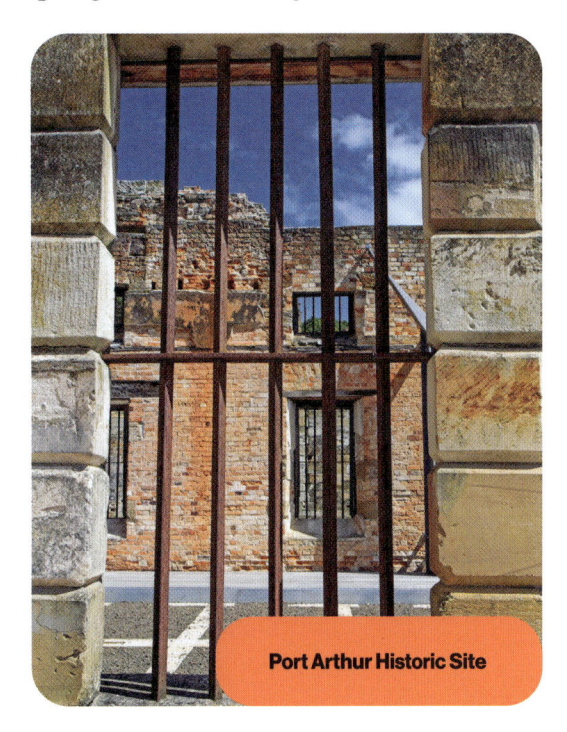

Port Arthur Historic Site

GHOSTED BY HISTORY

FARINA, SA
KUYANI COUNTRY

The ghost town of Farina
Opposite **The remains of a stone fort on West Wallabi Island**

From Port Essington in the Northern Territory's far north to Adamsfield in Tasmania's Southwest wilderness, Australia is littered with hundreds of ghost towns – settlements that arose in great hope but faded from maps when minerals and riches dried up, or when the realisation struck that they'd been built in unsuitably arid or challenging locations. Farina was one such town.

One of the most evocative of the country's abandoned towns, Farina was proclaimed in 1878, with fanciful dreams of endless wheat fields for this railway town in the desert. When the fields didn't materialise and the Ghan railway shifted its line 300km (186 miles) to the west, Farina, once a town of 300 people, went belly-up.

Today, Farina is an atmospheric outdoor museum of abandoned buildings and ruins. Set beside the Oodnadatta Track, midway between Leigh Creek and Marree on the lands of the Kuyani People, its chimneys rise like the legs of upturned stools, and bricks are strewn about like a toppled game of Jenga.

Among the ruins, which are free to visit, you'll find the likes of the post office, Exchange Hotel and Granny Davies' cottage still standing. There's a campground on the banks of Farina Creek and one very surprising detail to a winter visit (when conditions are most comfortable) – for eight weeks, volunteers from the Farina Restoration Group operate Farina's underground oven inside the 1888 bakery. It's likely the most remote bakery you'll ever visit. Check the Restoration Group's website for opening dates.

farinarestoration.com

AUSTRALIA'S OLDEST EUROPEAN BUILDING

HOUTMAN ABROLHOS ISLANDS, WA

Australia's oldest structure built by Europeans predates European settlement by almost 160 years. In 1629, the Dutch merchant ship *Batavia* wrecked on a reef in the Houtman Abrolhos Islands, 60km (37 miles) off the coast of Geraldton. A small group of survivors built a stone fort among the wind-pruned scrub on West Wallabi Island to defend themselves against a *Lord of the Flies*-style mutiny among other wreck survivors on nearby Beacon Island. Almost 400 years on, the low remains of the two-room dry-wall fort still stand on the east coast of the hard-to-reach island.

The surest way here is on a five-day Houtman Abrolhos cruise with Eco Abrolhos Cruises. Diving of the scant *Batavia* wreck – its cannons and anchor still visible – can be arranged in Geraldton. The ship, rediscovered in 1963, sits in less than 5m (16ft) of water.

ecoabrolhos.com.au

THE GREAT AUSSIE PUB

VARIOUS LOCATIONS

If there's one single structure that defines an outback town, it's the pub. Typically the most imposing building in town (and sometimes just about the only building in town), it's the very image of outback life, wrapped in mercifully shady verandas and often with a grandness that hints at a town's past wealth.

Here are some of the finest of the genre.

Birdsville Hotel, Queensland

With the Simpson Desert reaching its doors and the nearest capital city more than 1000km (621 miles) away, this revered Channel Country pub is the epitome of remote. Standing beside the Queensland–South Australia border since 1884, it's typically decorated in Australiana memorabilia – road signs, licence plates and a Hat Wall, featuring Akubras and caps from those who've achieved the goal of living in Birdsville for more than a year. If Birdsville, with its population of 110, is too crowded for you, head two hours east to Australia's smallest town, Betoota, where there's only a pub and an official population of zero.

 birdsvillehotel.com.au

Palace Hotel, NSW

Famously a key location in the cult Aussie movie *Priscilla Queen of the Desert*, Broken Hill's Palace Hotel was built in 1889 as a coffee palace but turned from beans to beer within three years. The pub's most striking feature is the 500 sq m (5381 sq ft) of interior murals by First Nations artist Gordon Waye. Each painting features water, making the Palace an oasis of the desert.

 thepalacehotelbrokenhill.com.au

William Creek Hotel, SA

Welcome to South Australia's smallest town – population six – encased by the largest cattle station in the world. Once a siding on the old Ghan railway, and now a popular stop along the unsealed Oodnadatta Track, the pub's ceiling is scrawled with names and hung with business cards, hats, banknotes, stubbie holders and a coffee pot. It's the closest town to Kati Thanda–Lake Eyre North and, with the opening of a nearby solar array in 2023, it's the only fully solar-powered town in SA (and possibly the country). There's a makeshift nine-hole golf course right beside.

 williamcreekhotel.com

Daly Waters Pub, NT

Enter past Australia's most remote traffic lights (granted, they don't work) and it's like stepping through the looking glass. IDs of past patrons decorate the bar of the Northern Territory's oldest pub (1930), alongside bank notes and dozens of bras hanging overhead. There's the Junk Yard museum out back, and through the dry season (April to October) a nightly Beef 'n' Barra BBQ. Step outside and ponder the fact that this 'town', six hours drive from Darwin, was the site of Australia's first international airfield, used as a necessary refuelling stop for flights between London and Sydney/Warrane.

 dalywaterspub.com.au

Great Western Hotel, Queensland

Taking beef to new levels, this Rockhampton stalwart, opened in 1862, is a pub that doubles as a rodeo venue. There's a mechanical bull in one of the four bars, but also an arena with regular musical performers and events. As you'd expect in the town that claims itself as Australia's beef capital, the steak is revered, with a steakhouse among its dining options.

 greatwesternhotel.com.au

Top **Daly Waters is the Northern Territory's oldest pub**
Bottom **The solar-powered William Creek Hotel**

EUREKA!

BALLARAT, VICTORIA
WADAWARRUNG & DJA DJA WURRUNG COUNTRY

One of the pivotal events in modern Australian history was indeed a Eureka moment. In 1854, disgruntled miners in the rich goldfields of Ballarat took a stand against authorities. In the Eureka diggings, they built a wooden fort – the Eureka Stockade – which was stormed by soldiers on 3 December. At least 22 miners and five soldiers were killed in Australia's most celebrated rebellion.

Rising today from what's believed to be the site of the uprising is the Eureka Stockade Monument, erected in 1884, and the Eureka Stockade Memorial Park. At its heart is Lake Penhalluriak – once a sludge pond for the Eureka diggings – and the Eureka Centre, a museum telling the story of the famous siege. The centre's prize item is the original Eureka flag with its white cross and stars of the Southern Cross on a blue background. Measuring 2.6m (8.5ft) by 4m (13.1ft), it was allegedly souvenired by a soldier and donated to the Art Gallery of Ballarat by his family in the 1890s.

To Australians, this flag is almost as familiar as the nation's own flag, and though it's been appropriated by a number of causes over the decades – most prominently trade unions and, in recent years, white nationalist groups – the original remains one of the country's most treasured and storied historic artefacts.

When you're done at the Eureka Centre, head across town to find the statue of rebellion leader Peter Lalor on the corner of Sturt and Dawson Sts. Lalor survived the attack on the stockade – he was shot but hidden under the rubble by rebels – and went on to become a member of Victoria's parliament.

eurekacentreballarat.com.au

CASTING LIGHT ON DARK DAYS

◉ MELBOURNE/NAARM, VICTORIA
BOONWURRUNG/BUNURONG & WURUNDJERI COUNTRY

Left and right The Melbourne Holocaust Museum
Opposite The Eureka flag flies at the Eureka Centre

Victoria has Australia's largest population of people who identify with Jewish ancestry – more than 46,000 people at the last census – with more than half of the community settled in the council area of Glen Eira in Melbourne/Naarm's south-eastern suburbs.

It's here, just a few steps from Elsternwick railway station, that you'll find the remarkable blend of light and historic darkness at the Melbourne Holocaust Museum. Created in 1984 by Holocaust survivors, the museum underwent extensive renovations in 2023, emerging as both an expanded museum and an architectural statement.

Incorporating transparent glass bricks, the white building is intended to draw in natural light, which, combined with the blonde timbers inside, is intended as a symbol of hope as the story of the Holocaust is told from the years leading up to WWII, through the war and on to the trauma, loss and freedom beyond.

Central to the museum's experience is the permanent exhibition, Everybody Had a Name. Choose one of six postcards with an image of a Holocaust survivor and follow their life journey as you walk through the collection of historical items and documents – all donated by members of Melbourne/Naarm's Jewish community – that tell the chilling story of life under the Nazis.

Australia's own connections aren't overlooked, including the story of a protest by Yorta Yorta activist William Cooper against the persecution of Jews in Nazi Germany, the only private protest of its kind in the world. William Cooper is also recognised in Yad Vashem, the World Holocaust Rememberance Centre in Israel.

◉ mhm.org.au

THE DOG FENCE

⬤ KANKU-BREAKAWAYS CONSERVATION PARK, SA
ANTAKIRINJA MATUNTJARA YANKUNYTJATJARA COUNTRY

The world's longest fence marches across Australia from Jimbour in Queensland's Darling Downs to the cliffs of the Nullarbor in South Australia. Known as the Dog Fence, it stretches 5300km (3293 miles) – and once ran to 9600km (5965 miles) – across three states (Queensland, New South Wales and South Australia).

Standing 1.7m (5.6ft) high, the wire fence cuts a seam through deserts and the outback, most spectacularly along the foot of the Kanku-Breakaways, 30 minutes drive north of Coober Pedy. These colourful, flat-topped peaks are part of the traditional country of the Antakirinja Matuntjara Yankunytjatjara Peoples and are cared for by the Antakirinja Matu-Yankunytjatjara Aboriginal Corporation.

Stained orange, white and black, the Kanku-Breakaways' peaks were once islands in an inland sea and form an otherworldly landscape that's become a cinematic favourite, with movies such as *Mad Max Beyond Thunderdome*, *Priscilla Queen of the Desert* and *Pitch Black* filmed here. But descend from its hilltop lookouts and the road meets and runs beside Australia's most impressive fence on the drive back towards Coober Pedy.

Built from 1947 to protect the sheep industry south of its line, the Dog Fence continues to separate northern and southern Australia even more effectively than state borders. The fence costs around $10 million a year to maintain, with a portion of every sheep sold in South Australia going towards its maintenance across that state – owners of property through which the fence runs must inspect it every 14 days.

The lengthy Dog Fence

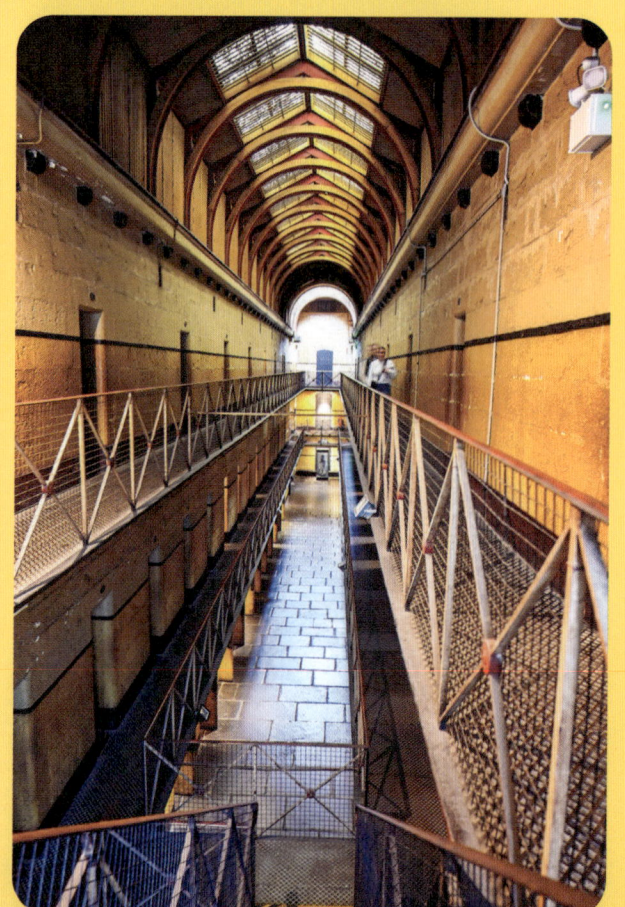

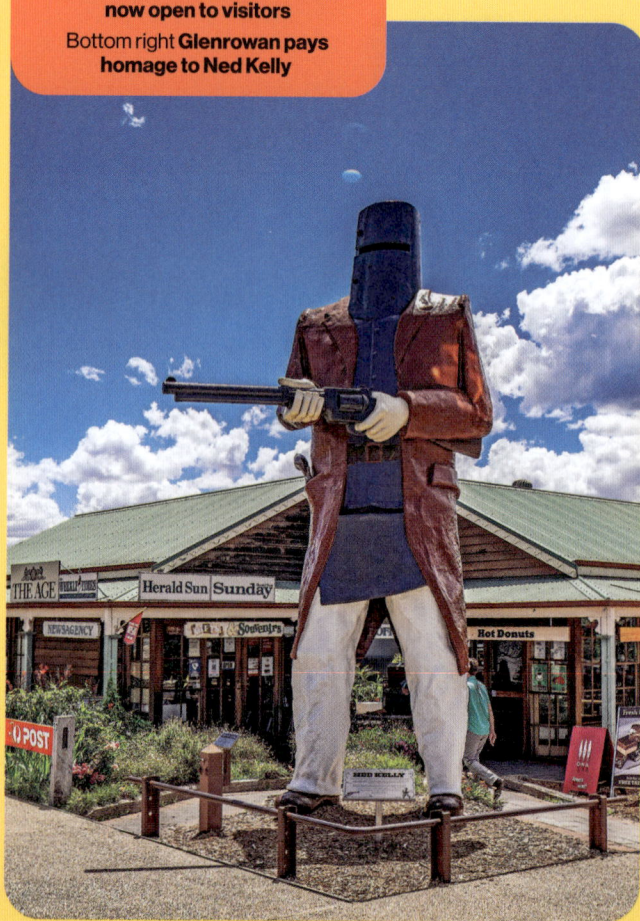

Top **Old Beechworth Gaol**

Bottom left **Old Melbourne Gaol, now open to visitors**

Bottom right **Glenrowan pays homage to Ned Kelly**

AUSTRALIA'S FAVOURITE BAD BOY

VARIOUS LOCATIONS, VICTORIA

Australia has a deep and irreverent love for antiheroes, and few come more celebrated than the bushrangers who roamed the countryside and roads through the 19th century. Their crimes and legends were manifold and their names live large in local folklore – Captain Moonlight, Ben Hall, Martin Cash, the Clarke Gang. But Australia's favourite bad boy was unquestionably the armour-clad Ned Kelly, who terrorised areas of northern Victoria and southern NSW in the 1870s.

Delve into the life and crimes of Kelly – the subject of one of Australia's most famous art series (by painter Sidney Nolan) and a Booker Prize-winning novel (by Peter Carey) – at the following sites.

Beveridge
Kelly's childhood home, built by his father Red, still stands in this tiny town just north of Melbourne/Naarm. It's closed to the public, but swing by for a look from the outside.

Stringybark Creek Reserve
Kelly's true infamy began when his gang killed three police officers at Stringybark Creek in 1878. A plaque on the so-called Kelly Tree marks the spot of the shootout.

Benalla Costume and Kelly Museum
The centrepiece of this collection is a transportable cell in which Kelly was once imprisoned, along with the blood-stained sash he was wearing in his final shootout with police.

- home.vicnet.net.au/~benmus

Glenrowan
The scene of Kelly's final siege and arrest, and now home to the Ned Kelly History Museum and Kellyland, a multimedia re-enactment of the final stand.

- katescottageglenrowan.com.au/ned-kelly-museum
- kellylandglenrowan.com

Old Beechworth Gaol
The prison that variously interred Kelly, his mother and all the members of his gang.

- oldbeechworthgaol.com.au

State Library of Victoria
Step into the Redmond Barry Reading Room to view Kelly's steel armour (complete with dents from bullets) and his Enfield rifle, its barrel inscribed 'NK son of RED'.

- slv.vic.gov.au

Old Melbourne Gaol
Before this prison closed in 1929, it executed 133 prisoners, including Kelly. Tours run daily.

- oldmelbournegaol.com.au

THE FOSSILS FANTASTIC

◉ WINTON, QUEENSLAND
KOA COUNTRY

In the 1990s, western Queensland farmer David Elliott regularly set out to muster sheep but encountered dinosaurs instead … or at least their bones, scattered across the grass plains of his property near Winton.

'All of the discoveries I ever made were while mustering,' says the founder of the Australian Age of Dinosaurs (AAOD). 'It's always when you're in a bloody hurry, when you don't have time to stop. We found quite a few sites in the '90s – I think about 14 sites.'

Among them, in 1999, was the remains of Australia's largest-known dinosaur, a 21m (69ft) sauropod christened Elliot. 'It was pretty exciting, this big piece of dinosaur bone. That used to get you going in those days – now not so much because we're getting fussy,' he says with a laugh.

It was the discovery of Elliot that led to the establishment of AAOD, which was originally just a working laboratory squeezed into a farm shed on David's property, in 2002. Now positioned atop a mesa known as the Jump Up, 25km (15 miles) east of Winton, AAOD has developed and grown to become one of the world's premier dinosaur museums, home to the largest collection of Australian dinosaur fossils.

Among the impressive displays, AAOD continues its work of unearthing and unveiling dinosaurs. The museum has two laboratories, including a fossil preparation lab that runs a Prep-a-Dino program, in which visitors can join in the meditative and meticulous work of preparing and restoring bones. You can sign on for as little as a day in the lab, or spend 10 days on the tools to become an honorary technician.

More immersive still is the Dig-a-Dino experience, joining an AAOD team on a dig for fossils in the Winton Formation – the geological area surrounding Winton. Participants spend eight days in the field (usually including five or six days of digging and a day visiting the museum and laboratories).

'The vast majority of Australia's dinosaurs have been found in the Winton Formation,' David says. 'We usually have four weeks of digging a year. A lot of people come every year – there are two people who did their 19th dig this year.'

MORE ROAR

The AAOD might be the apex of fossil museums, but it's not the only keeper of dinosaur tales in this part of Queensland.

* **Lark Quarry Dinosaur Trackways** The mud-hardened footprints of a 95-million-year-old dinosaur stampede when around 150 small dinosaurs were spooked by a larger beast at a waterhole 110km (68 miles) south of Winton. dinosaurtrackways.com.au

* **Kronosaurus Korner** Richmond museum with a collection of more than 1000 fossil specimens, predominantly marine reptiles from the time when the area was submerged by an inland sea. kronosauruskorner.com.au

* **Muttaburra** Pay homage to the country town that gave its name to a dinosaur species – Muttaburrasaurus – uncovered by a local grazier in 1963. It was one of the most complete dinosaur skeletons ever found in Australia. There's a life-size statue of the creature in town, while the original skeleton is in the Queensland Museum in Brisbane.

Outside the Australian Age of Dinosaurs

Top **The National Museum of Australia**
Bottom **The museum houses many local and international treasures**

NATIONAL TREASURES

CANBERRA/KAMBERRA, ACT
NGUNNAWAL COUNTRY

In the national capital, Canberra/Kamberra, national icons abound. Visit the National Museum of Australia and, within its collection of 21 million items, you'll find a sprinkling of national treasures as Australian as bulldust and beaches.

A water bottle used by Burke and Wills

The explorers made an ill-fated 1860 inland expedition. The collection also includes the breastplate awarded to the Yandruwandha People who came to the explorers' help.

The shears used by Jack Howe

In 1892 Jack Howe, Australia's greatest shearer, sheared 321 sheep in a day – still an Australian record.

The Bedford truck used at Wave Hill

First Nations workers walked off Wave Hill Station in 1966 to protest unequal pay and conditions, leading to the beginning of land rights for Australia's First Nations population.

The black dress worn by Azaria Chamberlain

The baby Azaria was taken by a dingo at Uluru in 1980, sparking one of the country's highest-profile court cases.

The preserved body of a thylacine

The emblematic Tasmanian tiger that was last officially sighted in 1936 became a symbol of the loss of Australian native species.

The fleece of Chris the Sheep

Shorn in 2015 and weighing in at a world-record 41.1kg (90.6lb) from the planet's woolliest sheep.

The two Wimbledon trophies of Wiradjuri tennis player Evonne Goolagong Cawley

Along with one of her racquets from the 1970s.

nma.gov.au

232	Pottering through the Desert
233	Bundanon: An Art Gift to the Nation
234	Warm Hospitality in the Torres Strait
236	The Art of Wine
238	The World's Greatest Concentration of Rock Art
241	Mad About Max
242	A Rockstar Gallery
244	The Great Barrier Reef's Underwater Art Gallery
247	The Mysterious Giant of the Desert
248	Sydney Harbour through First Nations' Eyes
251	Desert Sculptures
252	Against the Grain
253	Yarra Yarns
254	New Light on Uluru
256	The Most Australian Piece of Australia?
259	Picnic at Hanging Rock
260	Central Art
263	Where the Giant Things Are
264	Iga Warta: Home of the Native Orange
265	Life in the Art Lane
266	The Outback Town Where Art Trumps Beer
268	Tasmania's Aboriginal Revival
270	Sculpting a Reef
271	Portrait of a Gallery
273	Spirited Art

"The strangest thing of all? Nobody claimed credit for its creation, and even today its origins are unknown"

ART & CULTURE

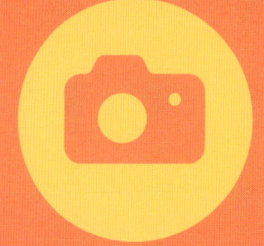

POTTERING THROUGH THE DESERT

◉ HERMANNSBURG, NT
ARRERNTE COUNTRY

The First Nations town of Hermannsburg is synonymous with art. It was here, 90 minutes drive west of Alice Springs/Mparntwe, that Arrernte artist Albert Namatjira inspired a celebrated style of watercolour landscapes that became known as the Hermannsburg School, and it's now home to one of the most recognisable of Australia's First Nations art centres, the Hermannsburg Potters.

Established in 1990, the art centre, which is open to visitors by appointment on weekdays, represents more than 20 artists – historically only women, but now with a few men under a men's development program. During the day, there can be four or five artists at work in the studio, painting the bulbous pots in their trademark designs, with a small showroom at the entrance. There's the chance to watch the artists at work, and the day I visited, one artist – Rona Rubuntja, who has been working with the Hermannsburg Potters since 1998 – downed brushes to provide an impromptu tour of the studio and backroom kiln.

A few minutes walk from the studio, the Hermannsburg Historic Precinct is an architectural record of the town's origins when Lutheran missionaries established the Finke River Mission Station in 1877. It was briefly the largest settlement in central Australia and is today a museum village fresh off a $5-million upgrade. Wrapped around the central Lutheran church is a collection of original whitewashed buildings, including a meat house, classroom and tannery. Note the visitor centre, which is a former bakehouse built after WWII from flattened and recycled 44-gallon drums.

◉ hermannsburgpotters.com.au

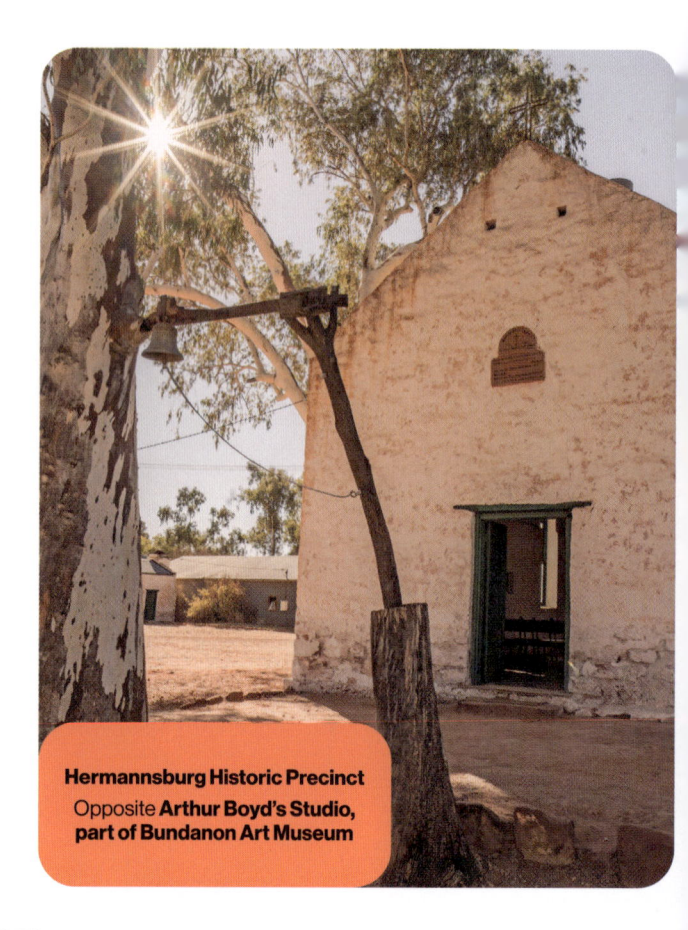

Hermannsburg Historic Precinct
Opposite **Arthur Boyd's Studio, part of Bundanon Art Museum**

BUNDANON: AN ART GIFT TO THE NATION

ILLAROO, NSW
DHARAWAL & DHURGA COUNTRY

Arthur Boyd was one of Australia's most acclaimed 20th-century artists, painting (among other themes) memorable Impressionist works of the Australian bush. In 1993, six years before his death, Boyd and wife Yvonne gifted their home, Bundanon, on the Traditional Lands of the Dharawal and Dhurga People on NSW's South Coast, to the nation, along with 1000 hectares (2471 acres) of bushland and their private art collection. This included many of Boyd's own paintings as well as works from other great Australian artists such as Sidney Nolan, Brett Whiteley and Joy Hester.

In 2022, after a major renovation, the site opened as the Bundanon Art Museum, with a collection of 4000 artworks, including works by Bundanon artists in residence, and an architectural design as artistic as anything on exhibition. The gallery is subterranean, built into a hill, but Bundanon's centrepiece is a 160m (525ft) bridge – a nod to the old railway trestle bridges so prevalent around Australia – spanning a gully beside the gallery. The bridge houses a cafe, a creative learning centre and 32 rooms of accommodation suspended high above the gully.

Boyd's studio and homestead, which are a 20-minute drive from the gallery, are open to visitors on weekends, with entry included in the gallery ticket price.

bundanon.com.au

WARM HOSPITALITY IN THE TORRES STRAIT

TORRES STRAIT ISLANDS

The islands of the stunning Torres Strait archipelago consist of over 250 coastal and volcanic islands, situated between the tip of Queensland's Cape York Peninsula and the waters of Papua New Guinea. This picturesque region is known for its crystal-clear, aqua-green seas and is home to 17 inhabited villages, each boasting its own unique language and culture. The Torres Strait is not only a cultural treasure but also serves as the gateway to the magnificent Great Barrier Reef, making it a prime destination for adventure and exploration.

If you're planning a trip to the Torres Strait, your journey can begin with an hour-long flight from Cairns to Horn Island, an entry point into this captivating area. From Horn Island, a short 10-minute ferry ride will take you to Thursday Island, the capital and most populated island in the Torres Strait. Here, you can immerse yourself in local culture by visiting an impressive gallery featuring artwork from across the islands, much of which is available for purchase. Additionally, don't miss Mona's Bizarre, where you can find unique souvenirs to commemorate your trip.

If you're seeking an authentic cultural experience, consider booking a program with Island Stars, to enjoy traditional dancing, savour an island feast, and embark on tours from Thursday Island to the outer islands. Each island offers its own unique charm and beauty, showcasing untouched landscapes that include volcanic peaks, turquoise waters brimming with marine life, and pristine beaches surrounded by vibrant reefs. While diving in these clear waters, be sure to seek out the famous painted crayfish – a true delicacy of the Torres Strait. You might even get the chance to dig up some yams from local gardens, giving you a taste of the region's rich agricultural heritage.

The local communities are known for their warmth and hospitality, welcoming visitors into their homes to share cultural traditions, stories and culinary delights. This experience provides a deeper understanding of the vibrant life and rich history that defines the Torres Strait Islands.

If you're searching for a getaway that offers a slower pace, friendly locals and breathtaking natural beauty, a trip to the Torres Strait Islands is perfect for you.

By Nornie Bero

HELP YOURSELF

Chef Nornie Bero founded Mabu Mabu (a Torres Strait saying that means 'help yourself') in 2018, aimed at hero-ing native ingredients and flavours in the kitchen. You can grab a plate of kami (emu) steak or bush spice fried artichokes at Big Esso by Mabu Mabu at Federation Square in Melbourne/Naarm, or explore the range of products online.

 mabumabu.com.au

Top **Welcome to Thursday Island**
Bottom **The stunning blue waters of the Torres Strait**

THINGS TO KNOW

* Bring sunscreen!
* Locals are often happy to take you out on their dinghies.
* Everything operates on island time.
* If you love fishing, the locals can take you to their favourite spots.
* You'll need to ask for permission from each council to enter the outer islands.
* Each island offers a unique experience, so try to see as many as you can.
* Taxi boats are available to take you to islands near Thursday Island.
* Surrounding islands feature art centres where you can purchase local works.

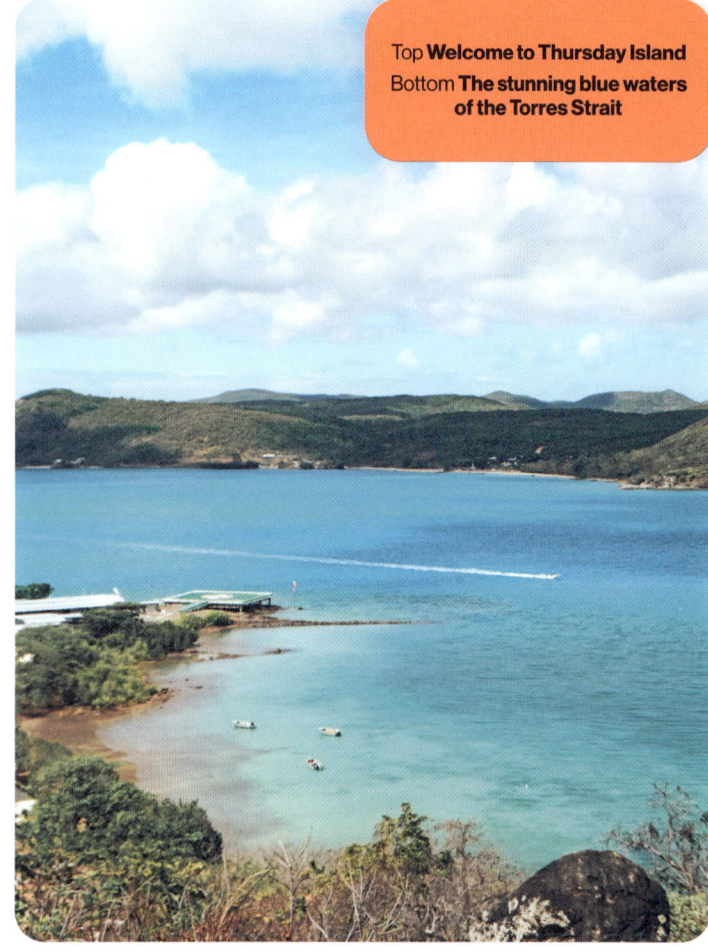

THE ART OF WINE

VARIOUS LOCATIONS

Make art your next wine pairing with a visit to a vineyard that doubles as an art gallery.

D'Arenberg

Arguably the most recognisable sight at an Australian winery is the D'Arenberg Cube, rising five storeys above the McLaren Vale vines. The building is an artwork in itself – a $16-million glass-and-steel representation of a Rubik's cube – and it houses D'Arenberg's tasting room, an Asian fusion restaurant and the winery's collection of 25 artworks and sculptures from the Surrealist Spanish artist Salvador Dali. The Modern Masters Marquee has also exhibited works from the likes of Picasso and Chagall. All that and more than 70 different wines from 30 varietals.

darenberg.com.au

Pt Leo Estate

Sprawling across 133 hectares (328 acres), this Mornington Peninsula vineyard's striking sculpture park contains around 60 works from some of the world's most memorable sculptors. Linked by a pair of walking trails (1.9km/1.2 miles and 3km/1.9 miles) are the cartoon-like figures of *KAWS*, Inge King's *Grand Arch*, one of Barry Flanagan's bronze hares and, added to the collection in 2023, one of the distinctive pumpkins from Yayoi Kusama, once dubbed 'the world's favourite artist'.

ptleoestate.com.au

TarraWarra Estate

With its cellar door dug into the earth, this leading Yarra Valley vineyard would be enticing enough, but throw in the on-site TarraWarra Museum of Art and it's downright compelling. Evolving from the private collection of the late Eva and Marc Besen, the gallery is best known for its collection of Australian paintings from the last century, featuring artists such as Arthur Boyd, Sidney Nolan, Brett Whiteley, Rosslynd Piggott, Charles Blackman, Richard Bell, Jeffrey Smart and John Olsen.

tarrawarra.com.au

Leeuwin Estate

This former cattle farm was one of Margaret River's founding vineyards in the 1970s and has been producing its Art Series wines from the outset. The first winery to use art on its labels, the series included specially commissioned works from Australian artists such as John Olsen, Sidney Nolan, Robert Juniper and a number of First Nations artists from the Kimberley region. The labels in turn led to an art gallery brimming with equally renowned artists. It now holds more than 140 works, with new acquisitions each year. The Leeuwin Concerts, held on the vineyard grounds every year since 1985, attract an equally impressive line-up – past performers have included Sting, Shirley Bassey, Ray Charles and Dame Kiri Te Kanawa.

leeuwinestate.com.au

Montalto

Since 2003, this Mornington Peninsula winery has run the acquisitive Montalto Sculpture Prize, one of Australia's richest sculpture prizes – currently awarding $50,000 to the winner. Two decades on, every winner of the prize dots the vineyard grounds, all linked on a 1km (0.6-mile) sculpture trail through the vines and along wetland boardwalks.

montalto.com.au

Mitchelton Gallery of Aboriginal Art | Taungurung Country

This Nagambie winery's Mitchelton Gallery of Aboriginal Art contains works from artists from more than 15 different First Nations art centres, including the local Taungurung People. It's a member of the Aboriginal Art Association of Australia. It's also all things to all drinkers (and even non-drinkers), featuring a distinctive viewing tower, hotel, pool, day spa, restaurant and cabin accommodation.

mitchelton.com.au

Top **D'Arenberg Cube**
Bottom **Mitchelton Wines**

THE WORLD'S GREATEST CONCENTRATION OF ROCK ART

◉ MURUJUGA NATIONAL PARK, WA
MARDUDHUNERA, NGARLUMA, WONG-GOO-TI-OO, YABURARA & YINDJIBARNDI COUNTRY

Ask Clinton Walker whether the petroglyphs on Murujuga, aka the Burrup Peninsula, and Dampier Archipelago number in their thousands and he chuckles. 'In their millions,' he says. 'One of the rock-art locations I take people to has over 10,000, and there's more than 2500 sites across Murujuga.'

Hanging off the coast near Karratha, Murujuga suitably means 'hip bone sticking out' in the Ngarluma-Yaburara language and has the world's highest concentration of rock art, some of it estimated to be up to 47,000 years old. Protected as Murujuga National Park, it's WA's first park to be jointly managed by the government and Traditional Custodians (the Murujuga Aboriginal Corporation, representing the area's five Traditional Owner groups). Clinton, a Ngarluma-Yindjibarndi man, grew up on Country here, absorbing information from one of the most knowledgeable locals: his late uncle.

'He was a big influence on me as someone who used to teach us culture and used to take people out on Country to teach them about all the things that I do now,' Clinton says. 'He even took the current King of England when he was still a prince back in the '90s.'

In the early 2010s, Clinton worked delivering cultural training courses about First Nations engagement in the workforce, but he came to feel that it wasn't giving people enough sense of life on Country. So in 2013, he started Ngurrangga Tours.

'The name of the business means basically "On Country Tours",' he says. 'Murujuga is such a significant sight. For all the Aboriginal groups right across the continent, almost all of the major songlines actually begin in Murujuga, and that's part of the reason why there's so much rock art – it's full of stories.'

Ngurrangga Tours operates guided walks along the Yaburara Trail near Karratha and into Nganjarli Gorge (as well as longer 4WD tag-along tours), adding layers of First Nations stories to the gorge's petroglyphs, middens and grinding stones while also absorbing Murujuga's striking natural beauty. Around 30 per cent of all Pilbara plant and animal species are found in the national park, even though it covers an area of just 5134 hectares (12,686 acres), while the landscape has a very distinctive quality.

'The rock art is done on basalt, and the basalt forms massive stone piles that are like hills,' Clinton says. 'A lot of the people

Murujuga features more than 2500 sites of petroglyphs

who come here think it's put there by mining companies, but it's a natural formation.'

Murujuga National Park is day-use only – there's no camping or accommodation – but Karratha is little more than 30km (19 miles) from the park entrance. If visiting independently, the best time to head into Nganjarli (reached on a 700m/0.4-mile walking trail) is in the late afternoon, when shadowing from the low sun brings the engravings into the clearest view.

🔗 exploreparks.dbca.wa.gov.au/park/murujuga-national-park

🔗 ngurrangga.com.au

SONGLINES

Songlines have been used by First Nations communities since time immemorial. They are a complex set of interconnected stories informed by a deep understanding of Country that map safe passage by describing the landscape. Passed down by the generations, many are intertwined with the Dreaming, illustrating how Creator Spirits shaped the origins of landforms and features.

By Jamil Tye

Top *Mad Max* **is an Aussie classic**
Bottom **Just one of many vehicles on display at The Mad Max 2 Museum**

MAD ABOUT MAX

SILVERTON, NSW
WILYAKALI COUNTRY

When Adrian Bennett was dragged to a cinema in northern England by two friends in 1982 to watch *Mad Max 2*, he thought he was going to see a movie about motorbikes.

'I wasn't really interested; I hadn't even heard of Mad Max,' he says. 'Anyway, I ended up going to see it with them and I was blown away. I was just so taken by what I'd seen on screen.'

To say it was a screening that changed his life is no hyperbole. His first visit to Australia from the UK was to visit *Mad Max* movie sites, and in 2009 he moved to the tiny outback town of Silverton, 25km (15.5 miles) west of Broken Hill on the Traditional lands of the Wilyakali People, where so much of *Mad Max 2* (and the 2024 prequel, *Furiosa*, the most expensive film ever made in Australia) was filmed. Here, one year later, he opened the Mad Max 2 Museum, paying homage to one of Australia's first great international successes on the screen.

'I had nothing (when we started),' Adrian says. 'I'm not a collector. My interest lies in the movie. Since we've been open, we've constantly added as we've come across things – some things from crew members, some things from locals and some things I've found and excavated from location sites, with permission of course.'

The end result is what Adrian calls a 'rust and dust museum', a 1980s period piece in the desert with a compound of largely original *Mad Max* vehicles – the Gyro, buggies, the stunt double's Interceptor and the bus, among others – under camo netting. In the room in front, the collection includes some of Adrian's most treasured movie pieces, including the silver boomerang, the music box and the silver fork Mel Gibson used to eat dog food from a can.

A ROCKSTAR GALLERY

◉ HOBART/NIPALUNA, TASMANIA
PALAWA COUNTRY

On the restaurant floor of Faro, Mona's glass-walled restaurant, one of the art gallery's most mind-bending artworks is hidden in plain sight. *Unseen Seen* resembles nothing more than a giant egg rolled into the space between tables, but this is an artwork you step inside – lying back on a bed to witness a strobing, psychedelic creation from American artist James Turrell that, experienced between lunch courses, is less a palate cleanser and more a sensory cleanser.

A five-course lunch at Faro, jutting out over the River Derwent, is one element of an indulgent Mona Like a Rockstar day at Hobart/nipaluna's subversive, subterranean gallery. For me, it began two hours before, on the central docks of Hobart/nipaluna, stepping onto the Mona ferry and into its Posh Pit, with its VIP black leather chairs, open bar and food. It's a 20-minute cruise upstream – just time for a mid-morning wine and a tapas-style snack before ascending the 99 cliff-lined steps to the gallery entrance (there is a stair-free tunnel through the cliffs for less-mobile guests).

Atop the steps, 'rockstars' are met by a tuxedoed staff member (with rockstar-style lanyards on heavy metal chains) and escorted into the gallery. From ground level, stairs (or an elevator) spiral down into the cliffs and the gallery within. Opened in 2011, Mona houses the private art collection of David Walsh, the local lad who made his fortune gambling and built his hometown a world-class gallery from the winnings. When Mona opened, Walsh described it as a 'subversive adult Disneyland', housing art often connected to sex and death. The so-called 'Mona effect' transformed Hobart/nipaluna, sparking the city's now-celebrated dining scene and wealth of quality accommodation.

After a welcome cocktail on the chaise lounges of the Void bar, set beneath the gallery's smooth sandstone walls (i.e. the inside of the cliffs), rockstars have the day to freely roam the labyrinthine gallery. Notable artworks include Wim Delvoye's Cloaca Professional (a machine that replicates the human digestive system) and Sidney Nolan's gargantuan Snake, composed of

1620 paintings that together form the figure of a rainbow serpent – Mona was designed especially to fit this enormous artwork, which had previously never been able to fit inside an Australian gallery.

The lunchtime date with Turrell art is a lingering one. The 15-minute *Unseen Seen* is a separate, but worthwhile, addition to the rockstar experience, and is one of five mesmerising Turrell artworks-in-light at Mona. Among the others are the *Beside Myself* corridor (which you walk through to access Faro) and *Event Horizon*, which is included in the package. In this work, you step through a hole in a wall into a room disorientatingly lit to feel like the inside of a cloud or a whiteout.

Lunch courses are paired with local wines, and the meal can stretch across two or three hours before more time wandering through the gallery and back onto the day's last return ferry at 5pm.

mona.net.au

Top and bottom **Installations at Mona Museum of Old and New Art**

THE GREAT BARRIER REEF'S UNDERWATER ART GALLERY

⦿ TOWNSVILLE, QUEENSLAND
WULGURUKABA OF GURAMBILBARRA & YUNBENUN, BINDAL, GUGU BADHUN & NYWAIGI COUNTRY

When sculptor Jason deCaires Taylor visits one of his greatest creations, he often feels bested by nature. Part of the Museum of Underwater Art (MOUA), off the coast of Townsville, the *Coral Greenhouse* is a 12m (40ft), 100-tonne (2204lb) A-frame sculpture sat on the ocean floor. It's listed by Guinness World Records as the planet's largest underwater art structure, but when Jason dives at the John Brewer Reef site, he sees the coral usurping his own artistic endeavour.

'The whole idea with *Coral Greenhouse* was that it was a skeletal design and it relies on nature to paint it and give it its structure and fully form it,' says the British artist who has created other underwater artworks in places such as Mexico, the Maldives and Canary Island. 'When I went back last year, the *Greenhouse* had these amazing, huge pink chandeliers of soft coral hanging down. And they're so spectacular.

'They've got these tiny little pink and purple flecks, they've got veins that run through them and some of them are almost a metre long. And they sway slightly in the current. That's something that you could never make with the human hand.'

Great art galleries typically guard themselves against water damage, but MOUA is all about water. *Coral Greenhouse* was installed at John Brewer Reef, 70km (43 miles) offshore from Townsville, in 2019, followed four years later by the *Ocean Sentinels*, a series of eight sculptures blending human and marine forms, just a short swim away.

The colossal *Coral Greenhouse*, which is also inhabited by a series of human sculptures, was the largest project of Jason's artistic life. 'It was pretty daunting, but the infrastructure is so good in Australia and some of the companies working in the Great Barrier Reef are so professional that it was something I could attempt,' he says. 'It was a really complicated install.'

Sitting 16m (52ft) below the ocean surface, *Coral Greenhouse* is most suitable for divers, but the *Sentinels* are in 5m (16ft) of water, bringing them also into view for snorkellers. A third sculpture, the 4m (13ft) *Ocean Siren*, stands above the sea immediately beside Townsville's Strand Promenade.

'*Ocean Siren* gives real-time data of what's happening to the reef,' Jason says. 'If the reef is suffering prolonged, warm temperatures, then the sculpture turns red. The idea is that it's a sort of warning siren.'

Adrenalin Snorkel and Dive (adrenalindive.com.au) and Yongala Dive (yongaladive.com.au) run diving and snorkelling day trips to *Coral Greenhouse* and the *Ocean Sentinels* from Townsville. At times, travelling incognito as a tourist, Jason has been aboard these boats, stepping back to observe the installations and divers' reactions to them.

'People have a range of different emotions,' he says. 'Some think it's a sort of archaeological experience. Some people find it strange and odd, bumping into people underwater. Some people love the colours and the interaction with the marine life.

'I speak often to the dive guides who take people to the sites, and they say that every day, something is a little bit different. It's constantly evolving.'

moua.com.au

The Great Barrier Reef's underwater art gallery

Look closely to spot Marree Man

THE MYSTERIOUS GIANT OF THE DESERT

◉ MARREE, SA
ARABANA & DIERI COUNTRY

In 1998, a mysterious figure appeared on a desert mountaintop outside the South Australian town of Marree on Arabana and Dieri Country. On one day, aerial photos showed an empty natural plateau, but a month later a pilot spied the outline of a man holding a stick or boomerang carved into the earth. Dubbed Marree Man, the figure, outlined by trenches up to 30cm (12in) deep, was 3.5km (2.2 miles) in length and covered an area of around 2.5 sq km (1 sq mile), making it one of the world's largest works of art. The strangest thing of all? Nobody claimed credit for its creation, and even today its origins are unknown.

'A hand hasn't been put up yet as to who did it,' says Phil van Wegen, owner of the local Marree Hotel. 'There's all sorts of theories and rumours about the military being involved – which I think they were – with GPS positioning. If you talk to different locals, they've all got a different theory on who did it. I think I know people that know who did it, but nobody says.'

The only way to view Marree Man, which was given a facelift in 2016 (a task that took five days), is from the air. Operating out of the Marree Hotel, Arid Air scenic flights take in Marree Man as well as vast Kati Thanda–Lake Eyre, the salt lake that is Australia's lowest point (15m/49ft below sea level) and its largest lake.

aridair.com.au

SYDNEY HARBOUR THROUGH FIRST NATIONS' EYES

◎ SYDNEY/WARRANE, NSW
GADIGAL COUNTRY

Circular Quay is perpetually busy with cruise ships, ferries and foot traffic – scenes symbolic of the busy, future-looking city that is Sydney/Warrane. But in the early afternoon, slipping quietly through the midst of it all, is a boat named *Mari Nawi*, taking a journey back in time.

Meaning 'Big Canoe' in the Gadigal language, Tribal Warrior's *Mari Nawi* sails around Sydney Harbour to Goat Island/Me-mel, with guides providing Gadigal, Wangal, Gammeraigal and Wallunedegal stories of this place now known as Sydney. They tell of the human and cultural layering of Sydney/Warrane – the traditional uses of places such as Fort Denison/Muddawahnyuh and the harbour's fishing grounds before they were seized by European settlers.

Sailing out past the Sydney Opera House, built atop a First Nations ceremonial site (and where a seal named Charlie is often sighted), the *Mari Nawi* heads east into Farm Cove/Wuganmagulya, where the narration recalls the arrival of the First Fleet – a scene of First Nations people fishing in canoes as the mysterious larger 'canoes' of the English sailed into the harbour – and swings past the Prime Minister's residence in Kirribilli.

Docking on Goat Island/Me-mel brings a celebratory feeling, with the small island, which peers into Darling Harbour, returned to First Nations ownership in 2023. A guided walk on the island commences with a dance from crew members and rounds the shores to the home of Eora couple Bennelong and Barangaroo during the early years of European contact.

 tribalwarrior.org/cultural-cruise

FIVE WAYS TO VIEW THE SYDNEY OPERA HOUSE

Sydney/Warrane, NSW | Gadigal Country

* **Catch a Performance** With seven performance spaces, Australia's most famous building has around 1800 shows every year, attended by more than 1.5 million people. Show listings and ticket sales are available through the Opera House website. ◉ **sydneyoperahouse.com**

* **Take an Architectural Tour** One of the Opera House's greatest performances is its own design by Danish architect Jørn Utzon. Completed in 1973, its 'sails' contain around one million white tiles and it surprisingly reaches 9m (30ft) higher than the Sydney Harbour Bridge roadway, with treasures such as the world's largest mechanical organ – all 10,154 pipes of it – inside. Absorb its structural beauty on daily one-hour tours, or get even more nuts and bolts on dedicated architectural tours on Saturday mornings (8.15am and 10am). There's also a daily Mobility Access Tour.

* **House Dining** With five eating and drinking spaces in addition to its theatre bars, the Opera House is a dining destination in its own right. Headlining the offerings is exquisite Bennelong, one of Australia's top restaurants, under the watch of celebrated chef Peter Gilmore. Equally enticing is Midden by Mark Olive, which focuses on native Australian ingredients and cooking from the namesake Bundjalung chef

  If you're dining outside at the likes of the Opera Bar, keep an eye out for the Opera House's cute seagull patrol dogs, tasked with keeping seagulls from stealing your food.

* **Diva for a Day** Opera Australia (OA) calls the Opera House home, and runs this tour with a difference. OA's makeup artist does your hair and makeup, then it's into a limo to the Opera House for a photo shoot on the steps, dinner at one of the restaurants and seats at OA's evening performance. Diva decadence.

* **Viewpoints** Seek out new angles on the Opera House at the following locations: the Sydney Harbour Bridge, Mrs Macquarie's Chair, Hickson Road Reserve, Shangri-La Sydney's Blu Bar on 36 (*see* p. 134), the Kirribilli foreshore, Manly ferry and the glass walls of the Park Hyatt Hotel for Opera House reflections.

Sydney's famed Harbour Bridge and Opera House

Top **Mutonia Sculpture Park**
Bottom **Sandstone sculptures of Living Desert**

DESERT SCULPTURES

◉ **VARIOUS LOCATIONS**

Travel through almost any desert on Earth and you'll find landscapes sculpted by wind and erosion, but venture into the deserts of Australia and you'll also find a curious assortment of sculptures created by human artists. Here are three outback sculpture parks to add to your travel plans.

Lake Ballard, WA

This remote salt pan, 130km (80 miles) north of Kalgoorlie, is dotted with 51 stainless-steel-alloy human figures cast by British sculptor Sir Antony Gormley (most famous for the *Angel of the North* sculpture at Gateshead in north-east England). Spread across 10 sq km (4 sq miles), each figure of this *Inside Australia* installation was modelled on a resident of Menzies, the one-pub town on Ballard's shores.

Living Desert, NSW

The Living Desert is foremost a nature reserve on the outskirts of Broken Hill, but in 1993 it was also the site of a sculpture symposium that left a legacy of 12 sandstone sculptures – carved from blocks weighing as much as 50 tonnes – that have become a de-facto symbol of the outback town. Wander the 1km (0.6-mile) walking trail through the artworks atop Sundown Hill or drive between them.

Mutonia Sculpture Park, SA

Little changes in the landscape along the Oodnadatta Track north of Marree, at least until you spy a pair of Beechcraft Baron airplanes rising out of the flatlands, their noses pointing at the sky. Known as Plane Henge, they form a gateway into Mutonia, where former mechanic Robin Cooke has puzzled together a host of sculptures from scrap metal, such as a windmill flower (Mutonia's very first sculpture, from 1997) and a person created from parts of a vehicle engine.

AGAINST THE GRAIN

◉ VARIOUS LOCATIONS

One of the newest art phenomena in Australia is silo art – enormous murals wrapped around the grain silos that dominate so many country towns, turning them into vivid outdoor art galleries. The first silo mural appeared only in 2015 in Northam, WA, but there are now more than 60 of them sprinkled across the country.

These curved concrete canvases have transformed the utilitarian silos into epic story boards – portraits and landscapes that depict local scenes and people: First Nations figures, boys leaping from a jetty, a water diviner, wildlife. Many were painted by internationally renowned street artists.

There are silo murals across every mainland state, and a pair of Silo Art Trails that connect two clusters of them on opposite sides of the country. The PUBLIC Silo Art Trail (publicsilotrail.com) is a 1070km (665-mile) journey past seven rural murals in WA's southern wheatbelt, from the prototype in Northam, to the Southern Hemisphere's largest grain storage bins in Merredin (an artwork that required 200L of paint), to a cute ruby seadragon swimming across the silos in coastal Albany.

In Victoria, the state with the great number of murals (29 at the time of writing), the Silo Art Trail links more than a dozen towns through the western Wimmera Mallee region on a 700km (435-mile) road trip in art that's invigorated small communities – the likes of Brim (home to Victoria's first silo mural), Sheep Hills and Arkona – previously undiscovered by tourism.

australiansiloarttrail.com

YARRA YARNS

📍 MELBOURNE/NAARM, VICTORIA
WURUNDJERI & BOONWURRUNG COUNTRY

Koorie Heritage Trust at Federation Square in Melbourne/Naarm

Opposite **Impressive silo art in Australia's rural towns**

Commanding space on Melbourne/Naarm's puzzle-like Federation Square, the Koorie Heritage Trust is primarily a First Nations gallery with two floors of art, but it also runs short walking tours along the bank of the Birrarung Marr (river of mists in Woiwurrung language), aka the Yarra River, immediately below the square.

The river is the setting for an oral re-creation of Melbourne/Naarm before European contact, with the tour bringing to life the scene of hills that were flattened to reclaim the wetlands on which Melbourne/Naarm now stands – an area that was traditionally under water for two to eight months of the year.

The Birrarung Wilam (River Camp) Walk heads a few hundred metres upstream to a pair of public art installations: a series of larger-than-life spears and shields, and a mosaic depicting local First Nations art styles.

The walk is more than a look back at pre-colonial times. It recounts details such as the mistaken European interpretation that gave the river its Yarra name and the waterfall that once poured over a 1m (3.2-ft) basalt ledge at the site of the present Queen Street Bridge (it was dynamited by settlers in 1883 to allow ships to sail further up the river), creating a beautifully clear river upstream.

The hour-long tour returns to the Koorie Heritage Trust building for an overview of Koorie weapons and tools – a hands-on display of shields, woomeras and the famous returning boomerang, an instrument favoured among Victoria's First Nations countries.

🌐 koorieheritagetrust.com.au

NEW LIGHT ON ULURU

📍 **ULURU-KATA TJUTA NATIONAL PARK, NT**
ANANGU COUNTRY

In the evening sky above Uluru, an ancient story is unfolding in light. Hundreds of drones hover in the sky, their lights forming the figure of a devil dog from an Anangu ancestral story, while projections and lasers illuminate the desert sand, mulga trees and desert oaks on the ground.

For nine minutes, the world's largest permanent drone show will portray the Anangu's chapter of the Mala (rufous hare-wallaby) ancestral story between Uluru and Kaltukatjara (Docker River), 240km (150 miles) to the west. Known as Wintjiri Wiru (or 'beautiful view out to the horizon' in the Pitjantjatjara language), the show is a modern telling of an ancient creation story and the brainchild of Uluru's Traditional Custodians. Working with Voyages Indigenous Tourism Australia (the operator of the hotels and services at Uluru's tourism centre, Yulara) and Canadian-born light artist Bruce Ramus, a working group of senior Anangu spent three years creating the Wintjiri Wiru show, which lights the sky above Uluru – the great red rock that rises 348m (1142ft) above the desert plains – twice a night (weather conditions permitting) from April to October.

'When we saw the result of all that work, we were quite overcome,' says Anangu woman Rene Kulitja, a member of the Wintjiri Wiru working group. 'We felt immensely proud and happy. How we saw it bring things to life for us was amazing and that it came from our *tjukurpa* – from our story – and from our understanding of the world.'

'What we've experienced (in the past) is often people rushing in with ideas and developing them', adds working group member Sammy Wilson. 'And suddenly there's this happening thing that we haven't felt part of. So it was really important and great that we were acknowledged as having the cultural understanding of this place, having an understanding of the country and its ancestors, and that we were involved in working together to bring this to life.'

Visitors to Wintjiri Wiru have three options: dinner and twilight show, with a menu featuring native ingredients such as smoked emu, pepper leaf kangaroo, native celery and quandong; the twilight show alone; or a later after-dark show (the latter pair with wine, cheeses and dessert). For the Anangu, it's hoped that the show is the first big step in new experiences of First Nations tourism around Uluru.

'One thing that would be really great to come out of it is for people to want to see more of our country beyond just here, out to other parts of the country,' Rene says.

Already, in addition to tours and walks around the rock, visitors can join a SEIT tour (seittours.com/tour-cultural) to spend a day travelling with a member of the Uluru family – descendants of patriarch Paddy Uluru – to Patji, the family's desert homeland south of the rock.

In addition to this, there are dot-painting workshops led by Anangu artists at Maruku Arts (maruku.com.au), displays and galleries in the Uluru-Kata Tjuta Cultural Centre and Anangu-led walking tours to learn about the Kuniya creation story and view cave art at the base of the rock.

- **ayersrockresort.com.au/wintjiri-wiru**
- **parksaustralia.gov.au/uluru**

Watch the sunset and Wintjiri Wiru show at Uluru

THE MOST AUSTRALIAN PIECE OF AUSTRALIA?

◉ WINTON, QUEENSLAND
KOA COUNTRY

Search the country for Australian cultural icons and you'll inevitably come to a cluster of sites around the outback Queensland town of Winton. Drive 150km (93 miles) north of town on the well-named Matilda Way and you come to a turning to Combo Waterhole. The name itself might mean little, but this mud-brown waterhole is said to be the billabong eulogised in Australia's unofficial national anthem, 'Waltzing Matilda'. 'Banjo' Paterson, the poem's author, visited the waterhole in 1895 and soon after penned his tale of a jolly, sheep-rustling swagman.

Combo Waterhole is well signed from the highway and reached on a 2.6km (1.6-mile) return walking trail that ends at the billabong, surrounded by the coolabah trees of the poem, their branches often strung with those most Australian of birds – galahs.

From the waterhole, it's just a 20km (12.4-mile) drive into Kyuna and the Blue Heeler Hotel, where 'Waltzing Matilda' was first performed by Paterson. It's also claimed that the swagman who inspired Paterson's poem took his last drink here before heading to his death at Combo Waterhole.

You can bring together all the pieces of the poem and Banjo Paterson's life at Winton's Waltzing Matilda Centre, claimed to be the world's first museum dedicated to a song. Or you can continue another 75km (47 miles) north from Kyuna to McKinlay and the Walkabout Creek Hotel, a pub that starred in a more modern Australian classic – *Crocodile Dundee*. The century-old pub, with its saloon-like façade, was Mick Dundee's boozer and the bar in which Paul Hogan's character first meets Sue Charlton (Linda Kozlowski), a fact still celebrated in the memorabilia and photos throughout the bar.

◉ matildacentre.com.au

Top left **Banjo Paterson sculpture at the Waltzing Matilda Centre**
Top right **Blue Heeler Hotel**
Bottom **Combo Waterhole is featured in the classic song**

Hanging Rock is an iconic Australian setting

PICNIC AT HANGING ROCK

⦿ HANGING ROCK, VICTORIA
WURUNDJERI, DJA DJA WURRUNG & TAUNGURUNG COUNTRY

Take the most Australian picnic of all, just an hour drive north of Melbourne/Naarm at storied Hanging Rock. This small hill, bubbling out of the earth beside Mount Macedon, is an enduring part of the Australian cultural psyche, synonymous with Joan Lindsay's eponymous 1967 novel *Picnic at Hanging Rock* and Peter Weir's 1975 film adaptation, which was one of Australia's first great international successes on the big screen.

Suitably, Hanging Rock is now ringed with picnic areas. Stock up for your own picnic at Hanging Rock at local providores such as Mount Macedon Trading Post, or settle in for a picnic platter and a glass of red or white at nearby Hanging Rock Winery, looking over the vines to Hanging Rock.

The 'rock' itself is the remains of an extinct volcano that rises more than 100m (328ft) above the surrounding plains. It was used as a ceremony site for Wurundjeri, Dja Dja Wurrung and Taungurung People for at least 25,000 years, and later as a reputed hideout for bushrangers. Today, a 1.8km (1.1-mile) wheelchair-accessible (albeit steep) track ascends to its peak, climbing through and among the cockscomb of boulders that furnish the summit. It was in this maze of boulders – a world of crawl spaces and cubby holes – that three students disappeared in the *Picnic at Hanging Rock* story, never to be found. Watch the movie, climb through the rocks and join in the chorus of 'Miranda!'.

⦿ visitmacedonranges.com/tourism-listing/hanging-rock

CENTRAL ART

ALICE SPRINGS/MPARNTWE, NT
ARRERNTE COUNTRY

Alice Springs/Mparntwe is claimed to have more galleries per capita than any other Australian city, and much of this art from the heart is centred on First Nations artists and the surrounding art centres of their desert communities.

There are more than half a dozen galleries in Alice that are owned and governed by First Nations people, each with a distinctive style and presence. Iltja Ntjarra Many Hands Art Centre (29 Wilkinson St, manyhandsart.com.au) has been operating for two decades and brings the Hermannsburg School style of art to the fore. Among the most famous of Australian art styles, the watercolour landscapes of the Hermannsburg School are inspired by famed Arrernte artist Albert Namatjira, who painted much of the desert landscape around the region. Namatjira's descendants are among the 20 artists who work with the gallery, where each day (Monday to Thursday) you can find up to eight artists at work in the studio.

There's a particular beauty to the creations at Tjanpi Desert Weavers (3 Wilkinson St, tjanpi.com.au), a social enterprise of the Ngaanyatjarra Pitjantjatjara Yankunytjatjara Women's Council. 'Tjanpi' means grass in Pitjantjatjara language, and its artists – some 400 women from 26 communities – weave native desert grasses and contemporary fibres into figures such as dogs, lizards and birds, as well as baskets.

Tangentyere Artists (16 Fogarty St, tangentyere.org.au/tangentyere-artists) brings together art from Alice Springs/Mparntwe's town camps, including the renowned Yarrenyty Arltere Artists with their distinctive soft sculptures made from recycled, hand-dyed woollen blankets. Bindi Mwerre Anthurre Artists (47 Elder St, bindiart.com.au) is an art centre providing supported studio space to First Nations artists with disabilities. In the centre of town, Papunya Tula Artists (63 Todd Mall, papunyatula.com.au) stems from an art movement that began in Papunya, north-west of Alice, in 1971, with artists using a style that derives from traditional body and sand painting among Pintupi and Luritja People. The gallery's rotating exhibitions represent around 120 artists. The Waltja Tjutangku Palyapayi Aboriginal Corporation (3 Ghan Rd, waltja.org.au), with its board of entirely First Nations women, works with remote Central Australian communities on community issues and has an art shop on site.

ETHICAL ART PURCHASES

It sounds obvious, but be certain that any Indigenous artwork you buy was created by a First Nations person – ask for a certificate or statement of authenticity to avoid the risk of purchasing unauthorised copies of First Nations art.

Where possible, buy from First Nations–owned galleries (Desart publishes a list of such galleries around Central Australia at desart.com.au) and ensure that the gallery is a member of the Aboriginal Art Association of Australia and the Indigenous Art Code. The Code (indigenousartcode.org) sets rules and guidelines that dealers and galleries (First Nations–owned and otherwise) commit to follow, ensuring fair treatment of artists, many of whom have historically been carpetbagged (exploited) and seen little of the money from the sale of their art. The Art Association (aboriginalart.org.au) is an advocate for artists, galleries and dealers, and can be consulted for advice on purchasing First Nations Art. Its website lists member artists and galleries.

Overlooking Alice Springs/ Mparntwe

Top **Santi Ikto – one of Mandurah's giants**
Bottom **Each giant is around five metres (16 feet) tall**

WHERE THE GIANT THINGS ARE

◉ MANDURAH, WA
BINDJAREB NOONGAR COUNTRY

Looking like an out-take from the classic children's book *Where the Wild Things Are*, the Giants of Mandurah is an art installation of six giants from world-renowned Danish recycle artist Thomas Dambo. Five of the giants reside within a 40km (25-mile) radius of Mandurah, an hour drive south of Perth/Boorloo on the lands of the Bindjareb Noongar People, with another in the Perth/Boorloo suburb of Subiaco.

Each of the whimsical creations is constructed from recycled wood and stands up to 5m (16.4ft) tall. Collectively, they've been designed as a hide-and-seek-type game by Dambo and project producer FORM Building a State of Creativity. Visitors must download a digital 'Travellers' Companion' from the Giants of Mandurah website and then follow its clues in search of each giant – they're all reached at the end of walking trails between 500m (0.3 miles) and 3.6km (2.2 miles) in length (the giants that are most wheelchair accessible are the seaside Yaburgurt Winjan Cirkelstone and Seba's Song).

Once you've visited the five giants detailed in the Travellers' Companion, recording a unique symbol found at each one, return to the Mandurah Visitor Centre where a code reveals the location of the sixth 'secret' giant.

Local tours that take in the giants include a Bike Kiosk (thebikekiosk.rezdy.com) ebike 'hunt' for two or three of the figures, and a Mandurah Cruises' (mandurahcruises.com.au) dolphin-watching boat trip that swings past Seba's Song.

◉ giantsofmandurah.com.au

IGA WARTA: HOME OF THE NATIVE ORANGE

◉ VULKATHUNHA-GAMMON RANGES, SA
ADNYAMATHANHA COUNTRY

Beside an evening campfire, guitar at his side, Terry Coulthard explains to a group of visitors the compelling logic behind the location for his accommodation and tourism business, Iga Warta.

'In business they say "location, location, location",' the Adnyamathanha man says. 'We thought about setting up Iga Warta beside Arkaroola or Wilpena Pound, but my family totem is the iga (native orange) tree, and the mother of all the iga trees is just over there, so in the end I felt it had to be here.'

Tucked into a fold in the Vulkathunha-Gammon Ranges, on the road between Copley and Arkaroola, Iga Warta – which translates as 'Home of the Native Orange' – was established by the welcoming Terry, wife Josie and Terry's late brothers Cliff and Clarrie in 1996. The idea came after hearing stories from their father, who was working as a driver-guide on Arkaroola's Ridgetop Track, of newfound interest among visitors in First Nations culture.

Almost 30 years on, guests at Iga Warta, with its campground, cabins, bunkhouses and glamping-style safari tents with decks looking onto the mountains, are welcomed to country around the campfire by Terry, who also tells stories from Adnyamathanha Culture and almost certainly will play a few songs on the guitar – Terry was once guitarist for the Artoowarapana Band, which supported the likes of Australian country-music powerhouses Lee Kernaghan and Troy Cassar-Daley.

Iga Warta also has an on-site museum about family history and Adnyamathanha culture, and cultural tours include half-day trips to an ochre pit or engravings at Red Gorge and a walk into a narrow gorge to the Malki rock-art site with Josie's nephew, Vinnie Coulthard.

◉ igawarta.com

Learn about Adnyamathanha culture at Iga Warta

Opposite **Street art in Melbourne/Naarm**

LIFE IN THE ART LANE

◉ MELBOURNE/NAARM, VICTORIA
WURUNDJERI COUNTRY

Not all of Melbourne/Naarm's best artworks are found inside galleries, with the city's multitude of laneways serving as canvases for a wealth of street art. Peer down any lane and you'll likely find murals looking back at you, but not all laneways are art equals, with a select few worth taking the time to seek out.

A trio of the most colourful laneways are clustered just off Flinders St, including Hosier Lane, which is the lynchpin of Melbourne/Naarm murals. There's not a space in the cobbled lane that isn't beaming with colour, from walls to doors, posts, bins and the footpath. Look up to see Adnate's 23m (75ft) portrait of a First Nations boy.

Nearby, Duckboard Pl's myriad murals present a collage of themes and figures as it winds around to meet art-splashed AC/DC Lane, which is watched over by a sculpture of rock band AC/DC's original frontman Bon Scott.

Switch to the northern end of the city to find Guildford Lane, where art is planted as much as painted. Enter past a mural of a green dog to find a lane just as memorable for its wall-to-wall greenery. In 2017, residents came together to create an urban oasis – plant boxes hang from every window, and the lane itself is a mini-forest of pot plants, tall and small, and also sprinkled with murals.

Finally, take a moment (or a train or tram in this case) to head north to Collingwood where famed New York artist Keith Haring painted one of the city's first murals in 1984. The 7.4m (24ft) artwork remains on the side wall of the Collingwood Yards on Johnston St and is one of only around 30 surviving Haring murals around the world.

◉ whatson.melbourne.vic.gov.au/things-to-do/walks/street-art

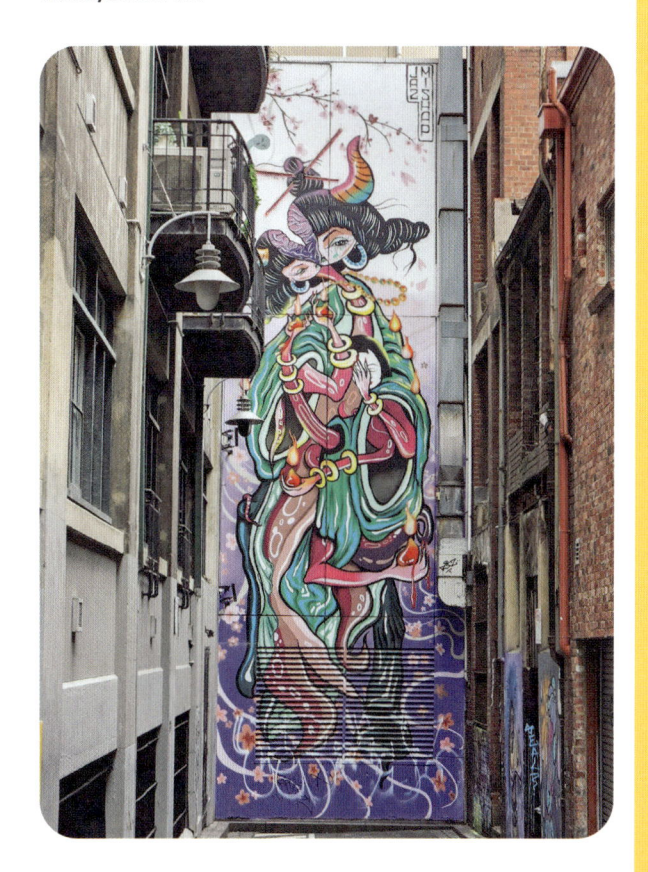

THE OUTBACK TOWN WHERE ART TRUMPS BEER

BROKEN HILL, NSW
WILYAKALI COUNTRY

Broken Hill is that rarest of outback towns where art galleries outnumber pubs (though it did, in its mining heyday, sport more than 70 hotels). Home to around 20 galleries, this city on the Traditional Lands of the Wilyakali People is a place where imagination is often as artistic as the landscape.

Broken Hill City Art Gallery

NSW's oldest regional gallery sits inside what was the city's longest-running business – Sully's Emporium – and has ever-rotating exhibitions from its collection. Expect First Nations art, modern masters such as John Olsen and plenty from the so-called 'Brushmen and Co' – the local collective of Pro Hart, Jack Absalom, High Schulz, Eric Minchin and John Pickup – and one of their mentors, local artist and art teacher Florence May Harding.

bhartgallery.com.au

Pro Hart Gallery

Immortalised in a 1980s TV carpet commercial, the late Hart's gallery fills the garage of what was his family home. Among three floors of his distinctive naïve art and a re-created studio, there's one room of works for sale – some original and some digital reproductions – and a park filled with his sculptures across the road. Hart's daughter Julie is also an accomplished artist, with a gallery on nearby Williams Street.

prohart.com.au

Absalom Gallery's

Classic outback landscapes from a celebrity outback artist. Scenes range from the nearby Mundi Mundi Plains to the distant Kimberley, all surrounding what's billed as the largest opal collection in the Southern Hemisphere. All works are for sale.

jackabsalom.com.au

The Big Picture

The world's largest acrylic painting on canvas – all 100m (328ft) by 12m (39ft) of it – wraps around a circular room inside the Silver City Mint and Art Centre. It took nine tonnes of paint to create the landscape, which you almost literally step into – it encircles a timber viewing platform and a sandy re-creation of a desert environment. The work features landmarks within a 300km (186-mile) radius of Broken Hill, including the Flinders Ranges, Silverton, White Cliffs and Mungo and Mutawintji National Parks.

silvercitymint.com.au

John Dynon Gallery

Skip town to find this gallery in a colourful tin shed behind a paint-splashed Volkswagen

Beetle in Silverton. Dynon is known as the Emu Man for his depictions of wiry, wide-eyed emus – aka Silverton bush chooks – and quirky outback scenes.

◉ store.johndynon.com.au

Outdoor galleries

Drive to a hilltop 10km (6.2 miles) out of town to find the chess-piece-like Living Desert Sculptures (see p. 251), and range further afield to Mutawintji National Park, 150km (93 miles) north, to find one of NSW's most extensive First Nations rock-art sites. Visits to the engravings and ochre stencils at Mutawintji Historic Site, inside the park, are by guided tour only.

◉ nationalparks.nsw.gov.au/visit-a-park/parks/mutawintji-historic-site

This colourful Volkswagen Beetle is found at the John Dynon Gallery

TASMANIA'S ABORIGINAL REVIVAL

TASMANIA
PALAWA COUNTRY

Allan Mansell's story is a harrowing one, but it's overlaid with the beauty of his artwork. Raised on Cape Barren Island, the palawa (Tasmanian Aboriginal) man is a member of the Stolen Generations – Aboriginal children removed from their families by the state – spending eight years in a boys' home. More than 50 years on, the emotional pain remains, finding expression in the printmaking that's seen his art acquired by major galleries and international collectors.

'I was with the original Tasmanian Aboriginal Legal Service for a while as an activist, but it got too political, so I changed tack and I've become a political activist in artwork,' Allan says. 'I do this because I need to express what Aboriginality is (to me).'

As Mansell speaks, he turns the press on his newest print, explaining the printmaking process and recounting his own story to a group of guests at Hobart/nipaluna's Henry Jones Art Hotel. For Australia's first art hotel, it's a new visitor experience called Palawa Connection (thehenryjones.com/palawa-connection-stories-with-artist-allan-mansell), combining Mansell's art with his compelling life story. It's one of a range of palawa visitor experiences that have emerged across Tasmania in recent years, defiantly setting the record straight on the survival of the Tasmanian Aboriginal people.

For decades, a myth was perpetuated by many non-Indigenous people that a Nuenonne woman named Truganini, who died in 1876, was the last Tasmanian Aboriginal – a race of people subjected to murder, disease and genocide by Europeans who collectively suffered extreme loss of life, Country, Culture and language on an immeasurable scale in the 80 years following European Invasion. But the people and the culture hadn't disappeared, and in the 2021 national census, 5.4 per cent of Tasmania's population identified as Aboriginal and/or Torres Strait Islander, a rate higher than many mainland states.

Today, visitors can sit with Mansell at the Henry Jones Art Hotel and learn about palawa history and art, which is different in style from mainland art forms. They can also experience a variety of palawa tours around the state.

The four-day wukalina Walk (wukalinawalk.com.au) is a guided hike along the Bay of Fires, seeing its brilliant white beaches, blazes of orange lichen and granite headlands through the lens of culture, story and bush tucker. The first two nights are spent in the architect-designed krakani lumi camp, with its sleeping pods designed to replicate the shape of early palawa shelters (the final night is spent in the lighthouse keeper's cottage at larapuna/Eddystone Point). Meals feature traditional palawa ingredients and recipes.

A distinct moment in Hobart/nipaluna's history is explored on takana nipaluna (blackledtours.com). This 90-minute guided walk, led by palawa and Warlpiri woman

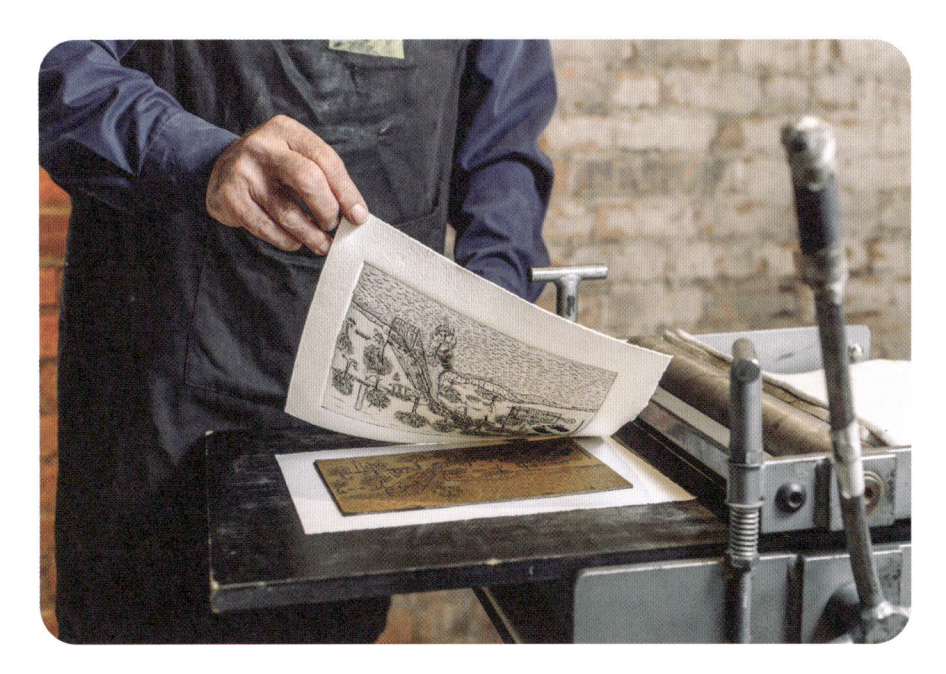

Nunami Sculthorpe-Green, follows in the steps of members of the Tasmanian Aboriginal resistance as they walked to Government House in 1832 in hope of negotiating an end to the Black War that had been raging between Europeans and the palawa since 1824.

At Risdon Cove, a culturally significant site that was also the first attempted (and failed) settlement of Hobart/nipaluna by Europeans in 1803, kipli takara is a 90-minute bush tucker tour, exploring the bush flavours with palawa woman Kitana Mansell, owner of local catering company palawa kipli (palawakipli.com). The walk concludes with tastings of distinctly local tucker such as wallaby, muttonbird and kunzea.

In the state's north, Kooparoona Niara Tours explore culturally significant sites such as Launceston's Cataract Gorge and tulampanga/Alum Cliffs, outside of Deloraine, with trawlwoolway man Greg Murray.

Top **palawa art at Henry Jones Art Hotel**
Bottom **Artist Allan Mansell**

SCULPTING A REEF

⊙ BUSSELTON, WA
WADANDI COUNTRY

The Busselton jetty pylons are covered in coral

Opposite Finalists of the Archibald Prize

It's a long walk to the end of the Busselton jetty – it is, after all, the Southern Hemisphere's longest timber-piled jetty. But once you reach its end, 1841m (6040ft) from shore – a solar-powered train also makes the journey – there's magic underfoot.

Since its construction in 1865, one of the largest artificial reefs in Australia has formed around the jetty, with 13 sculptures added to the marine landscape in 2023. Each sculpture – among them a mermaid, a diver's helmet and a southern right whale – was commissioned from a West Australian artist, and the gallery sits in 8m (26ft) of water to form a snorkelling trail over the reef and sculptures. They are living works of art, intended to be colonised by the reef, extending its size and beauty.

A dive and snorkel pass (available from the jetty website) is required to access the trail, while Swan Dive (swandive.com.au) runs guided diving and snorkelling tours beneath the jetty.

busseltonjetty.com.au

PORTRAIT OF A GALLERY

◉ SYDNEY/WARRANE, NSW & MELBOURNE/NAARM, VICTORIA

Sometimes described as 'the face that stops a nation' (in a cheeky nod to the Melbourne Cup's moniker as 'the race that stops a nation'), the Archibald Prize for the best portrait painted by an Australian resident is the country's most famous art prize.

Attracting close to 1000 entrants some years, the field is narrowed down to a selection of finalists (57 of them in 2023) that are hung in the Art Gallery of NSW from June to September.

Visited by more than one million people each year, this art gallery overlooking Sydney/Warrane's Domain comes in two distinct parts: its original 19th-century classical building, Naala Nura, which was modelled on the National Gallery of Scotland building; and the light-filled Naala Badu, opened in 2022 and home to the Yiribana Gallery, the gallery's collection of First Nations art.

Head through Naala Badu to find the Tank, a WWII-era oil bunker, four storeys underground and repurposed into gallery space in 2022. It's also worth visiting the gallery-owned studio of artist Brett Whiteley in Surry Hills (2 Raper St).

The gallery's Melbourne/Naarm counterpart is the National Gallery of Victoria (NGV), Australia's oldest (1860) and most visited art gallery, with a collection of more than 76,000 works.

Behind a pond featuring an 8m (26ft) bronze eel trap from Wurundjeri artist Aunty Kim Wandin and the gallery's signature Waterwall is the four-level NGV International, featuring the gallery's collection of international art. Australian art, including the Wurrdha Marra First Nations space, is displayed at the nearby Ian Potter Centre: NGV Australia.

◉ artgallery.nsw.gov.au

◉ ngv.vic.gov.au

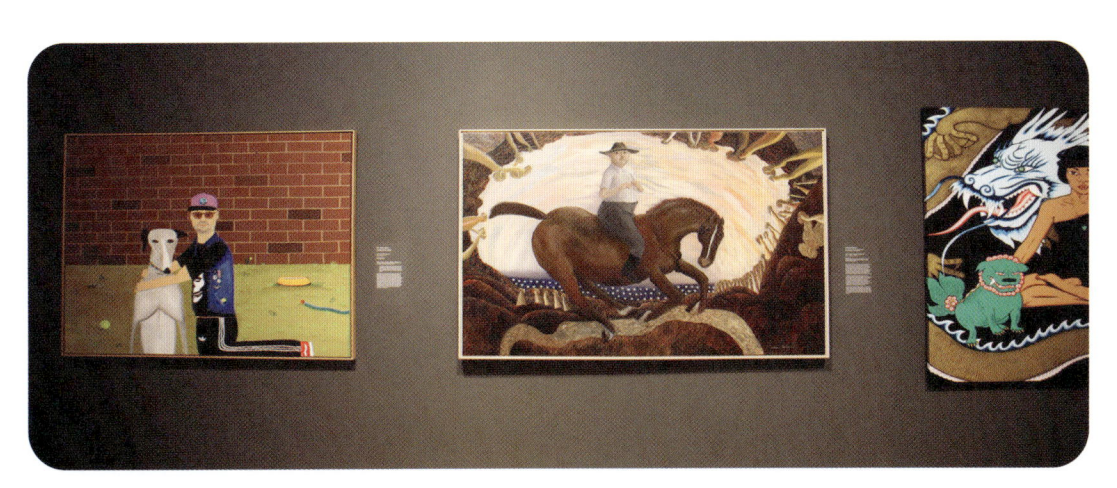

DANCE PARTNER

One great artform deserves another, and in the case of the Quinkan rock art, it comes in the shape of the biannual Laura Quinkan Dance Festival. Held in odd-numbered years, the three-day July festival has been running since the early 1980s, making it one of Australia's longest-running First Nations cultural festivals. It's a celebration of local song and dance, with troupes from Cape York communities competing for a shield awarded to the troupe judged the best dancers. Johnny Murison has been a regular attendee at the festival.

'With the songs and the music and the didgeridoo, it sends shivers up your spine,' he says. 'It's a great spectacle and a great exhibition of Aboriginal culture through song and dance.'

lauraquinkanfestival.com.au

Laura, Quinkan Country

SPIRITED ART

LAURA, QUEENSLAND
QUINKAN COUNTRY

When Johnny Murison goes to work, he feels a bit like he's stepping into a natural equivalent of the Louvre. As the Western Yalanji man tours through Quinkan Country – which is likely a word derived from 'guwin-gan' from the Aboriginal Kuku-Yalanji language – around Laura, 330km (205 miles) north of Cairns on Cape York Peninsula, he's surrounded by rock art that UNESCO has rated among the 10 most significant such sites in the world.

'There's a real wow factor – the sunrises, the sunsets, the environment and the rock art,' Johnny says. 'Then you've got the stories associated with it.'

Growing up in Townsville and the Atherton Tablelands, Johnny was a regular visitor to Laura on childhood family holidays to his Traditional Country. Almost a decade ago, he started Jarramali Rock Art Tours, wanting to share the region and its art with the world.

'The grandeur and magnificence of the escarpment country and how beautiful and rugged it is … I was pretty much like, "I have to bring people here",' he says.

There are an estimated 10,000 rock-art sites in what's become known as Quinkan Country, named for the stick-like spirit beings depicted in much of the sandstone art. What sets Quinkan Country apart, says Johnny in his trademark cowboy hat, is the condition and sheer number of the paintings.

'When people have seen the Kimberleys and Arnhem Land and they come to ours, there's nothing can match it,' he says. 'It's because of the quality of the art and the quantity and the grandeur of the place. Just being there automatically takes your breath away.'

Johnny's 4WD trips (either tagalong or in his vehicle) range from a day exploring the region and art to a two-day tour staying at his Jarramali campground on the bank of the Little Laura River, 35 minutes drive outside of Laura.

'My goal is that people leave as a better version of themselves,' he says. 'After they've spent time with us on country, that they leave with a greater, deeper understanding and appreciation of Aboriginal culture.'

The best time to visit Quinkan Country is in the cooler months from around May to October.

anggnarra.org.au

jarramalirockarttours.com.au

276	Rooftop Ramble at Adelaide Oval
277	Australia's Grandest Library Space
278	Night Lights: Australia's Lighthouse Stays
280	Australia's True 'Down Under'
282	A Bridge Too Far?
283	Outdoing the Sydney Opera House

"Another less-heralded structure beat it to the punch to become Australia's first World Heritage-listed building"

ARCHIT-
ECTURE

ROOFTOP RAMBLE AT ADELAIDE OVAL

ADELAIDE/TANDANYA, SA
KAURNA COUNTRY

Conduct a straw poll among cricket fans on the world's most beautiful stadiums, and Adelaide Oval will invariably figure highly. Set in the city's leafy ring of parklands in Kaurna Country, and backed by the spires of St Peter's Cathedral, a line of massive Moreton Bay figs and the oval's nostalgic Edwardian scoreboard, it's a scene as genteel as it is hoarse on match days.

You can catch international and domestic cricket games at the oval throughout the summer, or AFL matches most weekends of that competition's winter season (March to September), but the most immersive way to view the stadium is on a RoofClimb tour.

These guided day and evening adventures ascend to the billowing rooftops, wandering atop the 140-year-old stands, up to 50m (164ft) above the playing surface (all while safely harnessed to the stadium).

roofclimb.com.au

Top **RoofClimb offers 360 degree views of Adelaide**
Bottom **Adelaide Oval**
Opposite **The striking La Trobe Reading Room**

276

AUSTRALIA'S GRANDEST LIBRARY SPACE

◉ MELBOURNE/NAARM, VICTORIA
BOON WURRUNG/BUNURONG & WURUNDJERI COUNTRY

Nowhere does Melbourne/Naarm's standing as Australia's first UNESCO City of Literature feel more germane than in the La Trobe Reading Room at the heart of the State Library of Victoria. A hallowed monument to words and knowledge, the octagonal room was modelled jointly on the British Museum in London and Washington's Library of Congress and was the world's largest reinforced concrete structure when it was opened in 1913.

Rising six storeys to a glass dome, the reading room is best observed from the three levels of Dome Galleries that ring the walls (accessed by stairs or elevator), looking down onto the reading desks (containing up to 320 reading spaces) that radiate out from a central hub. With its walls inscribed with bookish quotes from the likes of Kafka, Dickinson and Borges, the room is every representation of a grand library you've ever conjured, in perfect architectural symmetry.

🌐 slv.vic.gov.au/visit/our-magnificent-spaces/la-trobe-reading-room

NIGHT LIGHTS: AUSTRALIA'S LIGHTHOUSE STAYS

◎ VARIOUS LOCATIONS

The Australian coastline is lined with more than 350 lighthouses. Standing atop headlands, cliffs and islands, and casting their beams over rocks and reefs, they are the night lights of the nation – literally so when you spend a night inside one of several that offer accommodation.

Troubridge Island, SA

It's just you, a few thousand seabirds and some very chatty little penguins when you stay in the lighthouse keeper's cottage at this candy-striped lighthouse off the Yorke Peninsula coast. Reached by boat from Edithburgh.

◉ troubridgeislandescapeandcharters.au

Wilsons Promontory, Victoria

Mere steps from mainland Australia's southernmost point, this granite lighthouse can only be reached on foot. Its three keeper cottages provide a night out of the tent for hikers on the popular Southern Prom Circuit.

◉ parks.vic.gov.au/places-to-see/parks/wilsons-promontory-national-park/where-to-stay/wilsons-promontory-lightstation

Cape Otway, Victoria

This 1859 lighthouse, midway along the Great Ocean Road, has a lighthouse keeper's cottage and lodge (both sleeping up to 10) and a renovated studio for two. Stays come with the addition of a morning climb of the lighthouse.

◉ lightstation.com/stay

Gabo Island, Victoria

Victoria's only island lighthouse is also the country's second-tallest (47m/154ft), with accommodation for up to eight people in the assistant keeper's cottage. Charter boats from Mallacoota run transfers.

◉ parks.vic.gov.au/places-to-see/parks/gabo-island-lighthouse-reserve

Barunguba Montague Island, NSW

Bed down on an island that's home to hundreds of seals and a plethora of seabirds, including around 12,000 little penguins. Accommodation is in two lighthouse keeper's cottages.

◉ nationalparks.nsw.gov.au/visit-a-park/parks/barunguba-montague-island-nature-reserve

Cape Byron, NSW

Standing on mainland Australia's most easterly point, this lighthouse's cottages guarantee you'll be the first person in the country to see the sunrise. And it's just the spot to keep a vigil for humpback whales, turtles and dolphins.

◉ nationalparks.nsw.gov.au/camping-and-accommodation/accommodation/assistant-lighthouse-keepers-cottages

Troubridge Island Lighthouse

AUSTRALIA'S TRUE 'DOWN UNDER'

◉ COOBER PEDY, SA
ANTAKIRINJA MATU-YANKUNYTJATJARA COUNTRY

Zoe Pollard remembers growing up, like many young children, around horses. They wandered her family's stables, roamed the plains and even won local thoroughbred races. What sets Zoe's story apart is that she lived underground in the opal-mining town of Coober Pedy, in the country of the Antakirinja Matu-Yankunytjatjara People, and so did her horses.

'Mum loved horses growing up and always wanted a hobby farm, so my parents built an underground stable for the hot days,' Zoe says.

Coober Pedy is Australia's true 'down under', a place where more than half the population lives underground in homes, known as 'dugouts', excavated into the slopes of the town's hills to escape the relentless desert heat. And like Zoe's stables, Coober Pedy is a place where things are done differently.

Until about 1995, explosives (used to blast out the opal mines) were sold in the town's supermarkets, and SA's last remaining drive-in cinema sported signs asking patrons not to bring said explosives into screenings. And while the town population is less than 1600, it's comprised of people from 47 different nationalities.

It's the kind of town where Zoe's mum ran an underground beauty studio and also painted crosses for the cemetery, while her stepdad was a miner, explosives distributor, undertaker and carpenter. When he wanted to extend their underground home (or put in those stables), he simply cut new rooms into the rock with the tunnelling machines used by miners. It's a common practice around town – one underground home contains 21 rooms – with home renovations often netting a bounty of opals (95 per cent of the world's opals come from Australia and the bulk of them from Coober Pedy) that more than cover the cost of the work.

'A motel here extended to put in some new rooms and found $1.2 million worth of opals,' says Zoe, who works as a guide at the Umoona Opal Mine and Museum. Set inside a mine that was first worked in the 1920s, just a few years after opal was discovered in the area by a young boy in 1915, the museum presents just one of the many chances to experience underground Coober Pedy. There are said to be 1.5 million holes in the vicinity of the town – the dune-like mounds that cover the plain are the mullock heaps from mines – including the narrow St Peter and Paul Catholic Church and the larger Serbian Orthodox Church with its colourful stained-glass windows set among the mullock heaps at the edge of town.

Motels such as the Comfort Inn and Desert Cave Hotel have underground rooms, and you can even pitch a tent underground at Riba's Underground Camping and Caravan Park.

Since returning to Coober Pedy during the Covid pandemic, after a few years living in Western Australia, Zoe has bought a dugout and settled back into life underground. In the crazy, quirky world that is Coober Pedy, it's good to be home.

'I really appreciate the town for its unique lifestyle. There really is nothing else like it in the world.'

cooberpedy.com

Top **Zoe Pollard polishing opals**
Bottom **The underground town of Coober Pedy**

A BRIDGE TOO FAR?

📍 **PERTH/BOORLOO, WA**
WHADJUK NOONGAR COUNTRY

Zipling above the Swan River

Perth/Boorloo's Matagarup Bridge is a symbol as much as a structure. Spanning the Swan River from East Perth to Burswood, the footbridge, built in 2020, has braided arches that represent the intertwined necks of black and white swans. The curving lines are further inspired by the flowing shape of Wagyl, the rainbow serpent that carved the Swan River in the creation story of the Whadjuk Noongar People. The colours – black and white – also symbolise the meeting of cultures: First Nations and European.

The bridge is one of three in Australia (along with the Sydney Harbour Bridge and Brisbane's Story Bridge) that can be climbed on tours, though the Matagarup Zip+Climb has a significant point of difference – once you've climbed to its top, 72m (246ft) above the river, you zipline off, skimming 400m (1312ft) over the river at speeds up to 75km/h (47mph).

🔸 zipclimb.com.au

OUTDOING THE SYDNEY OPERA HOUSE

◉ MELBOURNE/NAARM, VICTORIA
BOON WURRUNG/BUNURONG & WURUNDJERI COUNTRY

Three years before the Sydney Opera House was inscribed on UNESCO's World Heritage list, another less-heralded structure beat it to the punch to become Australia's first World Heritage-listed building.

Rising out of Carlton Gardens, at the northern edge of Melbourne/Naarm's city centre, the Royal Exhibition Building was constructed as a 'Palace of Industry' for an international industrial exhibition in 1880. Built on the highest point overlooking a bend in the Yarra River (now blocked from view by the city), it was, at the time of construction, the largest and tallest building in Australia.

With its dome modelled on Florence's Duomo and its cathedral-like cruciform shape, the 61m (200ft) building has had a varied life. Australia's first parliament sat in its Great Hall in 1901, and after WWI it was used as a temporary hospital as Spanish flu raged across the globe. It held Melbourne/Naarm's first aquarium and first motor show, and it staged the basketball, wrestling and weightlifting events in the 1956 Olympic Games. Today it remains an exhibition venue and an exam hall for high school and university students.

In its early years, the building's rooftop promenade was a favourite haunt for locals, providing the finest view in town. The promenade eventually closed, remaining off-limits for nearly a century, but in 2022 it reopened to guided tours. These begin in the foyer of the neighbouring Melbourne Museum, descend into a mini-museum in the Exhibition Building's basement (stepping over a glass-covered shaft that drove Australia's first elevator and was rediscovered only when stairs were put in for this tour) and then climb to the promenade to eyeball the city towers of Melbourne/Naarm.

Note that tours don't operate during school and university exam periods.

🌐 museumsvictoria.com.au/melbournemuseum/whats-on/royal-exhibition-building-dome-promenade

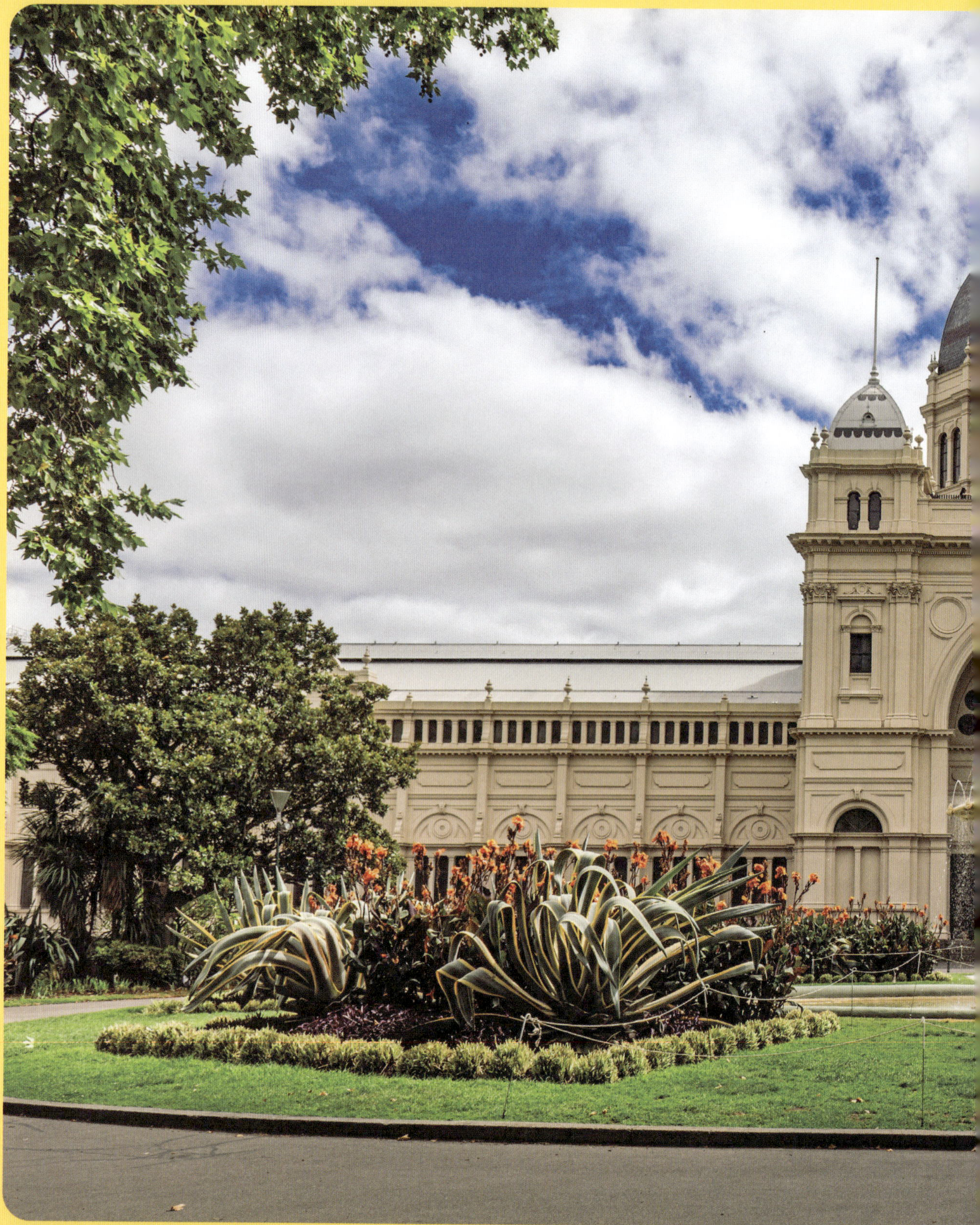

Melbourne/Naarm's Royal Exhibition Building

288	Greater than Australia's Most Famous Road?
289	The Aussie Camino
291	Extreme Sauna
294	Transcontinental Train
295	Pieman Perfection
297	The World's Greatest Desert Hike?
298	Rocking the Cradle
302	Riding the Rivers
303	Tingles All Over
305	Outback Springs
306	Camp in Sydney Harbour
307	You've Got Mail
309	Ride the Railway Inspired by Afghan Cameleers
310	A Caped Crusade
311	Pedals and Produce
312	Traversing the Gramps
315	Starry, Starry Nights

"The Overland Track is a moving slideshow of some of the country's most beautiful and craggy mountains"

SLOW TRAVEL

GREATER THAN AUSTRALIA'S MOST FAMOUS ROAD?

GREAT OCEAN ROAD, VICTORIA
GUNDITJMARA & GIRAI WURRUNG COUNTRY

If you think the Great Ocean Road is impressive in its beauty, wait till you meet its hiking equivalent. Stretching from Apollo Bay to the Twelve Apostles, the 110km (68-mile) Great Ocean Walk mirrors the course of its namesake road, but is always at least a few steps closer to the country's edge.

Pinched between the road and the coast for its entire length, the walk unveils much that the drive misses. Rounding Cape Otway instead of weaving over its inland slopes, it passes by Victoria's oldest working lighthouse to reach Rainbow Falls, where a freshwater spring pours into the sea amid a colourful mosaic of mosses. And as the road continues to hang back from the coast, the walk stays true to it, crossing little-visited strands such as Station Beach and Milanesia Beach and passing the rusted anchors of two ships wedged into the sand on Wreck Beach – this is the Shipwreck Coast, after all.

The Great Ocean Walk is designed to be hiked over eight days, or it can be sampled in sections. Seven hiker-only campgrounds are no more than 15.3km (9.5 miles) apart, each one containing eight tent pads (book sites ahead through the Parks Victoria website).

Walking options aren't limited to shouldering all your gear in a backpack and sleeping on tent pads. Several companies operate guided walks along the trail, as well as self-guided options with transport to and from the trail each night and transfers of your luggage between accommodation stops.

V/Line buses stop at Apollo Bay and the Twelve Apostles car park, the walk's start and finish points, making the walk accessible on public transport.

parks.vic.gov.au/places-to-see/parks/great-otway-national-park/things-to-do/great-ocean-walk

The Great Ocean Road features some of Australia's best hiking trails
Opposite Hikers on Bridgewater

THE AUSSIE CAMINO

PORTLAND (VICTORIA)–PENOLA (SA)
GUNDITJMARA & BINDJALI COUNTRY

Not all great Christian pilgrimages end in Santiago de Compostela – even Australia has its own *camino*, inspired by the revered Camino de Santiago across northern Spain. Unofficially known as the Aussie Camino, Australia's only true pilgrimage celebrates the life and work of Mary Mackillop, the country's first and only saint.

A walk of around 160km (100 miles), it connects Portland, the south-west Victorian town where Mackillop served her last posting as a teacher, to Penola, where she first worked as a governess and later founded the Sisters of St Joseph order.

The first part of the walk follows the coastal section of Victoria's 250km (155-mile) Great South West Walk, rounding Capes Nelson and Bridgewater – home to a seal colony and a bare, rocky moonscape known as the Petrified Forest – and making the long beach traverse to Nelson along Discovery Bay.

Crossing the border into South Australia, the walk turns away from the coast at Port MacDonnell, where some pilgrims choose to begin their hike. Tradition already dictates that pilgrims pause at the jetty in Port MacDonell, from where Mackillop sailed to Adelaide in 1867.

Passing through Mount Gambier, the walk continues north to Penola and a fitting finish post – the Mary Mackillop Penola Centre, a museum devoted to the life of the saint who was canonised in 2010, inside the schoolroom where she taught.

The Aussie Camino borrows several customs from its more famous counterpart, including the ritual of carrying a shell (as per the scallop shell of Camino de Santiago traditions) and a pilgrim's passport that can be stamped at towns and parishes along the walk.

Several travel companies run guided hiking tours along the Aussie Camino, typically taking in highlight sections, with bus connections in between.

walkingsa.org.au/news/the-aussie-camino

Top **Taking a dip in Lake Derby**
Bottom **Floating Sauna**

EXTREME SAUNA

◉ DERBY, TASMANIA
PALAWA COUNTRY

The north-east Tasmanian town of Derby might be well-known for its mountain biking, but that's not its only extreme pursuit. Head to a pontoon at the edge of the town's lake and there's another form of extremes on offer – a floating sauna that will take you on a rollercoaster of temperatures.

Modelled on the water-top saunas that line the shores of Oslo, Norway, the Floating Sauna Lake Derby is a southern outpost of Scandinavian sauna methods – get yourself absurdly hot, then get yourself shockingly cold. Rinse and repeat.

Hour-long sessions at Australia's only floating sauna alternate between the hotbox of the sauna and plunges into the icy lake. With temperatures reaching up to 90°C (194°F) in the wood-fired sauna, and the lake as frigid as 10°C (50°F), this means temperature variations as great as 80°C (176°F). Floating Sauna founder Nigel Reeves describes the effect on the body as a natural high that resets your nervous system.

'The shock of going from a hot environment into cold means your body responds by releasing a whole lot of endorphins and adrenaline into your system to fight the "tiger in the jungle" that might have appeared,' he says.

The steam and the swims aren't the only therapeutic features of the sauna. One wall is floor-to-ceiling glass, providing soothing views across the lake and surrounding hills as you bake. Mountain bikes whirr past, but there's a hard-to-shake sense of removal – it's just you, this sauna and that next dive off the pontoon. Extremes have never felt so good.

🌐 floatingsauna.com.au

Reflections on Lake Derby

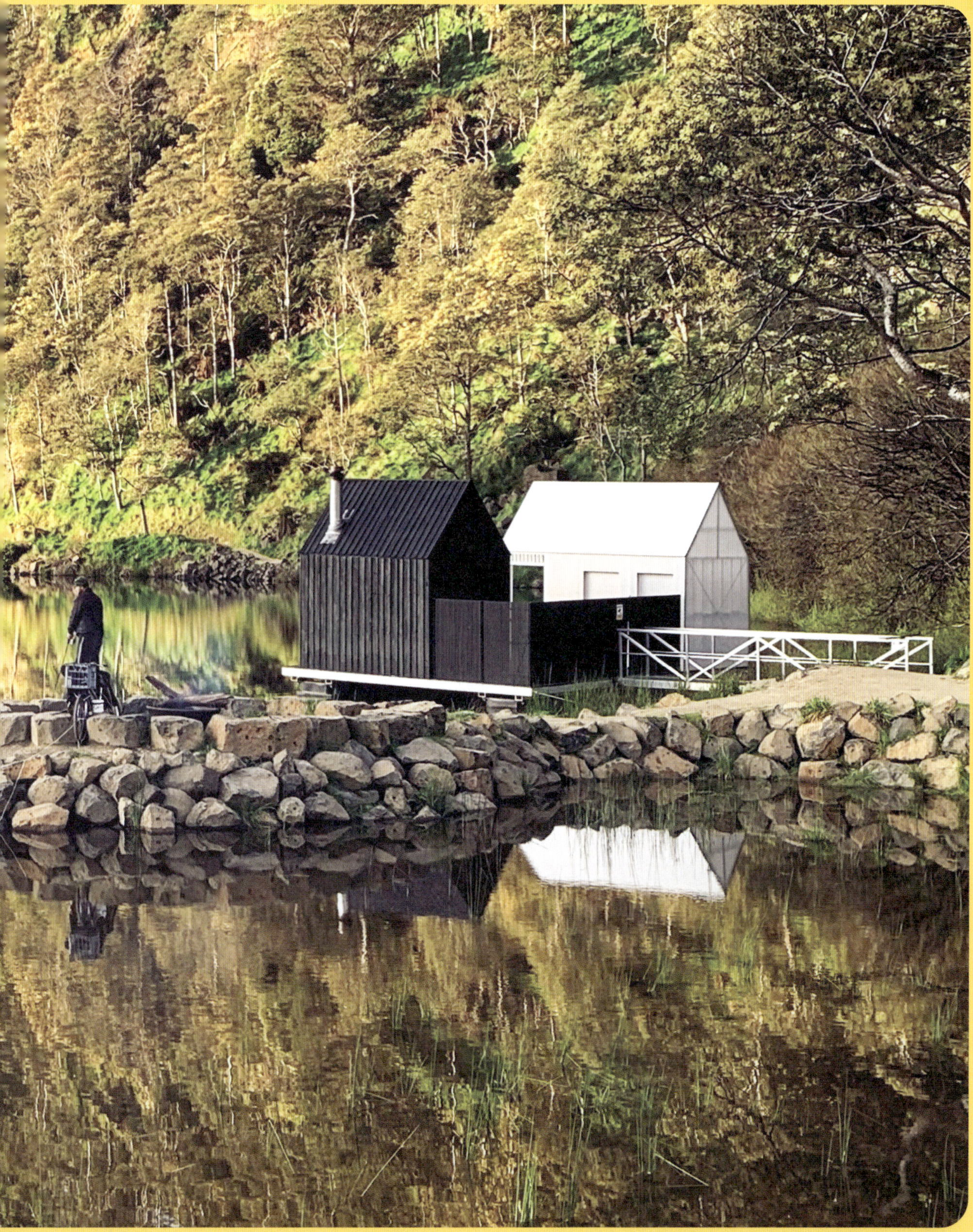

TRANSCONTINENTAL TRAIN

PERTH/BOORLOO (WA)–SYDNEY/WARRANE (NSW)
WHADJUK COUNTRY–GADIGAL COUNTRY COUNTRY

Australia's longest rail journey – all 4352km (2704 miles) of it – is a shore-to-shore transcontinental chug from Perth to Sydney (or vice versa) on the *Indian Pacific*. Completed as a railway line in 1917, it didn't carry its first passenger service until 1970 but is today considered one of the world's great rail journeys.

Departing weekly (from Perth on Sundays and Sydney on Wednesdays), it's a four-day journey from ocean to ocean (hence the name *Indian Pacific*). If setting out from the west, it's a day of travel to a sunrise wake-up on the Nullarbor and its seemingly endless horizons. Here, the *Indian Pacific* traverses the world's longest straight stretch of railway – a 478km (297-mile) stretch that's so unnaturally straight it can be seen from space. The next day there's a stop in Adelaide before the train powers on towards Sydney.

Station stops bring the chance for off-train experiences in Kalgoorlie, Adelaide (heading out to the Barossa Valley), Broken Hill, the Blue Mountains and Cook, a secluded station in the middle of the Nullarbor where passengers can take a stargazing tour (try to imagine empty Cook as it once was … home to just 50 railway workers).

The *Indian Pacific* features the Queen Adelaide Restaurant and Outback Explorer Lounge, with all food, drinks and off-train experiences included in the fare.

journeybeyondrail.com.au/journeys/indian-pacific

The *Indian Pacific* crosses through Cook
Opposite A peaceful morning in Corinna

PIEMAN PERFECTION

CORINNA, TASMANIA
PALAWA COUNTRY

At dawn on Tasmania's Pieman River, you could almost be convinced that the world has stopped turning. Australia's largest temperate rainforest, takayna/Tarkine, smothers the river's northern bank, and the surface of the water is as smooth as silk and as reflective as a mirror. The only things that stir are the paddles of kayaks as they head downstream from Corinna in the first light.

Established as a gold-mining settlement near the end of the 19th century, Corinna is now an isolated tourist centre gift-wrapped by nature. Its rustic miners' cottages, steps from the banks of the river and encased by the rainforest, serve as visitor accommodation, with sit-on-top kayaks available for hire.

Dawn is the time to take to the river. Regular sightings of thylacines (Tasmanian tigers) were claimed along these banks up to 20 years after the animal had supposedly died out, and a detour of just a few metres up the Savage River will have you paddling over the wreck of the steamship *Croydon*. Australia's most inland shipwreck, the hull of the *Croydon* is still filled with Huon pine logs, more than a century after it sank.

The prime lure for kayakers is another few hundred metres downstream, where a set of much-photographed wooden stairs disappear into the rainforest, accessing a track to the base of Lovers Falls, a quixotic waterfall that pours down among some of the state's tallest and most impressive ferns.

corinna.com.au

Hiking Mount Sonder/ Rwetyepme

✱ DESERT OR COAST?

If your tastes run to the more leisurely (and watery) walking experiences, Sydney/Warrane's glittering beaches are the setting for one of the city's most popular walking tracks, connecting Bondi Beach to Coogee Beach across a line of cliffs furnished with a string of other beaches.

Though just 6km (3.7 miles) in length, the Bondi to Coogee walk, on Bidjigal and Gadigal Country, incorporates six beaches – Bondi, Tamarama, Bronte, Clovelly, Gordons Bay and Coogee – rising to ocean views along the sandstone cliffs between.

Beginning by the Bondi Icebergs (see p. 195), Sydney/Warrane's most famous ocean pool, and finishing on the sands at Coogee, the walk is fully paved (though a series of steps prevent it from being fully accessible) and would take walkers two to three hours, if only it wasn't so full of distractions.

Don't forget to pack your swimmers.

🌐 bonditocoogeewalk.com

THE WORLD'S GREATEST DESERT HIKE?

TJORITJA/WEST MACDONNELL NATIONAL PARK, NT
ARRERNTE COUNTRY

A two-week walk through a desert should, by rights, be filled with hardships. But not if that walk is on the Larapinta Trail. Stretching 223km (139 miles) from Alice Springs/Mparntwe to the summit of shapely Mount Sonder/Rwetyepme, this trail runs the length of Tjoritja/West MacDonnell Ranges, connecting a string of peaks, gorges and waterholes.

There's so much that's compelling about this trail. The ancient Tjoritja/West MacDonnell Ranges were once as tall as the Himalayas, and the Finke River, which is crossed near Ormiston Gorge, is often claimed to be the world's oldest waterway. There's also a likely familiarity in the 'sleeping woman' shape of Mount Sonder – seen along so much of the western end of the trail – because it was a favourite scene for the celebrated Western Arrernte artist Albert Namatijira.

The waterholes and gorges are the literal coolest moments of the hike, with days often ending beside the likes of Ormiston Gorge/Kwartatuma, Ellery Creek Big Hole/Udepata and Birthday Waterhole.

There are 34 official campsites strung along the trail, with sites ranging from bare earth to covered sleeping shelters at the likes of Jay Creek and Serpentine Gorge. There are food storage rooms at Ellery Creek/Udepata, Serpentine Gorge/Ulpma and Ormiston Gorge/Kwartatuma (storage can also be arranged at the visitor centre at Standley Chasm/Angkerle Atwatye), cutting down on the amount of gear you need to carry along the trail. Larapinta Trail Trek Support (treksupport.com.au) can make food drops at these sites, and also runs trail transfers.

Book your campsites up to 12 months ahead through the Northern Territory Parks Booking System (parkbookings.nt.gov.au), or hike with the many companies that run guided walks along the trail, from highlight sections to end-to-end traverses.

larapintatrail.com.au

ROCKING THE CRADLE

◉ CRADLE MOUNTAIN-LAKE ST CLAIR NATIONAL PARK, TASMANIA
PALAWA COUNTRY

Long Australia's most famous bushwalk, the Overland Track is a moving slideshow of some of the country's most beautiful and craggy mountains. Connecting Tasmania's most famous peak (Cradle Mountain) to Australia's deepest lake (Lake St Clair), it's 65km (40 miles) of alpine magic passing four of the state's five tallest mountains (or 82km/51 miles if you choose to finish the walk along the shores of Lake St Clair, which most hikers skip in favour of a ferry crossing).

Hiker huts neatly partition the track into six days, with no day any longer than 16.8km (10.4 miles) – most days are less than 10km (6.2 miles). The track has the kindness to thread between the mountains rather than over them, with only two climbs of note – a 300m (984ft) ascent to Marions Lookout at the very start of the hike, and another 300m (984ft) climb on day four to Pelion Gap – but it's also stitched with side trails that ascend a host of surrounding summits: Cradle Mountain, Barn Bluff, Mount Oakleigh, Mount Pelion East and an acrobatic scramble to Tasmania's highest peak, 1617m (5305ft) Mount Ossa.

From October through May, a permit system applies on the track, with a maximum of 34 independent (and 26 guided) walkers permitted to set out each day. Bookings for each season open on 1 July and fill fast.

During this season, the Overland Track can only be walked from north to south, setting out from Ronny Creek or the shores of Dove Lake, where an old boatshed with the bowed figure of Cradle Mountain behind provides one of the classic images of Tasmania. The initial climb takes walkers straight into the alpine zone and the promise (on good days) of vast mountain views before the track disappears into the wilderness of Tasmania's most famous national park, passing lakes and waterfalls in addition to its collection of mighty mountains.

I've walked the Overland Track in most conditions and circumstances – through a blazing summer, in the middle of winter, with my kids when they each turned eight years of age, and guided on the plush Cradle Mountain Huts Walk that offers a comfortable (and well fed) alternative to the heavy backpacks and public huts of an independent hike. Winter – outside the booking season – is my favourite time, though it's unquestionably a far more challenging task, bringing the likelihood of snow and the guarantee of bitterly cold conditions (putting your feet into frozen socks each morning is hard to talk up as a pleasurable experience).

That said, expect changeable weather at any time of year – snow in summer is common – so pack prepared. Huts are sparsely fitted out, featuring tables and benches, heaters, rainwater tanks, composting toilets and wooden bunks. You'll need to carry a sleeping bag and mat, stove and all cooking equipment. Hikers must also carry a tent in case huts are full or you get caught out between huts.

◉ parks.tas.gov.au/explore-our-parks/cradle-mountain/overland-track

Top **Cradle Mountain**
Bottom **A trail through scenic Cradle Mountain-Lake St Clair National Park**

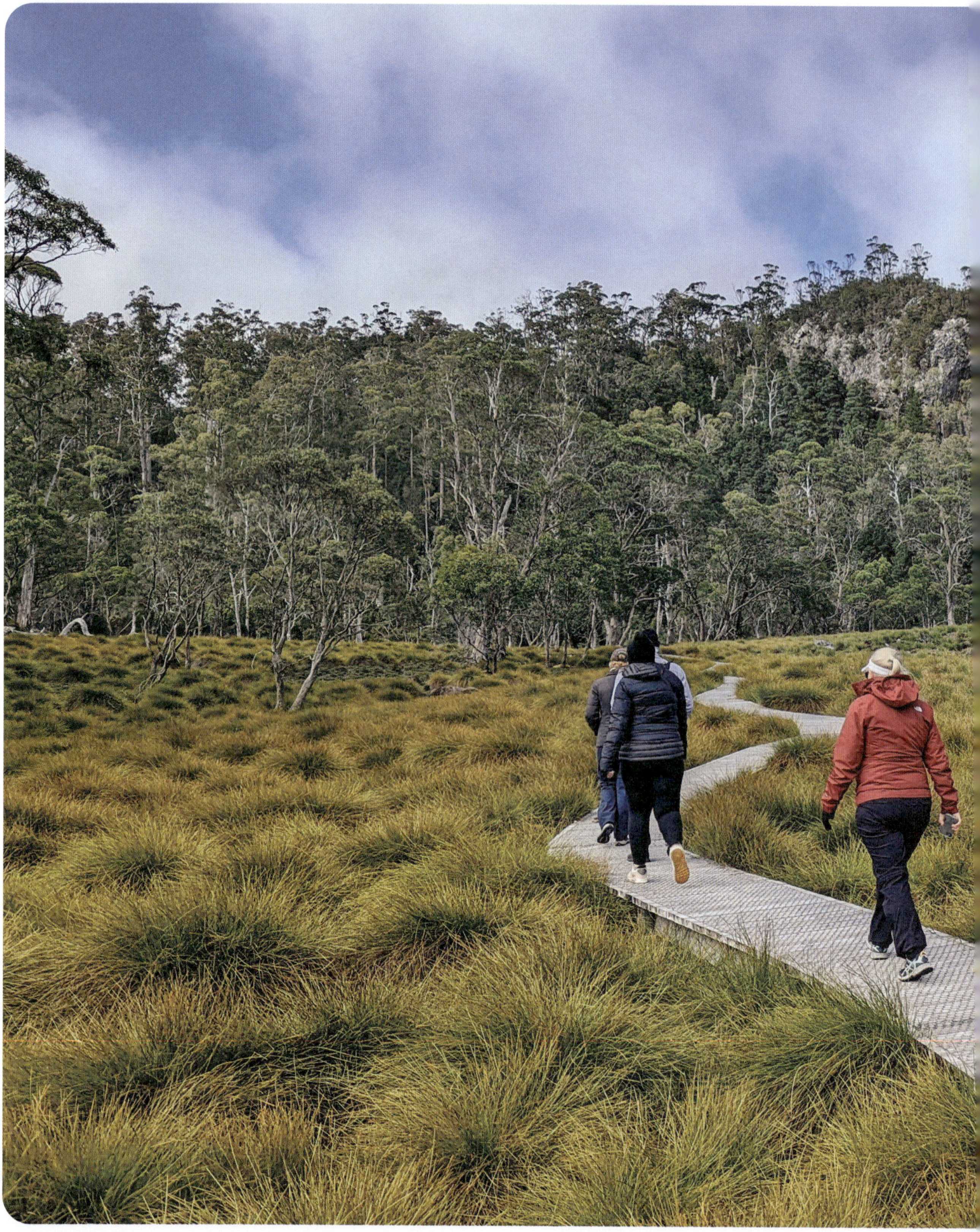

The Overland Track, one of Australia's favourite bushwalks

RIDING THE RIVERS

◉ NORTHERN RIVERS RAIL TRAIL, NSW
BUNDJALUNG COUNTRY

The Northern Rivers Rail Trail
Opposite **Cycling through a karri forest on the Munda Biddi**

New South Wales didn't get its first rail trail along a public rail corridor until 2020 when the 21km (13-mile) Tumbarumba to Rosewood Rail Trail at the foot of the Snowy Mountains was launched. But it was the arrival of the Northern Rivers Rail Trail in 2023 that catapulted the state into the minds of cyclists.

The first of the trail's four stages opened in March 2023, and within seven months more than 100,000 people had used the trail. Immediately, it had become one of the most popular cycling paths in the country.

Planned to stretch for 132km (82 miles) from Murwillumbah, near the Queensland border, to Lismore, making a horseshoe journey via Byron Bay, Northern Rivers will eventually become one of Australia's longest and most scenic rail trails.

For now, two sections are open: the original 24km (15-mile) stage from Murwillumbah to Crabbes Creek, and a 13.4km (8.3-mile) stretch from Bentley to Casino at the trail's far opposite end that opened in 2024. The two stages between remained in planning and funding at the time of writing.

Northern Rivers' popular Murwillumbah stage passes the doors of the Tweed Regional Gallery and Margaret Ollie Art Centre (one of regional Australia's top galleries) and follows the course of the former railway through a trio of pretty towns – Stokers Siding, Burringbar and Mooball – as it edges towards the coast over a host of old rail bridges and through two tunnels.

Sharp-tipped Wollumbin is an ever-visible (if distant) mountain presence, and look up as you pedal through the 500m (1640ft) Burringbar Range Tunnel – those tiny lights across the ceiling are glow-worms.

◉ northernriversrailtrail.com.au

TINGLES ALL OVER

◉ MUNDA BIDDI TRAIL, WA
NOONGAR COUNTRY

In the southern forests of WA – a mesmerising place of karri, tingle, marri and jarrah trees (all endemic to this south-west corner of Australia) – it's not hard to see the trees for the forest, especially at cycling speed. Pedalling slowly beneath trees that grow up to 90m (295ft) in height, or with trunks more than 20m (65.5ft) in circumference, the world seems mighty, as does the trail on which you're cycling.

Stretching more than 1000km (621 miles) from Mundaring in the Perth Hills to faraway Albany on the south coast, the Munda Biddi Trail (a name meaning 'path through the forest' in the Noongar language) is one of the longest purpose-built cycling trails in the country. It's also one of the best equipped. Between the 16 towns that dot its green course, offering civilising interludes such as motels, restaurants and wine and whisky bars, are 12 trail campsites. With covered sleeping shelters, bike lockers and tent sites, they're spaced a comfortable day's ride apart and are mostly exclusive to trail users.

The trail is off-road but not particularly technical, requiring a mountain bike or gravel bike, and can be comfortably cycled in around three weeks. Shorter rides of a few days between towns are also possible. Favourite options include Pemberton to Walpole (three to four days) and Manjimup to Northcliffe (three days), both lined with tall timber.

◉ mundabiddi.org.au

MORE AUSSIE CYCLE TRAILS

If one challenging long-distance ride isn't enough, check out these other options

* **Mawson Trail** (Adelaide/Tandanya to Blinman, SA; 900km/559 miles)
* **Tasmanian Trail** (Devonport to Dover; 480km/298 miles)
* **Bicentennial National Trail** (Cooktown, Queensland to Healesville, Victoria; an epic 5330km/3312 miles).

Top **Wabma Kadarbu Conservation Park**

Bottom **Swimming in the Dalhousie Springs**

OUTBACK SPRINGS

VARIOUS LOCATIONS

The Australian outback might look dry, but deep beneath the ground is one of the world's largest underground bodies of freshwater. Spanning more than 20 per cent of the country, the Great Artesian Basin holds around 130,000 times the volume of water in Sydney Harbour.

In a few places of oasis-worthy relief, it rises to the surface as springs and pools, creating welcome stops on outback travels.

Dalhousie Springs

On the edge of the Simpson Desert, Witjira National Park encases more than 120 mound springs (where underground water rises through mounds), including the Dalhousie Main Spring, which is naturally warmed to around 37 degrees (98.6°F). Soak and stay – there's a campground at the springs.

Coward Springs

Formed when a bore was drilled in the 1880s, overflowing to create a wetland in one of the driest spots in the country. A 1.3m (4.3ft) tub with 29°C (84.2°F) water has been formed by old railway sleepers, and there's a campground and museum telling of Coward Springs' days as a station on the Ghan railway line (see p. 309).

Wabma Kadarbu Conservation Park

About 10 minutes drive south of Coward Springs are the twin Bubbler/Pirdali–nha and Blanche Cup/Thirrka mound springs. True to its name, the Bubbler belches and bubbles as though created by geothermal activity, and while there's no swimming, the water creates a beautiful delta of green grasses. It's a good spot to sight dingoes. Signs on site tell the First Nations' story of the country's creation.

Lightning Ridge Bore Baths

The vintage – two-million-year-old water – is perfect at this large circular pool outside the opal-mining town of Lightning Ridge. Lie back at the end of a day of noodling and let the 41.5°C (106.7°F) waters do their thing. Free entry; open 24 hours.

Moree Artesian Aquatic Centre

Sure, it looks like a standard aquatic centre, but its waters flow from springs, creating two artesian pools naturally heated to 41°C (105.8°F).

CAMP IN SYDNEY HARBOUR

⊙ SYDNEY/WARRANE, NSW
GADIGAL COUNTRY

Waterfront in Sydney/Warrane is Australia's most prized real estate, and you can get no closer to the water than an island in the middle of the harbour. First a meeting place for First Nations people and then a convict prison and shipbuilding facility, World Heritage–listed Cockatoo Island/Wareamah has been reborn again as the ultimate urban camping destination.

Set below the cliffs of the Cockatoo Island/Wareamah plateau and peering across Sydney Harbour to the Woolwich Marina, the island has several camping options, from pitching your own tent, to staying in a pre-pitched tent that can hold two adults and two children, to a pair of waterfront glamping tents with double beds and outside decks. All less than 4km (2.5 miles) from the Harbour Bridge.

Access the island by public ferry from Circular Quay or Barangaroo.

⊙ cockatooisland.gov.au/en/stay

YOU'VE GOT MAIL

◎ HAWKESBURY RIVER/DYARUBBIN, NSW
DARUG COUNTRY

The Riverboat Postman ticket office
Opposite **Overnight visitors pitch tents on Cockatoo Island/Wareamah**

The mail run on the Hawkesbury River/Dyarubbin beyond Sydney/Warrane's northern edge is more of a mail flow. Upstream from Brooklyn are tiny settlements such as Bar Point, Milsons Passage and Coba Point that can only be accessed by river. So how does their mail arrive? By water, on the Riverboat Postman.

Joining this postal service turned visitor cruise on its weekday mail runs offers a nostalgic glimpse into Australian postal life. From Brooklyn, which can be reached on a direct train from Sydney/Warrane (disembark at the Hawkesbury River station) in an hour, the mailboat makes a three-hour round trip through Darug Country, calling in to deliver its messages and parcels, with commentary from the local skippers and a ploughman's lunch.

🌐 riverboatpostman.com.au

The *Ghan* travels from southern Australia to the Top End

RIDE THE RAILWAY INSPIRED BY AFGHAN CAMELEERS

◉ **ADELAIDE/TANDANYA TO DARWIN/GARAMILLA**

In the 19th century, travel through the central deserts of Australia was a brutal and blistering undertaking, largely made possible only by the import of camels and their cameleers from Asia. Known as Afghans (even though many came from Pakistan) or simply Ghans, these cameleers opened up vast expanses of the country's interior and would lend their name to one of Australia's most evocative train journeys – the *Ghan*.

Spanning almost 3000km (1864 miles) from the continent's southern shores to the Top End, the railway first operated from Adelaide/Tandanya to Alice Springs/Mparntwe in 1929, extending to Darwin/Garamilla in 2004. The full journey takes three to four days, with two-day trips from Adelaide/Tandanya to Alice Springs/Mparntwe, or Darwin/Garamilla to Alice Springs/Mparntwe, also possible.

Heading north, there are stops at Marla (the small town most synonymous with the *Ghan* cameleers), Alice Springs/Mparntwe and Katherine, with free off-train experiences at the latter pair. Southerly trips stop at Manguri, outside of Coober Pedy, instead of Marla – this stop (like the stop in Marla) is more a leg-stretcher than an exploration.

In Alice, organised excursions include a cultural walk at Standley Chasm/Angkerle Atwatye, a visit to Simpsons Gap/Rungutjirpa, tours of the Alice Springs Desert Park or combined visits to the Telegraph Station (Alice's original raison d'etre), School of the Air and Reptile Centre. Katherine options revolve around cruises through the nearby Nitmiluk gorge, including with a Jawoyn guide to a rock-art site inside the gorge.

The *Ghan* only travels during the cooler months of March to November.

⊘ journeybeyondrail.com.au/journeys/the-ghan

A CAPED CRUSADE

📍 LEEUWIN-NATURALISTE NATIONAL PARK, WA
WADANDI COUNTRY

In Australia's far south-western corner, the country is staked to the ground by a pair of lighthouses on opposing capes to either side of Margaret River. In addition to sending their warnings to mariners, the Cape Naturaliste and Cape Leeuwin lighthouses double as the start and finish posts on Western Australia's top long-distance hike.

The Cape to Cape Track is a coastal extravaganza that stretches for 125km (78 miles) along the beaches, cliffs and forest in and around Leeuwin-Naturaliste National Park. Typically walked in five to seven days, it strings together famed surfing beaches, caves, dramatic sections of rocky coast, waterfalls and towering karri trees through Boranup Forest. And as you walk along the cliffs, your walking companions might well only be dolphins and whales – humpbacks migrate along this coast from October to December, with southern rights present from June to September.

The track is dotted with towns – Yallingup, Gracetown, Margaret River, Prevelly Park, Hamelin Bay – that can provide off-track accommodation options, with campsites dotted in between. Roads and vehicle tracks also regularly intersect with the track, making it possible to walk shorter segments. Personal favourites include half-day stretches from Redgate Beach to Contos Beach, Yallingup Beach to Injidup Beach (passing Canal Rocks), and Hamelin Bay to Cosy Corner Beach.

More than half a dozen companies offer guided and self-guided hiking itineraries on the track; see the Friends of the Cape to Cape Track website (capetocapetrack.com.au) for listings.

🌐 exploreparks.dbca.wa.gov.au/trail/cape-cape-track

PEDALS AND PRODUCE

MURRAY TO MOUNTAINS RAIL TRAIL, VICTORIA
DHUDHUROA, TAUNGURUNG, WAYWURRU & JAITHMATHANG COUNTRY

Rail trails have truly gathered steam around Australia. More than 100 sections of abandoned railway have been reborn as cycling trails, providing flat(ish), vehicle-free pedalling across the country. Some extend for a few kilometres, others for a few days.

Leading this peloton of rail trails is Victoria, a state with more than 30 such trails, including, most prominently, the Murray to Mountains Rail Trail.

The ride that first popularised Australian rail trails, Murray to Mountains stretches for 84km (52 miles) through the Ovens Valley from Wangaratta to Bright, with side trails radiating like spokes to Beechworth, Milawa, Yackandandah and Harrietville. It takes you to the very edge of the High Country without ever quite venturing into the fatiguing mountains.

That kindness isn't Murray to Mountains' only concession to pleasure. Done right, this is a journey of cycling indulgence – fine food and wine, cooling craft beer and plush accommodation, with a bit of pedalling thrown in. There are wineries such as Gapsted and Ringer Reef set beside the main trail, while side trails go in search of other wineries around Beechworth and Milawa. Pair this with a berry farm, walnuts, vineyard platters, excellent restaurants and Australia's only pumpkin-seed producer, and it's a picnic with pedals.

It's possible to ride Murray to Mountains in one single-minded day, but it's best stretched out like a long lunch. The presence of regular towns means you can draw a return ride out to four or five days, pedalling no more than about 50km (31 miles) a day.

ridehighcountry.com.au/rail-trails/murray-to-mountains

Cycling the Murray to Mountains Rail Trail

Opposite **Cowaramup Bay, part of the Cape to Cape Track**

TRAVERSING THE GRAMPS

📍 GRAMPIANS (GARIWERD) NATIONAL PARK, VICTORIA
DJAB WURRUNG & JARDWARDJALI COUNTRY

The chance to traverse an entire mountain range on foot is an uncommon one in Australia, reserved for the toughest range in the country (Tasmania's Western Arthurs), the longest range in the country (the Great Dividing Range on the 5330km/3312-mile National Trail) or, more manageably, the Grampians Peaks Trail (GPT).

Launched in 2021, the GPT is one of Australia's newest long-distance trails and makes a tip-to-toe crossing of the Grampians/Gariwerd, a compact and rugged sandstone range that rises out of the otherwise flat Western District plains on the Traditional Lands of the Djab Wurrung and Jardwardjali People.

Along the way, it systematically picks off many of the range's summits – from Mount Zero in the north to Mount Sturgeon in the south – with nights in dedicated GPT camps (and one gloriously civilised night in the town of Halls Gap). Camps feature tent platforms or granite sand pads, water tanks and a communal shelter (with charging points for phones) or open gathering area – these camps must be booked before setting out.

There are numerous points at which to hop on and off the trail, making it possible to hike sections rather than the whole trail. A favourite three-day sampler is through the popular Wonderland Range above Halls Gap, climbing to the Pinnacle and Mount Rosea and staying in the Bugiga and Barri Yalug campsites.

Grampians Peaks Walking Co (grampianspeaks.com.au) operates a hikers' shuttle and food drops to various points along the route, while several companies run guided hikes along the trail. Views are best if walked north-south.

🔗 parks.vic.gov.au/places-to-see/parks/grampians-national-park/things-to-do/grampians-peaks-trail

Top **Traversing MacKenzie Falls**
Bottom **Grampians Peaks Trail takes you past some impressive rock formations**

The Milky Way seen from Warrumbungles National Park

STARRY, STARRY NIGHTS

◉ **VARIOUS LOCATIONS**

They call it dark sky tourism – travelling to view the stars – and with an estimated 80 per cent of the world's population living in places where they can't see the stars, it's an elusive quality. But it's one that Australia has in spades, with so much of the country far from sources of light pollution.

Head anywhere into the outback and the sky will likely be strewn with stars and streaked with satellites and falling stars, but to really immerse yourself in the night sky, head to one of the country's four designated Dark Sky sanctuaries, parks and reserves.

Warrumbungles National Park, NSW

Australia's first Dark Sky Park, two hours drive north of Dubbo, is a rugged place of craggy, sharp-tipped peaks, but it shines even brighter at night. There are two observatories at its edge – tour the Siding Spring Observatory, home to more than 20 telescopes, including Australia's largest, by day (it's closed at night), and join a 90-minute stargazing session each night at Milroy Observatory.

➔ sidingspringobservatory.com.au

➔ milroyobservatory.com.au

Arkaroola Wilderness Sanctuary, SA

(*see* p. 114) Home to three observatories, including one at the heart of Arkaroola Village with a nightly big-screen presentation of precision live images of the universe.

➔ arkaroola.com.au

Australian Age of Dinosaurs, Queensland

The jump-up that's home to this stunning museum (*see* p. 226) outside of Winton doubles as a Dark Sky Sanctuary. Head to the free Star Gallery at the base of the jump-up with your own telescope and binoculars for a night-sky extravaganza.

➔ australianageofdinosaurs.com

Murray River Dark Sky Reserve, SA

The nightlife along this 80km stretch of Australia's longest river, from Bowhill to Blanchetown, involves more stars than an Oscars after party. Sit out by the river to quietly absorb the celestial scene, join a guided Dark Sky Night Tour atop the river's Big Bend Cliffs, or dine with the stars at Juggle House's Dark Sky Gold Stars Sunset Dinner, which includes a guided tour of the Ngaut Ngaut Cultural Site with a Traditional Custodian from the Mannum Aboriginal Community Association.

➔ jugglehouse.com.au/tours/dark-sky-gold

INDEX

Abbott, Peter 35
Absalom Gallery, Broken Hill NSW 266
Adelaide/Tandanya SA 46, 75, 95, 139, 161, 173, 276, 309
Adelaide Central Market SA 139
Adelaide Dolphin Sanctuary 95
Adelaide Festival SA 173
Adelaide Fringe Festival SA 173
Adelaide Oval rooftop ramble SA 276
Adelaide, HMAS (scuttled ship), Avoca NSW 186
Adnyamathanha Country 82, 114–15, 264
Afghan cameleers 309
Agrarian Kitchen, New Norfolk Tas. 150–1
Alice Springs/Mparntwe NT 163, 171, 175, 260, 309
Alpine National Park Vic. 60
Anangu Country 80, 254–5
Angus, Bob 130
animal migrations 98, 104–5
Antakirinja Mat-Yankunytjatjara Country 222, 280–1
Apollo Bay Vic. 117
Arabana Country 247
Arakwal Country 116
Archibald Prize (for portraiture) 271
Arkaroola Wilderness Sanctuary SA 114–15, 315
Arrernte Country 82, 163, 171, 175, 232, 260, 297
art galleries 233, 236–7, 260, 266, 271
Art Gallery of NSW, Sydney NSW 271
aurora australis 66
Auslan interpreters 177
Australian Age of Dinosaurs (museum), Winton Qld 226–7, 315
Australian Convict Sites World Heritage Area 214–15
Australian cultural icons, Winton Qld 256–7
Australian Kelpie Muster, Casterton Vic. 158
Australian Motorcycle Grand Prix, Phillip Island Vic. 191
Australian Open (tennis), Melbourne Vic. 191

Australian Rules Football (AFL) xviii
 Grand Final, Melbourne Vic. 190
 Queenstown Tas. 183
 Tiwi Islands grand final, Wurrumiyanga NT 181
Australia's Big Things 2–3
Ayr Qld 186

Bagala Country 155
Bailai Country 126
Balladonia WA 17
Ballarat Vic. 140, 220
Bandjin Country 18
Banyjima Country 20–1
Barngarla Country 98, 133
Barossa Valley SA 145
Barry, Michelle 108–9
Barunga NT 153
Barunguba Montague Island lighthouse NSW 278
Batavia (shipwreck), Houtman Abrolhos Islands WA 186, 217
Bay of Fires Conservation Area Tas. 38–9, 268
beaches
 state capitals 75
 whitest and brightest 30–1
Beanie Festival, Alice Springs NT 163
Belgrove Distillery, Kempton Tas. 146
Bells Beach Vic. 197
Benalla Costume and Kelly Museum, Benalla Vic. 225
Bendigo Vic. 149
Bennett, Adrian 241
Bero, Nornie 235
Beveridge Vic. 225
Bicentennial National Trail 303
Bidjara Country 68
Big Banana, Coffs Harbour NSW 2
Big Bulls, Rockhampton Qld 2
Big Cassowary, Mission Beach Qld 2
Big Galah, Kimba SA 2
Big Gumboot, Tully Qld 2
Big Merino, Goulburn NSW 2
Big Penguin, Penguin Tas. 2
Big Picture, The, Broken Hill NSW 266
Big Pineapple, Woombye Qld 2
Big Potato, Robertson NSW 2
Big Prawn, Ballina NSW 2
Big Wine Bottle, Rutherglen Vic. 2
Bindal Country 244–5
Bindjali Country 289
Bindjareb Noongar Country 263
Bininj/Mungguy Country 90–1

bird watching 17, 91, 95, 99, 103, 104, 119
Birdsville Hotel Qld 218
Birragung Wilam (River Camp) Walk, Melbourne Vic. 253
Blackman, Uncle Boyd 14
Blue Lake/Warwar, Mount Gambier SA 37
Blue Mountains National Park NSW 196
Blues on Broadbeach, Gold Coast Qld 160
Boandik Country 37, 67
boat building, Franklin Tas. 123
Bogangar NSW 204–5
Bondi Beach NSW 75, 195
Bondi Icebergs Pool, Bondi Beach NSW 195
Bondi to Coogee walk NSW 296
Boon Wurrung/Bunurong Country 221, 253, 283
Bourke NSW 10
Boyd, Arthur 233
Breaden, Christine 35
Brickendon and Woolmers Estates Tas. 214–15
bridge climbs 208, 282
Brisbane/Meanjin Qld 47, 75, 160, 161
Broken Hill NSW 11, 218, 266–7
Broken Hill City Art Gallery NSW 266
Brown, Bob 72–3
Bruny Island Tas. 103, 142–3
Budj Bim Cultural Landscape Vic. 212–13
Buley Rockhole, Litchfield National Park NT 44
Bundanon Art Museum, Illaroo NSW 233
Bundjalung Country 116, 204–5, 302
Bungle Bungle Range WA 86
Burrawa BridgeClimb (First Nations perspective), Sydney NSW 208
bush tucker foraging 130–1
bushrangers 225
Busselton WA 270
Butchulla Country 14–15
Byellee Country 92
Byron Bay NSW 116

Caiguna Blowhole WA 17
Cairns Qld 103
Callington Mill Distillery, Oatlands Tas. 147
camping 18, 39, 58, 68, 130, 155, 306

316

Canberra ACT 159, 229
canoeing 62, 63
 see also kayaking
canyons 35, 175, 196
Cape Byron lighthouse NSW 278
Cape Hillsborough National Park Qld 94
Cape Le Grand National Park WA 30, 94
Cape Leeuwin lighthouse WA 310
Cape Naturaliste lighthouse WA 310
Cape Otway lighthouse Vic. 278
Cape to Cape Track WA 310
Cape Tourville Tas. 41
Capertee Valley NSW 103
Capewell, Darren 'Capes' 100–1
capital cities
 beaches 75
 national parks 46–7
Capricorn Caves Qld 200
Carnarvon Gorge National Park Qld 53, 68–9
Carnarvon Great Walk Qld 52
Cascades, Litchfield National Park NT 44
Cascades Female Factory Tas. 214
Casterton Vic. 158
Casuarina Beach Qld 94
Cataract Gorge, Launceston Tas. 23
caves 57, 200
chocolate makers 138
Christmas Island 104–5
citizen science programs, Great Barrier Reef 120
climate xii
climbing 26–7
Coal Mines Historic Site Tas. 214
Cobbold Gorge Qld 51
Cockatoo Island/Wareamah NSW 215
Cod Hole, Ribbon Reef #10, Great Barrier Reef Qld 108
Coffin Bay SA 137
Combo Waterhole, Winton Qld 256
Conondale Range Great Walk Qld 52
convict sites 214–15
Coober Pedy SA 222, 280–1
Cooke, Robin 251
cooking schools 150–1
Cooloola Great Walk Qld 52
Cooper, Uncle William 210, 211
Coral Bay WA 6
Coral Greenhouse (underwater sculpture), John Brewer Reef Qld 244

CoralWatch 120
Corinna Tas. 294
Cottesloe WA 75
Coulthard, Terry 264
Coulthard, Vinnie 264
Coward Springs SA 305
Cradle Mountain-Lake St Clair National Park Tas. 4, 57–8, 298–9
Craig's Royal Hotel, Ballarat Vic. 140
craters 82–3
crocodiles 4, 18, 51, 91, 99
Crowdy Bay National Park NSW 94
Currumbin Alley Qld 205
cuttlefish migration 98
cycle trails/cycling 84, 202, 302–3, 311–12
 see also mountain biking trails

D'Aguilar National Park Qld 47
Daintree Rainforest Qld 41
Daintree Village Qld 99
Dalhousie Springs SA 305
Daly Waters Pub NT 218–19
Dambo, Thomas 263
Dandenong Ranges National Park Vic. 46
Dandongadale Falls Vic. 60
D'Arenberg winery, McLaren Vale SA 236
Dark Mofo, Hobart Tas. 75, 162
dark sky tourism 315
Darkinjung Country 196
Darlington Probation Station Tas. 96, 214
Darug Country 306
Darwin/Garamilla NT 170, 309
deCaires Taylor, Jason 244
Deni Ute Muster, Deniliquin NSW 167
Deniliquin NSW 167
Derby Tas. 189, 291
Desert Mob (Araluen Arts Centre), Alice Springs NT 171
desert sculptures 251, 267
Dharawal Country 196, 233
Dharug Country 196
Dhudhuroa Country 311
Dhurga Country 233
Diamond Head Beach NSW 94
Dieri Country 247
dingoes, K'gari Qld 15
dinosaur museums Qld 226–7
diving and snorkelling 37, 58, 84, 98, 104–5, 120, 186, 198, 217, 244–5, 270

Dja Dja Wurrung Country 149, 220, 259
Djabwurrung Country 312
Dog Fence 222–3
dolphins 95, 100, 172, 278, 310
driving safety xv
Dubbo NSW 10
Dunn, Rodney 150–1

East MacDonnell Ranges NT 33
Eastern Arrernte Country 33
Eastern Maar Country 132
Elliott, David 226
Elvis Festival, Parkes NSW 164–5
estuarine crocodiles 4, 18, 91, 99
Eungella National Park Qld 107
Eureka Centre, Ballarat Vic. 220
Ewamian Country 51, 87, 113
Exmouth WA 6
Explorers Way, SA & NT xiv
Eye on the Reef (app) 120
Eyre Bird Observatory WA 17

'fagus' turning (changing colour) Tas. 54–5
Falls Creek Vic. 202
Farina SA 216
Farm, the, Byron Bay NSW 116
Federation Peak, Southwest National Park Tas. 22
festivals xviii
 Adelaide SA 173
 Auslan interpretation 177
 Barunga Festival NT 155
 Beanie Festival, Alice Springs NT 163
 Dark Mofo, Hobart Tas. 75, 162
 First Nations light festival, Alice Springs NT 175
 Garma Festival, Gulkula, East Arnhem Land NT 168–9
 Sydney Gay and Lesbian Mardi Gras NSW 156–7
 Sydney Lunar Festival NSW 174
 Vivid Sydney NSW 166
 see also music festivals
film xix
First Nations Art, ethical purchases 261
First Nations galleries
 Alice Springs NT 260
 Desert Mob (Araluen Arts Centre), Alice Springs NT 171
 Hermannsburg NT 232
 Jabiru NT 90

317

Mitchelton Vic. 237
  Tiwi Islands NT 181
First Nations peoples x–xi
  Barunga Festival NT 155
  Budj Bim Cultural Landscape (World Heritage Site) Vic. 212–13
  creation stories 83, 213, 254, 255
  cultural experiences 14, 79, 100–1
  early history 64–5
  food *see* bush tucker foraging
  Garma Festival, Gulkula, East Arnhem Land NT 168–9
  history 208, 248, 252, 264, 268–9
  light shows 175, 254
  photographs 69
  rise of Yorta Yorta activism 210–11
  rock-art sites 32–3, 68–9, 90, 238–9, 264, 267, 273
Fitzgerald River National Park WA 71
Flinders Ranges SA 82, 114–15, 140
Florence Falls, Litchfield National Park NT 44
Floriade, Canberra ACT 159
flower shows 159
fly fishing 136
food and drink *see* bush tucker foraging; gourmet food; whisky distilleries; wineries
food festivals 173
Formula One Australian Grand Prix, Melbourne Vic. 191
fossil museums/fossil deposits 115, 226–7
Franklin-Gordon Wild Rivers National Park Tas. 72–3
Fremantle Prison WA 215
freshwater crocodiles 51

Gabo Island lighthouse Vic. 278
Gadigal Country 56, 144, 156–7, 166, 174, 195, 208, 248, 294, 306
Gadubanud Country 117, 132
Garma Festival, Gulkula, East Arnhem Land NT 168–9
geography xii
Ghan, the (train) 309
ghost mushrooms 67
ghost towns 216
Giants of Mandurah (art installation), Mandurah WA 263
Gibb River Road WA xiv
Gibson, Roy 79
Girai Wurrung Country 288
Girramay Country 18

Glencoe SA 67
Glenelg Beach SA 75
Glenrowan Vic. 225
Gold Coast hinterland Qld 76–7
Gold Coast Hinterland Great Walk Qld 52, 76
Golden Plains (rock and pop festival), Meredith Vic. 161
Goldfields Trail Great Walk Qld 53
golf 182
Gondwana Rainforests of Australia World Heritage Area 76
Gooreng Gooreng Country 92, 126
gorges 20–1, 23, 41, 51, 62–3, 68, 79, 297
Gormley, Sir Antony 251
Gosses Bluff/Tnorala NT 82
gourmet food 132–3, 136–42, 149
Grampians (Gariwerd) National Park Vic. 41, 312–13
Great Barrier Reef Qld 58–9
  citizen science programs 120
  diving and snorkelling sites 108–9
  sleeping a night on the Reef 24
  underwater art gallery, Townsville 244–5
Great Barrier Reef Marine Park Authority 126
Great Ocean Road Vic. xiv, 41, 117, 132, 197, 288
Great Ocean Walk Vic. 288
Great Reef Census 120
Great Sandy National Park Qld 14–15, 52
Great South West Walk Vic. 289
Great Western Hotel, Rockhampton Qld 219
Gugu Badhun Country 244–5
Gulkula, East Arnhem Land NT 168–9
Gumatj Country 168–9
Gunditjmara Country 132, 158, 212–13, 288, 289
Gundungurra Country 196
Gurang Country 92, 126
Gureng Gureng Country 24, 120

Halls Gap Vic. 4
Hamilton Island Qld 59
Hanging Rock Vic. 259
Hawkesbury River/Dyarubbin NSW 306
Head of Bight cliffs SA 17
Hermannsburg NT 232
Heron Island Qld 126

Heron Island Research Station Qld 126–7
hiking trails 14, 18–19, 22, 23, 32–3, 35, 47, 52–3, 62–3, 76, 79, 84, 86, 91, 119, 202, 268, 288–9, 296–7, 298, 310, 312
  accessible 40–1
Hinchinbrook Island National Park Qld 18–19
Hobart/nipaluna Tas. 47, 75, 146, 162, 242–3, 268–9
Hobart Rivulet Tas. 107
Hodges, Rachael 79
honey producers 133
Hook Island Qld 59
Horn Island Qld 234
horseracing 191
hot springs 57, 113
Houtman Abrolhos Islands WA 186, 217
Huon Valley Tas. 123
Hutt Lagoon WA 43
Hyams Beach NSW 30
Hyde Park Barracks NSW 215
Hyden WA 61

Ian Potter Centre: NGV Australia, Melbourne Vic. 271
Iga Warta, Vulkathunnha-Gammon Ranges SA 264
Illaroo NSW 233
Indian Pacific (train) 294
Innawonga Country 20–1
Irlwentye NT 33
Irukandji jellyfish 4

Jaithmathang Country 311
James, Grampa Thomas Shadrach 210–11
Jardwadjali Country 312
Jaru Country 83
Jawoyn Country 62–3
Jim Jim Falls, Kakadu National Park NT 60
John Dynon Gallery, Silverton NSW 266
John Forrest National Park WA 47
John George Trail, Perth WA 41
Juicy Fest (hip hop and R&B) festival 160
Juru Country 186

Kabi Kali Country 192–3
Kakadu National Park NT 60, 90–1, 103

318

Kalbari National Park WA 41
Kangaroo Island SA 4, 133
Kangaroo Valley NSW 4
kangaroos 4, 94
Kanku-Breakaways Conservation Park SA 222
Kara Kara Country 68
Karijini National Park WA 7, 20–1, 26
Karingbal Country 68
Karkaganujaru Country 86
karri (trees) 78
Kata Tjuṯa, Uluṟu-Kata Tjuṯa National Park NT 80
Kaurna Country 95, 133, 139, 145, 173, 276
kayaking 52–3, 58, 95, 100–1, 192–3, 294
  see also canoeing
Kelly, Ned 225
K'gari Qld 14–15, 52
K'gari Great Walk Qld 52
Kimberley Dreaming, East Kimberley WA 130
Kimble, Belén Alvarez 204
Kings Canyon NT 35, 175
Kings Park and Botanic Garden, Perth WA 71
Kingston and Arthur's Vale Historic Area, Norfolk Island 215
Kingston on Murray SA 119
Koa Country 226–7, 256–7
koalas 4
Koongurrukun Country 44–5
Koorie Heritage Trust, Melbourne Vic. 253
Kosciuszko National Park NSW 27, 57
Kronosaurus Korner, Richmond Qld 227
Kuku Yalanji Country 79, 99
Kuku Yalanji Cultural Habitat Tours Qld 131
Kulitja, Rene 254
Kurrama Country 20–1
Kuyani Country 216

Lady Musgrave HQ (pontoon), Lady Musgrave Island, Great Barrier Reef Qld 24
Lake Ballard human figure sculptures WA 251
Lake Bumbunga SA 43
Lake Burley Griffin ACT 40
Lake Elizabeth Vic. 107
Lake Hillier WA 43
Lake Macdonnell SA 43
Lamington National Park Qld 52, 76
Lark, Bill 146
Lark Distillery, Hobart Tas. 146
Lark Quarry Dinosaur Trackway Qld 227
Larrakia Country 170
Launceston Tas. 23, 147, 149
Launceston Distillery Tas. 147
Laura Qld 272, 273
Laura Quinkan Dance Festival Qld 272
lava tubes, Undara Qld 87
Leeuwin Estate, Margaret River WA 236
Leeuwin-Naturaliste National Park WA 310
Lesueur National Park WA 71
LGBTQIA+ events 156–7
libraries 277
light shows/festivals
  Alice Springs Desert Park NT 175
  Vivid Sydney NSW 166
  Wintjiri Wiru, Uluṟu-Kata Tjuṯa National Park NT 174, 254
lighthouse stays 278
Lightning Ridge NSW 8, 305
Lightning Ridge Bore Baths NSW 305
Litchfield National Park NT 44–5
Living Desert Sculptures, Broken Hill NSW 251, 267
Lord Howe Island NSW 84–5
Lucky Bay WA 30, 94

Mabel Island, Frankland Islands Group, Great Barrier Reef Qld 108
Mackay Highlands Great Walk Qld 52
MacKenzie Falls Lookout, Grampians/Gariwerd Vic. 41
Mad Max museum, Silverton NSW 241
Magnetic Island Qld 4
Mahon Pool, Maroubra NSW 195
Mak Mak Marranunggu Country 44–5
Malgana Country 100–1
Mandurah WA 263
Manly NSW 75
Mansell, Allan 268
Mansell, Kitana 269
Mapleton Public House, Mapleton Qld 140
Mardi Gras, Sydney NSW 156–7
Mardudhunera Country 238–9
Margaret River WA 138, 140
Mari Nawi (First Nations boat cruise), Sydney Harbour NSW 248
Maria Island National Park Tas. 4, 96–7
marine sculptures 270
markets
  Adelaide Central Market SA 139
  Mindil Beach Sunset Market, Darwin NT 170
  Sydney Fish Market NSW 144
Marree Man (giant mysterious figure), Marree SA 247
Martin, Sally 130
Martin, Samantha 130
Massey, Brian 117
Matagarup Bridge, Perth WA 282
Mawson Trail SA 303
McIver's Ladies Baths, Coogee NSW 195
Melbourne/Naarm Vic. 46, 75, 160, 161, 190–1, 221, 253, 265, 271, 277, 283–4
Melbourne Cricket Ground (MCG) Vic. xviii, 190
Melbourne Holocaust Museum, Elsternwick Vic. 221
Melbourne International Jazz Festival Vic. 160
Mersey River Tas. 107
meteorite craters 83
microbats 87
Millstream-Chichester National Park WA 7
Mindil Beach Sunset Market, Darwin NT 170
Minjungbal Country 116
Mirning Country 17, 182
Mitchelton Gallery of Aboriginal Art/ Tangurang Country, Nagambie Vic. 237
Mole Creek Karst National Park Tas. 200
Mon Repos Turtle Centre Qld 92
Mona (gallery), Hobart 242–3
monoliths 41, 254–5
Montalto winery, Mornington Peninsula Vic. 237
Montezuma Falls Tas. 60
Moore Reef, Great Barrier Reef Qld 108
Moree Artesian Aquatic Centre NSW 305

Moreton Island/Mulgumpin Qld 198–9
Morialta Conservation Park SA 46, 60
Mossman Gorge Qld 79
motorcycle racing 191
Mount August National Park WA 32
Mount Bartle Brere Qld 26
Mount Bogong Vic. 26
Mount Buller Vic. 202
Mount Field National Parak Tas. 54–5
Mount Gambier SA 37
Mount Meharry/Wirlbiwirlbi WA 26
Mount Ossa Tas. 26
Mount Woodroffe SA 26
mountain ash 78
mountain biking trails 33, 189
 see also cycle trails/cycling
mountain climbing 26–7
movies xix
Munda Biddi Trail WA 303
Munga-Thirri-Simpson Desert National Park SA, Qld & NT 42
Mungo National Park NSW 4, 10, 64–5
Murison, Johnny 272, 273
Murramarang National Park NSW 94
Murray, Greg 269
Murray River Dark Sky Reserve SA 315
Murray-Sunset National Park Vic. 43
Murray to Mountains Rail Trail Vic. 311
Murujuga National Park WA 6, 238–9
mushrooms (bioluminescent) 67
music festivals xviii, 160–1
 Golden Plains (rock and pop festival), Meredith Vic. 161
 Juicy Fest (hip hop and R&B) festival 160
 Parkes Elvis Festival NSW 164–5
 Melbourne International Jazz Festival Vic. 160
 Port Fairy Folk Festival Vic. 160–1
 Splendour in the Grass (pop and rock festival), Byron Bay NSW 161
 Tamworth Country Music Festival NSW 160
 WOMADelaide SA 161, 173
Mutawintji National Park NSW 10, 267
Mutonia Sculpture Park SA 251
Muttaburra Qld 227
Mutthi Mutthi Country 64–5

Nambung National Park WA 81
Naracoorte Caves National Park SA 200
Narawntapu National Park Tas. 4
National Gallery of Victoria, Melbourne Vic. 271
National Museum of Australia, Canberra ACT 229
national parks (on the edge of capital cities) 46–7
Natural Bridge to Island Rock WA 41
Nauo Country 137
N'Dhala Gorge Nature Park NT 33
New Norfolk Tas. 150–1
Ngadjuri Country 145
Ngarigo Country 27, 57
Ngarluma Country 238–9
Ngaro Country 24, 58–9, 120
Ngarrindjeri Country 119, 133
Ngunnawal Country 159, 229
Ngyimpaa Country 64–5
Nhanda Country 100–1
Ningaloo Reef region WA 6–7
Nitmiluk National Park NT 62–3
Njaki Njaki Country 61
Noongar Country 303
Noosa National Park Qld 4, 192
Noosa Qld 192–3, 205
Nord, SS (shipwreck), Tasman Peninsula Tas. 186
Normanby Island, Frankland Islands Group, Great Barrier Reef Qld 108
Northern Rivers Rail Trail NSW 302
Nothofagus gunnii, changing colour 54–5
Nullarbor Links (golf course) SA & WA 182
Nullarbor Plain SA & WA xiv, 17, 182
Nurim Circuit Qld 41
Nywaigi Country 244–5

ocean pools 195
Ocean Sentinels (underwater sculpture), John Brewer Reef Qld 244
Ocean Siren (sculpture), Townsville Qld 244
Old Beechworth Gaol, Beechworth Vic. 225
Old Government House and Domain NSW 215
Old Great North Road NSW 215
Old Melbourne Gaol, Melbourne Vic. 225

oldest European building, Houtman Abrolhos Islands WA 217
Oodnadatta Track SA 216, 218, 251
opal-mining towns 10, 280–1
Orange NSW 136
Orizaba, RMS (shipwreck), Rockingham WA 186
Ormiston Gorge NT 41
Ormiston Pound NT 82
outback pubs 218–19
outback springs 305
outdoor galleries NSW 267
Overland Track Tas. 26, 298–9
Oxley Wild Rivers National Park NSW 60
oysters 137

Paakantji Country 64–5
Pacific Coast, NSW & Qld xiv
Palace Hotel, Broken Hill NSW 218
Palawa Country 57–8, 66, 72–5, 96–7, 123, 142–3, 146–7, 150–1, 162, 183, 189, 242–3, 268–9, 291, 294, 298
palawa kipli, piyrura kitina/Risdon Cove Tas. 130, 269
Parkes Elvis Festival, Parkes NSW 164–5
Pass, the, Byron Bay NSW 205
Paterson, 'Banjo' 256
Pebbly Beach NSW 94
Penola SA 289
Peramangk Country 145
Perrepa Perrepa Country 167
Perth/Boorloo WA 41, 47, 71, 75, 160, 161, 282, 294
Phillip Island Vic. 191
Pibleman Boodja Country 138
Pieman River Tas. 294
Pilbara region WA 6, 7
pink lakes 43
Pinnacles, the, Nambung National Park WA 81
platypus sites 107
Port Arthur Historic Site Tas. 214
Port Fairy Folk Festival Vic. 160–1
Port Macquarie NSW 4
Port River SA 95
Portland Vic. 289
pounds 82–3
Prairie Hotel, Parachilna SA 140
Preston, Lisa 104–5
Pro Hart Gallery, Broken Hill NSW 266
Pt Leo Estate, Mornington Peninsula Vic. 236

320

pub food 140–1
PUBLIC Silo Art Trail WA 252
Purnululu National Park WA 86

Quandamooka Country 198
Queenstown Tas. 183
Quinkan Country 273

rail trails 302, 311
rainforests 14, 41, 47, 52, 76–7, 79, 99, 189, 294
Ramindjeri Country 133
Red Centre Way NT xiv
red crabs, Christmas Island 104–5
Reef Check Australia 120
Reefworld Pontoon, Hardy Reef, Great Barrier Reef Qld 24
Reeves, Nigel 291
Remarkable Rocks SA 41
Ribbon Reef #9 1/3, Great Barrier Reef Qld 109
Riddle, Anthony 84
Riverboat Postman, Hawkesbury River NSW 306
road trips
Pilbara and Ningaloo WA 6–7
way out west NSW 10–11
Robe Coastal Walk SA 41
rock-art sites 32–3, 63, 68–9, 90, 238–9, 264, 267, 273
photographs 69
Rockhampton Qld 2, 200, 219
rooftop bars 134
Rottnest Island/Wadjemup WA 201
Royal Exhibition Buildings, Melbourne Vic. 283–4
Royal Mail Hotel, Dunkeld Vic. 140
Royal National Park NSW 46
Running River Qld 107
Russell Falls Tas. 41

sailing 58
saltwater crocodiles 4, 18, 91, 99
Salty Girls Surf School, Bogandar NSW 204
Sanctuary Loop ACT 40
Sandy Bay's Long Beach Tas. 75
saunas 291
Saunders, Joey 213
Sawn Rocks NSW 40
Secret Garden, Sydney NSW 56
Seppeltsfield Barossa (fortified wines) SA 145
Settlers Tavern, Margaret River WA 140

Shark Bay WA 100–1
sharks 100
Shelly Beach Pool, Cronulla NSW 195
shipwreck dives 186, 217
silo art 252, 253
Silo Art Trail Vic. 252
Silverton NSW 11, 241, 266
sinkholes 37
ski resorts in summer 202–3
Smith, Ben 130
snakes 4
snorkelling *see* diving and snorkelling
Snowy Mountains NSW 27, 57
South Curl Curl Rock Pool NSW 195
South Molle Island Qld 59
Southern Cross Cultural Tour, Ardyaloon WA 130
southern lights 66
Southwest National Park Tas. 23
Splendour in the Grass (pop and rock festival), Byron Bay NSW 161
sports arenas/sporting passion 190–1, 276
Sprigg, Doug 114
Spring Bay Distillery, Spring Beach Tas. 147
Spring Racing Carnival, Melbourne Vic. 191
Springbrook National Park Qld 52, 76
St Jerome's Laneway Festival (pop and rock) 160
St Kilda Beach Vic. 75
stand-up paddleboarding 51
Star of Greece (shipwreck), Port Willunga SA 186
stargazing 315
State Library of Victoria
La Trobe Reading Room, Melbourne Vic. 277
Redmond Barry Reading Room, Melbourne Vic. 225
Steele, Anne and Bob 164
Stevensons Falls Vic. 41
Stirling Range National Park WA 71
Story Bridge, Brisbane Qld 282
street art murals, Melbourne Vic. 265
Streets Beach, Brisbane Qld 75
Stringybark Creek Reserve Vic. 225
Sunshine Coast Hinterland Great Walk Qld 52
surfing 192, 197, 204–5
swimming 20–1, 44–5, 75, 195
swimming safety xvii

Sydney/Warrane NSW 46, 56, 75, 134, 144, 156–7, 160, 161, 166, 174, 195, 208, 248–9, 271, 294, 296, 306
Sydney Fish Market NSW 144
Sydney Gay and Lesbian Mardi Gras NSW 156–7
Sydney Harbour
camping NSW 306
through First Nations' eyes NSW 248
Sydney Harbour Bridge NSW 56, 208–9, 282
Sydney Lunar Festival NSW 174
Sydney Opera House NSW 249, 283

Tahune AirWalk Tas. 78
Talaroo Hot Springs Qld 113
tall timber Tas. & WA 78
Tamworth Country Music Festival NSW 160
Taribeland Bunda Country 92, 126
TarraWarra Estate, Yarra Valley Vic. 236
Tasmanian devil 96
Tasmanian Trail Tas. 303
Tasmanian Wilderness World Heritage Area 72–3
Tasmania's Aboriginal revival 268–9
Tasting Australia (food festival), Adelaida SA 173
Taungurung Country 259, 311
Thredbo NSW 202
Three Sisters NSW 40
Thursday Island Qld 234
Tiwi Country 181
Tiwi Islands/Yermalner NT 180–1
Tjaetaba Falls, Litchfield National Park NT 44
Tjaynera Falls, Litchfield National Park NT 44
Tjorita/West MacDonnell National Park NT 82, 175, 297
Tolmer Falls, Litchfield National Park NT 45
Tom Price WA 7
Torquay Vic. 197
Torres Strait Islands 234–5
Townsville Qld 244–5
train journeys 294, 309
Troubridge Island lighthouse SA 278
turtle hatching 92–3, 126
Twelve Apostles Vic. 132, 288
Twelve Apostles Food Artisan Trail Vic. 132
Two Towers, Ribbon Reef #10, Great Barrier Reef Qld 108

321

Uluṟu Base Walk NT 41
Uluṟu-Kata Tjuṯa National Park NT 41, 80, 254–5
Undara Volcanic National Park Qld 87
underground homes, Coober Pedy SA 280–1
underwater art gallery, Townsville Qld 244–5
UNESCO City of Gastronomy 149
UNESCO City of Literature sites 276, 283
University of Queensland 120, 126
ute muster, Deniliquin NSW 167

Valley of the Giants Tree Top Walk WA 78
Vivid Sydney (light festival) NSW 166
Vulkathunnha-Gammon Ranges SA 264

Wabma Kadarbu Conservation Park SA 305
Wadandi Country 138, 270, 310
Wadawarrung Country 132, 197, 220
Wajarri Country 32
Walgalu Country 57
Walkabout Creek Hotel, McKinlay Qld 256
Walker, Brandon 131
Walker, Clinton 238
Walker, Linc 131
Walker Creek, Litchfield National Park NT 45
walking trails *see* hiking trails
Waltzing Matilda Centre, Winton Qld 256
Wamba Wamba Country 167
Wanaruah Country 196
Wangkangurru Yurluyandi Country 42
Waray Country 44–5
Warrumbungle National Park NSW 8, 315
Watarrka National Park NT 35
waterfalls 18, 20–1, 41, 44–5, 46, 60, 76
Waubs Harbour Distillery, Bicheno Tas. 147
Wave Rock, Haydn WA 61
Waywurru Country 311
Webb, Mikey 177
Wellington Park Tas. 47
Wendy Whiteley's Secret Garden, Sydney NSW 56

Wentworth NSW 11
Werat Country 44–5
Western Treatment Plant Vic. 103
Wet Tropics Great Walk Qld 53
wetlands 119
Whadjuk Noongar Country 201, 282, 294
whale sharks 105
whales 14, 17, 41, 108, 192, 278, 310
whisky distilleries Tas. 146–7
white-water rafting 72–3
Whitehaven Beach Qld 30
Whiteley, Brett 56, 271
Whiteley, Wendy 56
Whitsunday Islands Qld 30, 52–3, 58–9
Whitsunday Ngaro Sea Trail Qld 52–3
Whyalla SA 98
Widjabul Country 116
wilderness sanctuaries, SA 114–15
Wildflower Way WA 71
wildflowers 7, 47, 71
wildlife watching
  cuttlefish 98
  dingoes 15
  dolphins 95, 100, 172, 278, 310
  estuarine (saltwater) crocodiles 4, 18, 91, 99
  freshwater crocodiles 51
  kangaroos 4, 94
  koalas 4
  microbats 87
  platypuses 107
  red crabs 104
  sharks 100
  Tasmanian devil 96
  turtle hatching 92–3
  whales 14, 17, 41, 108, 192, 278, 310
  wombats 4, 96
  yellow-footed rock wallabies 114
Wildlife Wonders (sanctuary), Apollo Bay Vic. 117
William Creek Hotel SA 218
Wilpena Pound/Ikara SA 82
Wilson, Sammy 254
Wilsons Promontory lighthouse Vic. 278
Wilsons Promontory National Park Vic. 4, 278
Wilyakali Country 241, 266–7
Wineglass Bay Tas. 30
wineries 77, 119, 133, 136, 138, 145, 236–7

Wintjiri Wiru, Uluṟu-Kata Tjuṯa National Park NT 175, 254
Winton Qld 226, 256–7
Wiradjuri Country 136, 164, 196
Witjira National Park SA 305
Wolfe Creek/Kandimalal WA 83
Wolgalu Country 27
Wollomombi Falls NSW 60
WOMAdelaide (festival) SA 161, 173
wombats 4, 96
Wong-goo-ti-oo Country 238–9
Wooden Boat Centre, Franklin Tas. 123
working dogs, Casterton Vic. 158
World Heritage listed sites 14, 64, 86, 90, 100, 114–15, 196, 212–15, 273
world's longest golf course, Nullarbor SA & WA 182
wukalina Walk Tas. 268
Wulgurukaba of Gurambilbarra Country 244–5
Wurundjeri Country 190–1, 221, 253, 259, 265, 277, 283

Yaburara Country 238–9
Yardie Creek WA 6
Yindjibarndi Country 238–9
Yingkarta Country 100–1
Yinyila Country 17
Yongala, SS (shipwreck), Ayr Qld 186
Yorta Yorta activism, rise of 210–11
Yued Country 81
Yugambeh Country 76–7
Yunbenun Country 244–5

ABOUT THE AUTHOR

Andrew Bain is a Hobart-based writer (Australia) who is passionate about the outdoors and remote places, having walked, cycled and kayaked his way across large parts of the world over the last 25 years.

Photo credits

Images © Andrew Bain with the exception of the following:
Pages ii, vi, xiii, xiv, xv, 5 (top), 39, 40, 300, 313 Intrepid Travel; xi, 169 Leicolhn McKellar/Yothu Yindi Foundation; xvi, 5 (bottom), 10, 11, 15, 25, 32, 33, 42, 45 (bottom), 47, 60, 65 (bottom), 66, 69 (bottom), 70, 73, 77, 78, 79, 80, 87, 91, 93, 94, 98, 99, 101, 102 (top), 106 (bottom), 121, 137, 138, 144, 148, 154 (bottom right), 157 (bottom), 161 (bottom), 174 (top), 194, 196, 200, 203, 205, 216, 219, 221, 224 (bottom left and right), 227, 228, 232, 240 (bottom), 243, 245, 253, 261, 262 (bottom), 267, 270, 277, 284, 288, 295, 299, 307, 310 Shutterstock; xix (top) Nina Franova/Yothu Yindi Foundation; xix (bottom), 43, 56, 57, 61, 67, 69 (top), 83, 100, 102 (bottom); 106 (top); 109; 115 (bottom); 116, 127, 141, 147 (bottom), 154 (top), 158, 161 (top), 162, 165 (bottom), 167, 170, 187, 191, 199, 217, 220, 224 (top), 237, 239, 246, 262 (top), 290 (bottom), 292, 294, 296, 302, 304 (bottom), 306, 308, 311, 314 Alamy; 8 Unsplash/Jamison Cameron; 9 Unsplash/Trevor McKinnon; 16 (top) Unsplash/Fiona Smallwood; 16 (bottom) Unsplash/Vince Russell; 31 Unsplash/Dmitry Osipenko; 45 (top) Unsplash/ Nick Dunn; 59 Unplash/Phill Graaf; 63 (top) Unsplash/ JL [julians_photos]; 63 (bottom) Unsplash/Tania Richardson; 65 (top) Unsplash/ Dylan Shaw; 74 (top) Unsplash/Alvin [heyalvin]; 74 (bottom) Unsplash/Nathan Hurst; 84 Unsplash/Dylan Shaw; 86 Unsplash/Sheila C; 97 M.Cuthbert; 105 Unsplash/Raphael Bick; 112 Courtesy Ewamian Limited; 117 Wildlife Wonders; 131 Samantha Martin; 132 Tourism Victoria; 135 (top) Jess Wyld; 135 (bottom) HER ROOFTOP; 143 (bottom) Unsplash/Tamara Thurman; 159 Unsplash/Masyitha Mutiara Ramadhan; 163 Alice Springs Beanie Festival; 166 Unplash/Srikant Sahoo; 172 (top right) Gary Francis/ZUMA Wire/Alamy Live News; 174 (bottom) Richard Milnes/Alamy Live News; 176 Auslan Stage Left; 180, 212 Wayne Quilliam; 197 Unsplash/Jamie Davies; 201 Unsplash/Tianlei Sun; 211 Monash University/William Cooper Institute; 233 Katherine Lu /Bundanon; 235 Emma Shaw; 237 Unsplash/Tom Kennedy; 240 (top) Destination NSW; 249 Unsplash/Luke White; 252 Unsplash/Mitchell Luo; 265 Unsplash/Dominic Kurniawan Suryaputra; 269 The Henry Jones Art Hotel; 271 Richard Milnes/Alamy Live News; 50, 92, 95, 124, 127 (top); 133, 136, 137, 143 (top), 145, 151, 154 (bottom left), 157 (top left and right), 165 (top), 172 (top left and bottom), 175, 209, 255, 272, 276 Tourism Australia.

Published in 2025 by Hardie Grant Explore,
an imprint of Hardie Grant Publishing

Hardie Grant Explore (Melbourne)
Wurundjeri Country
Level 11, 36 Wellington Street
Collingwood, VIC 3066

Hardie Grant Explore (Sydney)
Gadigal Country
Level 7, 45 Jones Street
Ultimo, NSW 2007

hardiegrant.com/explore

All rights reserved. No part of this publication may be reproduced, stored in a retrieval system or transmitted in any form by any means, electronic, mechanical, photocopying, recording or otherwise, without the prior written permission of the publishers and copyright holders.

The moral rights of the author have been asserted.

Copyright concept, text, maps and design © Hardie Grant Publishing 2025

The maps in this publication incorporate data from the following sources:

© Commonwealth of Australia (Geoscience Australia), 2006. Geoscience Australia has not evaluated the data as altered and incorporated within this publication, and therefore gives no warranty regarding accuracy, completeness, currency or suitability for any particular purpose.

Incorporates or developed using [Roads May 2023, Hydrology Nov 2012] © Geoscape Australia for Copyright and Disclaimer Notice see geoscape.com.au/legal/data-copyright-and-disclaimer

A catalogue record for this book is available from the National Library of Australia

Hardie Grant acknowledges the Traditional Owners of the Country on which we work, the Wurundjeri People of the Kulin Nation and the Gadigal People of the Eora Nation, and recognises their continuing connection to the land, waters and culture. We pay our respects to their Elders past and present.

Intrepid Australia
ISBN 9781741179316

10 9 8 7 6 5 4 3 2 1

Publisher
Megan Cuthbert

Editor
Monique Choy

Editorial assistance
Siena O'Kelly

Proofreader
Lyric Dodson

Cartographer
Emily Maffei

Design
George Saad Studio

Typesetting
Megan Ellis

Index
Max McMaster

Production manager
Simone Wall

First Nations consultant
Jamil Tye, Yorta Yorta

Colour reproduction and pre-press by Megan Ellis and Splitting Image Colour Studio

Printed and bound in China by LEO Paper Products LTD.

The paper this book is printed on is certified against the Forest Stewardship Council® Standards and other sources. FSC® promotes environmentally responsible, socially beneficial and economically viable management of the world's forests.

FSC® C020056

Disclaimer: While every care is taken to ensure the accuracy of the data within this product, the owners of the data do not make any representations or warranties about its accuracy, reliability, completeness or suitability for any particular purpose and, to the extent permitted by law, the owners of the data disclaim all responsibility and all liability (including without limitation, liability in negligence) for all expenses, losses, damages (including indirect or consequential damages) and costs which might be incurred as a result of the data being inaccurate or incomplete in any way and for any reason.

Publisher's Disclaimers: The publisher cannot accept responsibility for any errors or omissions. The representation on the maps of any road or track is not necessarily evidence of public right of way. The publisher cannot be held responsible for any injury, loss or damage incurred during travel. It is vital to research any proposed trip thoroughly and seek the advice of relevant state and travel organisations before you leave.

Publisher's Note: Every effort has been made to ensure that the information in this book is accurate at the time of going to press. The publisher welcomes information and suggestions for correction or improvement.